D0707704

Isaiah 40–66

Westminster Bible Companion

Series Editors

Patrick D. Miller
David L. Bartlett

Isaiah 40–66

WALTER BRUEGGEMANN

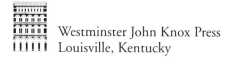
Westminster John Knox Press
Louisville, Kentucky

© 1998 Walter Brueggemann

All rights reserved. No part of this book may be reproduced or transmitted in any form or by any means, electronic or mechanical, including photocopying, recording, or by any information storage or retrieval system, without permission in writing from the publisher. For information, address Westminster John Knox Press, 100 Witherspoon Street, Louisville, Kentucky 40202-1396.

Scripture quotations, unless otherwise noted, are from the New Revised Standard Version of the Bible, copyright © 1989 by the Division of Christian Education of the National Council of the Churches of Christ in the U.S.A., and are used by permission.

Book design by Publisher's WorkGroup
Cover design by Drew Stevens

First edition

Published by Westminster John Knox Press
Louisville, Kentucky

This book is printed on acid-free paper that meets the American National Standards Institute Z39.48 standard. ♾

PRINTED IN THE UNITED STATES OF AMERICA

00 01 02 03 04 05 06 07 — 10 9 8 7 6 5 4 3 2

Library of Congress Cataloging-in-Publication Data

Brueggemann, Walter.
   Isaiah / Walter Brueggemann. — 1st ed.
      p.   cm. — (Westminster Bible companion)
   Includes bibliographical references.
   Contents: v. 1. 1–39 — v. 2. 40–66.
   ISBN 0-664-25524-8 (v. 1 : alk. paper). — ISBN 0-664-25791-7 (v. 2 : alk. paper)
   1. Bible. O.T. Isaiah—Commentaries. I. Title. II. Series.
BS1515.2.B669   1998
224′ .1077—DC21   98–16400

Contents

Series Foreword   ix

Introduction   1
  Models of Interpretation   3
  Directions of Interpretation   5

7. The God of All Comfort   8
  Isaiah 40—55

  The Indomitable Voice of Comfort (40:1–11)   15
  It Is Yahweh—Incomparable! (40:12–31)   22
    Yahweh without Parallel (40:12–17)   22
    Like Gods, Like Nations (40:18–24)   23
    The Incomparable Creator (40:25–26)   25
    The Creator as the Tireless God of Israel (40:27–31)   26
  Yahweh, Powerful and Merciful (41:1–29)   28
    Yahweh First and Last (41:1–7)   29
    Israel beyond Fear (41:8–13)   32
    News for the Worm (41:14–16)   34
    Yahweh's Transformed Landscape (41:17–20)   35
    More Adjudication (41:21–29)   38
  A Servant, a Warrior, a Dispute (42:1–25)   41
    A Called Agent (42:1–9)   41
    A New Song for a New World (42:10–17)   45
    A Rebuke from the Rescuing God (42:18–25)   48
  The Creator Who Redeems, Forgives, and Profanes (43:1–28)   51
    Yahweh's Decisive Love for Israel (43:1–7)   52
    Testimony to the Holy, True God (43:8–13)   55
    A Newness from Yahweh (43:14–21)   57
    A Wearying People (43:22–28)   60

God against the Gods (44:1–23)   64
   I Belong to the Lord (44:1–5)   64
   Witnesses to the Redeemer (44:6–8)   66
   The Nothingness of Idols and Their Witnesses (44:9–20)   67
   Israel Remembered and Forgiven (44:21–22)   71
   Once More Redeemer (44:23)   72
The Gentile Messiah (44:24–45:13)   72
   "The Lord Who . . . " (44:24–28)   73
   Cyrus Summoned (45:1–6)   74
   Lord of All These Things (45:7)   76
   A Doxological Interlude (45:8)   77
   Implied Questions, Explicit Answers (45:9–13)   78
Either Yahweh or . . . (45:14–25)   80
   Saved and Not Shamed (45:14–17)   80
   The Creator beyond Chaos (45:18–19)   82
   "No Other God" (45:20–21)   83
   The Ultimate Turn (45:22–23)   84
   Only Yahweh (45:24–25)   85
The Powerful, Active, Decisive "I" of Yahweh (46:1–13)   86
"You Say . . . but Evil Shall Come" (47:1–15)   92
"For My Own Sake" (48:1–22)   100
   Former and New Things, to the Glory of Yahweh (48:1–13)   101
   Wistfulness and Assurance (48:14–22)   105
A Servant as Light and as Covenant (49:1–12)   109
The Joy of Homecoming (49:13–26)   115
Yahweh's Power and Reliability (50:1–11)   119
"Listen, Listen, Listen" (51:1–8)   125
"I Am He . . . You Are My People" (51:9–16)   129
"Drink No More" (51:17–23)   132
"Awake . . . Depart" (52:1–12)   135
"My Servant . . . Who Prospers and Bears" (52:13–53:12)   141
Promises of Newness (54:1–17)   150
   A Wife Beloved and Blessed (54:1–8)   150
   Prosperity and Vindication (54:9–17)   155
"Go Out in Joy and Peace" (55:1–13)   158

8. "Maintain Justice, and Do What Is Right"   **164**
Isaiah 56:1–66:24

Life with the God Who Gathers (56:1–12)   167

Choosing for Peace or against Yahweh (57:1–13)   175
Once More the Gift of Comfort (57:14–21)   180
Faith in Its Demand (58:1–14)   186
Waiting for Justice (59:1–21)   194
   Israel's Failure (59:1–8)   194
   Israel's Need (59:9–15a)   197
   Yahweh's Response (59:15b–21)   199
"The Lord, Your Everlasting Light and Glory" (60:1–22)   203
"I Will Make an Everlasting Covenant" (61:1–11)   212
"No More Forsaken" (62:1–12)   219
"It Is I, Mighty to Save" (63:1–6)   225
"You, O Lord, Are Our Father" (63:7–64:12)   228
   "They Remembered the Days of Old" (63:7–14) 228
   "Turn Back . . . Come Down" (63:15–64:12)   231
"Here I Am, Here I Am" (65:1–16)   238
New Heavens; New Earth; New Jerusalem (65:17–25)   245
"I Am Coming" (66:1–24)   251

For Further Reading   **261**

Series Foreword

This series of study guides to the Bible is offered to the church and more specifically to the laity. In daily devotions, in church school classes, and in listening to the preached word, individual Christians turn to the Bible for a sustaining word, a challenging word, and a sense of direction. The word that scripture brings may be highly personal as one deals with the demands and surprises, the joys and sorrows, of daily life. It also may have broader dimensions as people wrestle with the moral and theological issues that involve us all. In every congregation and denomination, controversies arise that send ministry and laity alike back to the Word of God to find direction for dealing with difficult matters that confront us.

A significant number of lay women and men in the church also find themselves called to the service of teaching. Most of the time they will be teaching the Bible. In many churches, the primary sustained attention to the Bible and the discovery of its riches for our lives have come from the ongoing teaching of the Bible by persons who have not engaged in formal theological education. They have been willing, and often eager, to study the Bible in order to help others drink from its living water.

This volume is part of a series of books, the Westminster Bible Companion, intended to help the laity of the church read the Bible more clearly and intelligently. Whether such reading is for personal direction or for the teaching of others, the reader cannot avoid the difficulties of trying to understand these words from long ago. The scriptures are clear and clearly available to everyone as they call us to faith in the God who is revealed in Jesus Christ and as they offer to every human being the word of salvation. No companion volumes are necessary in order to hear such words truly. Yet every reader of scripture who pauses to ponder and think further about any text has questions that are not immediately answerable simply by reading the text of scripture. Such questions may be about historical and geographical details or about words that are obscure or so loaded with meaning that one cannot tell at a glance what is at stake. They may be about the fundamental meaning of a passage or about what connection a particular text might have to our contemporary world. Or a teacher preparing for a church school class may simply want to know: What should I say about this biblical passage when I have to teach it next Sunday? It is our hope that these volumes, written by teachers and pastors with long experience studying and teaching the Bible in the church, will help members of the church who want and need to study the Bible with their questions.

The New Revised Standard Version of the Bible is the basis for the interpretive comments that each author provides. The NRSV text is presented at the beginning of the discussion so that the reader may have at hand in a single volume both the scripture passage and the exposition of its meaning. In some instances, where inclusion of the entire passage is not necessary for understanding either the text of the interpreter's discussion, the presentation of the NRSV text may be abbreviated. Usually, the whole of the biblical text is given.

We hope this series will serve the community of faith, opening the Word of God to all the people, so that they may be sustained and guided by it.

Introduction

The book of Isaiah is like a mighty oratorio whereby Israel sings its story of faith. Like any oratorio, this one includes interaction among many voices, some of which are in dissent. Like any oratorio, this work requires a rendering; and because each interpretive rendering (including this one) takes on a peculiar character, no one rendering may claim to be the "correct" one. Like any oratorio, moreover, this one conveys its primary themes with great authority, so that they persist through the vagaries of many imaginative interpretations. In this oratorio, a primary theme is the predominant and constant character of Yahweh, who looms over the telling in holy sovereignty and in the faithful gentleness of a comforting nursemaid. All said, the book of Isaiah is a remarkable artistic achievement wherein the artistry is a match for the awesome, inscrutable Character whose tale it tells.

In broad sweep, the story told in the book of Isaiah is the long account of Israel's life in the midst of a demanding sequence of imperial powers. The book of Isaiah has in its purview an international geopolitical horizon. The book traverses the chronology of the Assyrian Empire from the incursions of Tiglath-pileser III (745–727 B.C.E. [Before Common Era—formerly known as B.C.]) to the miraculous deliverance of Jerusalem from Sennacherib in 701; the Babylonian Empire under the domination of Nebuchadrezzar; and the radically altered policies of the Persian Empire under Cyrus that resulted in a benign support of emerging Judaism. The interaction between Judah and the several imperial powers is a key element in the staging of the story.

The book of Isaiah, however, is not simply a telling of the political story of Judah, nor of the sequence of superpowers. It is not in the end an act of political theory or of history. What makes this rendering of Judah's life distinctive is that the story is told with unfailing attentiveness to Yahweh, who is reckoned to be the primal player in the life of Judah and in the life of the world around Judah. The book of Isaiah, with wondrous artistry, manages to hold together the realities of lived public history in that ancient world and the inscrutable reality of Yahweh, who is said here to impinge decisively in that history. Thus the book of Isaiah is neither "history" in any modern sense of the term nor "theology" in any conventional way.

The convergence of history and theology here results in a quite distinctive genre of documentation for which the best term we have is *prophecy*. Prophecy in this context may be understood as a *redescription* of the public processes of history through which the purposes of Yahweh are given in human utterance. As a consequence, any human decision—whether by Judean kings or by imperial overlords or by authorized priests—is reckoned to be penultimate, for what is ultimate is the resolve of Yahweh and the capacity of Yahweh to do something utterly new in such processes that appear to be settled and autonomous. Yahweh, as given us in the Isaiah tradition, is endlessly surprising, disjunctive, and elusive, so that the book of Isaiah does not yield a smooth presentation of sovereignty, but proceeds by disjunctive fits and starts, some unbearably harsh and some astonishingly healing. The hearer of the book of Isaiah must endlessly marvel at a text that dares to make this Disjunctive One available through artistic imagination, with the "nuts and bolts" of Judean history following meekly in the wake of that Holy Resolve.

The horizon of long-term *international history* and the *cruciality of Yahweh* for the telling of that history are even more focused, however, for in the end of the book of Isaiah is an oratorio about *the suffering and destiny of Jerusalem*. The city is regarded as the center of Yahweh's peculiar attentiveness, as the seat of the world's best hopes for well-being, and as the site of the most profound disobedience and recalcitrance. Jerusalem is taken in this tradition as an epitome of Yahweh's creation, which owes its life to Yahweh and which seeks with great resourcefulness to have a life other than the one Yahweh would give.

It is Jerusalem that is *under judgment* and that draws the negating attention of Yahweh (3:1, 8). It is Jerusalem that is *addressed in exile*, in recognition of its need and in assurance commensurate with its need (40:2; 44:28). It is Jerusalem that is imagined *healed, restored, ransomed, forgiven* (65:18–19). It is Jerusalem, the meeting place of divine will and historical reality, that is the recipient of Yahweh's judgment and Yahweh's renewing comfort and mercy. All of this is described at the outset, where the whole course of Jerusalem and the entire sequence of the book are laid out (1:21–27).

We late Western, Christian readers of course are not in Jerusalem. We read only at a distance. But we continue to pray for the peace of Jerusalem, for as peace comes there, we shall all be made whole.

MODELS OF INTERPRETATION

The book of Isaiah has been assessed through a variety of approaches, of which we may identify three quite distinct models:

1. *A pre-critical, or traditional, understanding*, still found in some quite conservative scholarship, keeps the entire book of Isaiah connected to the prophet Isaiah of the eighth century B.C.E. Much of the first part of the book refers beyond question to such a historical character. But with equal clarity it is certain that much of the later part of the book refers to circumstances and events long after the lifetime of the prophet. This reality poses no problem for what is essentially the traditional approach, for with the genre of "prophecy," it is entirely credible to judge that the eighth-century prophetic figure, by special grace as a prophet, was able to anticipate all that comes subsequently in the book. There is nothing intrinsically impossible about such an approach. It is nonetheless important to note that with the rise of modern theories of knowledge and specifically given "historical criticism," such an approach has been commonly rejected in the interpretive world represented by this series and by the church traditions related to it.

2. *A critical understanding* of the book of Isaiah is reflective of the intellectual world of the West in the eighteenth and nineteenth centuries that focused on historical issues. Scripture interpretation in such a posture sought to situate every book of the Bible and every major part of every book of the Bible in an appropriate historical context. As concerns the book of Isaiah, long and sophisticated historical study produced a long-standing scholarly consensus that is still found in most informed books on Isaiah.

According to that critical consensus, chapters 1—39 are linked to Isaiah of the eighth century B.C.E. in the context of the Assyrian Empire between 742 and 701. Chapters 40—55 are commonly dated to 540, just at the moment when the rising Persian Empire displaced the brutal and hated domination of Babylon. And chapters 56—66 are dated later, perhaps 520, when Jews who had returned from exile went about the critical and difficult task of reshaping the community of faith after its long, exilic jeopardy.

The judgments made in this approach concerning the divisions of the book of Isaiah, now referred to by the shorthand references First Isaiah, Second Isaiah, and Third Isaiah, largely continue to dominate scholarship. The gain of such an approach is the insistence that the theological claims of the text are evoked by and addressed to particular, sometimes recoverable, historical situations. Unfortunately, the assigning of parts of the book of Isaiah to particular historical contexts has led to an inadvertent judgment that the "Three Isaiahs" only exist back-to-back as an editorial convenience, but without integral connection to each other.

3. Although a critical understanding of the book continues to be nearly unanimous among interpreters, by the end of the twentieth century, with some critical distance from the assumptions about knowledge that seemed to be givens, it is not surprising that scholarly attention and energy have more recently moved away from common critical judgments in a canonical direction. *The canonical study of the book of Isaiah* continues to recognize that the book is a literary complexity. Representative of the newer approaches are the essays in *New Visions of Isaiah*, edited by Roy F. Melugin and Marvin A. Sweeney. A canonical approach is not a return to a traditional approach. The newer perspective seeks to understand the final form of the complex text as an integral statement offered by the shapers of the book for theological reasons.

This approach by scholars is relatively recent, and a great deal more work is yet to be done in this regard. To illustrate this perspective that seeks to relate elements of the book that critical judgment has separated, I cite two cases.

First, many scholars have pointed to the theme of "former things and new things," as in 43:18–19.

> Do not remember the former things,
> or consider the things of old.
> I am about to do a new thing;
> now it springs forth, do you not perceive it?

When attention is paid to this theme, it may be noticed in 9:1 ("former time . . . latter time"), in what is likely an early text, and in 65:16–17 ("former troubles . . . former things"), surely a late text. That is, the theme is evident in every major part of the book. It is argued in a canonical perspective that "former things" refers to the harsh judgments of Yahweh culminating in the destruction of Jerusalem and the Exile, and "latter things" are the promises of Yahweh for the restoration after the Exile. When these historical matters are related to the literature of the book of Isaiah, they correlate as "former things" in the judgment texts of chapter 1—39 and the "latter things" as the promises of chapters 40—66. Matters are much more complex than this, but the themes provide a guiding principle for interpreters that gives primary attention not to apparent historical contexts but to the shape of the canonical literature.

A second gain of the canonical approach is in a study of the call narrative of 6:1–10 (11–12). Whereas earlier scholarship has treated this text as the report of an intense personal experience of the prophet, canonical perspective takes the text as a literary-canonical marker whereby Yahweh's harsh verdict against Jerusalem is commended:

> "'Keep listening, but do not comprehend;
> keep looking, but do not understand.'
> Make the mind of this people dull,
> and stop their ears,
> and shut their eyes,
> so that they may not look with their eyes,
> and listen with their ears,
> and comprehend with their minds,
> and turn and be healed."

The intention that Israel should not "turn and be healed" is a governing motif of chapters 1—39. Such a perspective invites the thought that 40:1–11, also a report of a "heavenly consultation," announces the gospel of forgiveness (vv. 2–9) that governs chapters 40—66. Thus 6:1–10 (11–12) and 40:1–11 are taken as parallel declarations whereby the large themes of judgment and promise that permeate the book of Isaiah are rooted in visions of heavenly decision making. The assumption, moreover, is that whatever personal, psychological experience may lie behind these two texts, they now function primarily as literary points of reference in the larger canonical book.

The canonical approach, which is only at the beginning of its interpretive work, draws upon historical-critical gains but moves beyond them toward theological interpretation. This latter perspective is the one in which I have tried to work in this study.

DIRECTIONS OF INTERPRETATION

The book of Isaiah is such a rich, dense, and complex work that it is open for interpretation in various directions:

1. The book of Isaiah has been a fertile interpretive field for Christian theology. Positively, one may say that the book of Isaiah is enormously generative and suggestive, and therefore it is open for being drawn into a variety of interpretive molds, among them that of Christian faith. But it must always be recognized that much Christian reading has flatly

preempted the text and forced upon the text readings that are far removed from its seemingly clear intent. Readers of Isaiah who are situated in the Christian church would do well to read representative Christian interpreters. For example, John Calvin's impressive commentary moves, characteristically, directly into christological interpretation whereby references to Israel are routinely taken to refer to the church. We likely need to relearn both how to make such an interpretive move and to notice the preemptive quality of such a maneuver.

Consideration should be given to the remarkable book of John F. A. Sawyer, *The Fifth Gospel: Isaiah in the History of Christianity*, which explores Christian usage of the book of Isaiah through the history of reading. Sawyer traverses the entire theological-liturgical tradition of the church and pays attention to such focal themes as "Virgin Birth," "Suffering Servant," and "Messiah." The title of the book reflects the claim of early teachers in the church who concluded that along with the four Gospels of the New Testament, Isaiah is a "gospel" that fully contains the crucial claims of Christian faith.

2. It is a matter of considerable importance, in my judgment, that Christians should not preempt the book of Isaiah. It is legitimate to see how the book of Isaiah fed, nurtured, and evoked Christian imagination with reference to Jesus. But that is very different from any claim that the book of Isaiah predicts or specifically anticipates Jesus. Such a preemption, as has often occurred in the reading of the church, constitutes not only a failure to respect Jewish readers, but is a distortion of the book itself. It is strongly preferable, I suggest, that Jews and Christians together recognize that the book of Isaiah is enormously and generatively open in more than one direction. No interpretive tradition is able to monopolize and close interpretation. This is a difficult and important question to which respectful attention must be paid.

3. Beyond the particular Christian claims the church might make, it is important to recognize that the book of Isaiah provides a large rereading of historical reality that is strikingly pertinent to the current condition of Western culture. On that pertinence, I commend especially Daniel Berrigan's *Isaiah: Spirit of Courage, Gift of Tears*. Berrigan's rereading is uncommonly poignant and makes immediate contact with our human crisis.

The "map" of Israel's life in the book of Isaiah is broadly preexilic/exilic/postexilic. Although those labels refer to actual historical crises in the ancient world, it is possible to see that this sequence around *displacement* and *restoration* is peculiarly pertinent in our particular time and place. The displacement (and subsequent exile) is a credible way to characterize

Western culture, given the collapse of traditional certitudes and the demise of a covenantal social infrastructure (see Walter Brueggemann, *Cadences of Home: Preaching Among Exiles*). Western culture now faces a displacement that may indeed be expressed as an exile (see Frederick Buechner, *The Longing for Home: Recollections and Reflections*). And like the book of Isaiah, serious people are now disputatiously engaged in a struggle for the shape of the future, the outcome of whose struggles we are not able to see. One cannot, in reading Isaiah, disregard the concrete particularity of the text and simply *read past* that concreteness. But one can *read through* the concrete particularity into our own time and place, for it turns out that our time and place is much like that time and place. Believing people (Jews and Christians), moreover, dare to imagine that the same Holy One who acted in that time and place in disruptive and embracing ways still continues to disrupt and embrace even now. Thus the relevance of the text is evident. It cannot be arrived at too easily, but it is an insistent relevance that cannot be put off for too long either.

4. In the end, the book of Isaiah has continuing power among us, not because of historical critical judgments or because of canonical discernments, but because of the theological *stuff* of the text, given as image, theme, and phrase. This text tradition that insists upon the centrality of *the Holy One* is a *gospel* (40:9; 41:27; 52:7; 61:1). It is news about what God has decided, decreed, and is doing that makes a decisive difference in the world. It is a summons to *faith* (7:9; 30:15) that insists that Yahweh be relied upon in every circumstance of life. The *gospel* to be received in *faith* is an offer of *comfort* (40:1; 49:13; 51:3; 52:98; 61:2; 66:13) in the midst of every crisis. Such claims are endlessly problematic in a time and place such as ours, where the credibility of such gospel claims is difficult. I hazard that such claims are no more problematic now than they were when first asserted. But such a problematic does not deter the voice of the text and its claims. When circumstance is taken too seriously, either in self-confidence or in despair, the text keeps ringing in our doubting ears:

> For my thoughts are not your thoughts,
>   nor are your ways my ways, says the LORD.
> For as the heavens are higher than the earth,
>   so are my ways higher than your ways
>   and my thoughts than your thoughts.
>
> (55:8–9)

7. The God of All Comfort
Isaiah 40—55

As we finish chapter 39, we are permitted, by the shape of the book of Isaiah, to look into the defining abyss of the life and faith of Judah. In 39:1 we have been brought face-to-face with Babylon, a force that will dominate the book of Isaiah in the coming section (see also 13:1–14:23; 21:1–10). The prophet, moreover, anticipates that Jerusalem "shall be carried to Babylon, . . . shall be taken away; . . . shall be eunuchs in the palace of the king of Babylon" (39:6–7). Chapter 39 thus ends on an ominous note. The prophet looks to historical devastation deeply rooted in theological distortion.

The Long Pause

And then there is a pause—a long pause. The reader of the book of Isaiah must endure a very long pause before taking up chapter 40, for the space between 39:8 and 40:1 signifies the defining interruption in the life and faith of Israel as it is construed in the book of Isaiah. Chapter 39 is ostensibly enacted some time after 700 B.C.E., and chapter 40, according to common judgment, is voiced about 540 B.C.E. The gap between 39:8 and 40:1, reckoned in chronological time, is thus about 160 years, a long pause indeed. During that gap much happens: the collapse of Assyria, the rise of Babylon as the new superpower, the death of the good king Josiah, and the near-anarchy brought about by his royal sons. Most important, however, is the massive destruction of the entire Jerusalem establishment—city, dynasty, temple—and the complete infrastructure of that social and theological entity. What remains after the Babylonian incursion of 598 and the Babylonian devastation of 587 is a city in ruins, plus a scattering of Jews deported here and there. Among those deportees is the most influential concentration of displaced Jews in Babylon, Jews who sat "by the rivers of Babylon . . . and wept" (Psalm 137:1), Jews who are urged to "seek the welfare of the city where I have sent you" (Jer. 29:7). The move from *establishment* to *exilic displacement* is the story line that concerns the book of Isaiah.

The Rise and Fall of Superpowers

The internal history of Judah is matched by and impinged upon by the rise and fall of superpowers. During the seventh century B.C.E., the Assyrian Empire, the great vexation of Judah in the eighth century B.C.E. and in the early part of the book of Isaiah, disintegrated, and its capital city, Nineveh, was leveled (see Nahum). In the vacuum left by Assyrian demise, Babylon, the new dominant power in the Fertile Crescent, is led by Nabopolassar and then by his formidable and more famous son, Nebuchadrezzar. It is Nebuchadrezzar who enacts the devastation of Jerusalem in 587. Babylon, however, is in fact a brief blip on the geopolitical screen, for by 550, a new power begins to emerge to the east of Babylon—the kingdom of Persia, first led by Cyrus. (This Persia is to become the dominant power of the "known world" until the rise of the Greeks under Alexander the Great.) Thus Isaiah 39, soon after 700 B.C.E., anticipates the coming of Babylon, but chapter 40, on its heels, is able to speak of the demise of Babylon some decades later.

The geopolitical gap between chapters 39 and 40 is decisive for Judah's subsequent self-understanding; it is a self-understanding that makes exile a governing metaphor for all subsequent Judaism. But the sense of *theological* displacement and anticipation more fully concerns the book of Isaiah (and therefore us) than does the geopolitical component of the crisis. Speaking *theologically*, the book of Isaiah understands the coming of devastating, deporting Babylon as Yahweh's judgment upon the wayward city of Jerusalem and the failed public faith of Judah. The upshot of Isaiah 1—39, voiced in 39:6–7, is that Yahweh wills the destruction of the failed city and terminates the "most favored nation" status of Judah. Were the book of Isaiah to end there, the episode of Israel with Yahweh would be finished. But of course, if we wait long enough, chapter 40 will follow chapter 39. (That is known in Judah only later, not at the time of the destruction of 587.) In 40:1, the God of Israel once again speaks, after the long silence of disaster. The speaking of Yahweh now is in a quite changed tone. Now speaks the God of all comfort: "Comfort, O comfort my people" (40:1).

The burden of Isaiah 40—55 is that Yahweh is now to come powerfully among and in behalf of exilic Judah. Yahweh (in the form of Persian armies) will defeat Babylon, which defeat in turn will permit Judah, that part of Judah lodged in Babylon, to return in freedom and joy to beloved, unforgotten Zion. Happily, the theological anticipation of the poet is matched and enacted by the imperial policies of Persia that authorize and finance a return for those deported to Babylon. Thus Isaiah 40—55 is a counterpoint to Isaiah 1—39, good news of deliverance to resolve the unresolved bad news of judgment. The *literary arrangement* of 1—39 and 40—55 matches the *historical crisis* of expulsion and return that in turn is construed as a *theological verdict* of judgment and grace. The convergence of literary arrangement, historical crisis, and theological verdict makes the "final form" of the book of Isaiah, in its two contrasting, historically rooted parts, a most formidable scriptural testimony about this God who acts in and governs public history.

Consensus among Scholars

This way of interpreting the book of Isaiah represents a near consensus among critical scholars. Although the theological richness of such a view is enormous, it is important to understand the critical judgments that support and permit such a theological interpretation. Critical scholarship in general shares the judgment that whereas much of chapters 1—39 is connected to an eighth-century context (and personality), chapters 40—55 are indeed a piece of literature from a much later context (sixth century) that reflects the crisis and faith of that later time. The grounds for such a later dating are conventionally three:

1. In this material, we find very different *historical references*. The earlier chapters referred primarily to Assyria and the Judean kings, Ahaz and Hezekiah; here the references are to Babylon (43:14; 47:1; 48:14–20), the gods of Babylon (46:1), and the coming of Cyrus (44:28; 45:1). The text clearly has a different historical horizon.

2. The changed historical references correspond to a drastic change in *literary, rhetorical matters*. Whereas the older prophetic materials are concerned with woes and threats against Judah, here the rhetoric gives assurances (salvation oracles) and is primarily in dispute with competing gods and not with Judah. The agenda of this poetry is different and differently expressed.

3. Not surprisingly, the changed historical and rhetorical aspects of the book also yield a changed *theological message*, one now primarily (though not exclusively) positive, on a large screen asserting Yahweh's power as creator of heaven and earth. These elements together seem to make secure the interpretive judgment that this material is indeed later than chapters

1—39 and is concerned with a different theological crisis and a different historical possibility.

The Story Line of Chapters 40—55

The primary story line of these chapters is not very complex, even if it is developed with great rhetorical richness and imagination. The dramatic depiction of Judah's life in exile, according to this poetry, is concerned primarily with three characters: (1) *Babylon*, whether in the form of Babylonian rulers or Babylonian gods, is the oppressor agent who has deported and captured Judah; (2) *Judah*, whether the reference is to the community of Israelites or Zion the city presented as being in exile, is the helpless victim of Babylon; (3) The unequal and exploitative relation between Babylon and Judah is beyond challenge until the arrival of a third party into the crisis, namely, *Yahweh, the God of Israel.* It is this Yahweh who decrees emancipation for Judah, who offers assurances of solidarity with Judah, and who intervenes powerfully to assure the ineffectiveness of Babylon and the resultant well-being of Judah. The poetry revolves around the contest between Yahweh and Babylon, and the passionate bid for Judah to trust Yahweh rather than Babylon.

The Poetic Announcement of Yahweh's Power

The core claim of this poetry is that Yahweh has defeated the power of Babylon and now permits Judah to leave Babylon for its joyous, triumphant return home. This single assertion, that Yahweh has defeated Babylon and Judah is free to depart exile, is the primary theme of all of Isaiah 40—55. Indeed, the poet in the sixth century has a primal term for this announcement of victory for Yahweh, defeat for Babylon, and emancipation for Judah. The term is *gospel* (*baśar*). *The news is that Yahweh has won, Babylon has lost, Judah is free:*

> Get you up to a high mountain,
>> O Zion, herald of good tidings (*baśar*);
> lift up your voice with strength,
>> O Jerusalem, herald of good tidings (*baśar*) (40:9).

> I have first declared it to Zion,
>> and I gave to Jerusalem a herald of good tidings (*baśar*) (41:27).

> How beautiful upon the mountains

are the feet of the messenger (*baśar*) who announces peace,
who brings good news (*baśar*),
   who announces salvation,
   who says to Zion, "Your God reigns."

(52:7; cf. 60:6; 61:1)

It is this exilic Isaiah who makes the term *gospel* a theological usage, with news of the new governance of Yahweh (see a New Testament rendering in Mark 1:1, 15).

We should notice that the *announcement* of the gospel is a lyrical, poetic, imaginative one, likely enacted in a context of worship. But the actual *substance of the news*, the victory and the defeat, is an "event" to which exiles have no access. No one knows how or when or where it happened. It is *announced*, and Judah is here expected to trust the substance on the basis of the announcement. This usage of "gospel" to assert *a theological turn in the fortunes of the world* is a remarkable theological and rhetorical venture of this poet, an achievement that produces the taproot of the notion of *evangel*, so that release for captives who are held by exploitative powers has become the basis for what has belatedly come to be known as "evangelism" (see Walter Brueggemann, *Biblical Perspectives on Evangelism: Living in a Three-Storied Universe*).

Canonical Relatedness
of Chapters 1—39 and 40—55

The critical judgment, then, is that chapters 1—39 and 40—55 constitute quite distinct literatures in quite different modes from quite different contexts. That critical judgment is widely held. More recently, however, attention has been given to *canonical arrangement* concerning the relation of these two literatures. The emerging opinion of interpreters is that although chapters 1—39 and 40—55 seek to do very different things, they are intentionally and authoritatively placed together to make a single, bi-focal theological affirmation, and neither section of the book can be taken alone. That bi-focal theological affirmation specifically concerns the Jewish truth of *exile and homecoming* and, more broadly, *the judgment and deliverance of God*. Or in Christian cadence, this bi-focal presentation of reality, as the story of Israel is replicated in the story of Jesus, becomes an account of *crucifixion and resurrection*. Thus an interpreter must deal in turn with the *critical distinction* of chapters 1—39 and 40—55 and the *canonical relatedness* of the two.

The Servant of the Lord

Although the primary faith line of chapters 40—55 is clear enough, special notice may be made of one particular problem, "the servant of the Lord." For a century, scholars have suggested that the "servant songs" of 42:1–9; 49:1–7; 50:4–9; and 52:13–53:12 are a quite distinct literary grouping, referring to a special character identified as "the servant of the Lord." More recently, some scholars have concluded that this literature does not form a distinct part of Isaiah; rather, each text needs to be taken in its own immediate literary context.

The literary problems in these texts are acute. However they may be resolved, the reader of these texts is still left with the deep problem of the figure of the servant. The evidence of the text itself is not straightforward but offers various suggestions. Thus the servant appears to *be Israel*, but also to have a mission *to Israel*. The question is further complicated, moreover, by the long-standing Christian propensity to assume that this enigmatic figure is an anticipation of Jesus, who emerges as "servant."

Scholarship is not able to come to a shared conclusion about the identity of the servant nor about the role of the servant in this poetry. We can here only mark the problem. It may be enough to suggest that the servant songs provide an important and sobering qualification to the simple good-news proclamation of emancipation. "The servant" may function here to assert (a) that emancipation is linked to willing sufferers who suffer for the sake of the community and (b) that emancipation is perhaps for a larger purpose than simply the gift of homecoming—perhaps an invitation to mission that concerns the well-being of the world beyond Judaism.

With particular reference to the fourth and most crucial and most difficult of these poems, 52:13–53:12, I have taken a rather conventional theological reading, though I have not pressed a christological equation. It is important to recognize that there is a significant scholarly line of argument that concludes that this poem will not bear the theological freight familiarly assigned to it, and that its theological claims are rather minimal. A powerful representative of this reading is R. N. Whybray's *Thanksgiving for a Liberated Prophet: An Interpretation of Isaiah Chapter 53*. At the most, one must admit uncertainty about many of the vexing, critical questions related to the poem, as urged by David J. A. Clines in *I, He, We, and They: A Literary Approach to Isaiah 53*. One must in any case recognize a certain dis-ease about making a *maximal theological interpretation* (a large Christian inclination) on what are at best *unstable critical grounds*. I call the attention of the reader to this dis-ease that is reflected, to some extent, in my own comments on the text.

Conclusions

Chapters 40—55 are rich with theological resource. The lyrical quality of the text itself, plus the familiar renderings of Handel's *Messiah*, make this poetry almost a generic resource for faith, notably in ways presented by Christian theology and liturgy.

If, however, we are to take the text seriously as a contemporary theological resource, we must do more than enjoy its generic "evangelical" buoyancy. I do not think the text can be simply reapplied directly to our time and place. Nonetheless, I suggest an avenue of interpretation. If we take the triad of *Yahweh-Babylon-Judah* as the players in this dramatic enterprise and seek contemporaneity, it is easy enough to continue to acknowledge the identity of Yahweh, the same God who rules in judgment and deliverance. In parallel fashion, it is obvious enough to take Judah as the contemporary community of faith, surely the synagogue and by derivation the church. But it is with the third player, Babylon, that we are summoned to more disciplined reflection for an equivalence that is not obvious.

The term *Babylon* has become a code word for any rapacious social system. It is used in the book of Revelation to refer to imperial Rome and its demanding emperor worship (Revelation 18). Martin Luther used the term to refer to what he saw as the oppressive sacramental system of the Roman Church. In our time and place, as a believing community in the United States (or anywhere in the West), I suggest a powerful—though not precise—equivalence of Babylon in the ideology of *free-market consumerism* and its required ally, *unbridled militarism.* I refer not to particular players, parties, or leaders, but to the unexamined, dominant ideology that encompasses everyone, liberal and conservative, and that sets the limits of what is possible and what is good, what is to be feared and what is to be trusted.

There is no doubt that this powerful ideology is such that it robs the human community of its humanness and reduces all of life to commodity. The gospel question in our time, as it was for those ancient exiles, is whether there is or can be life outside the ideology and whether there is a good-news offer of such an option. The announcement of life emancipated from the endless demands of this ideology is indeed gospel news that the ultimate claims of the ideology are not credible and have been nullified. It is not easy to speak or hear or trust such a gospel, because the ideology is seemingly all pervasive. But it was not easy when this gospel of life beyond rapacious ideology was uttered in that ancient sixth century.

Perhaps that is why (a) the announcement is provisionally disputatious and (b) the figure of a suffering servant is, in the end, necessary to the credibility of the gospel. So it was then. So it is now—still a quite unattractive suffering, but one still needed. Only such suffering confirms the gospel news. We keep refusing the claim that we are healed by someone willing to accept the bruises (see 53:5). But we see it was so for the ancient Jews. We see it was so in the life and death of Jesus. And we dare face the staggering chance that it may continue to be so even to our time and place. It is this ancient yet contemporary text that insists that needed bruising is a present, inescapable reality. The text gives "comfort" from the God of all comfort, but not easily and not obviously—perhaps only hiddenly (see 45:15).

THE INDOMITABLE VOICE OF COMFORT
40:1–11

In 39:5–7, the prophet sounded an oracle to King Hezekiah anticipating Judah's exile into Babylon, which in due course occurred. As the book of Isaiah is arranged, there is a long silence after that oracle, a silence that lasts over 150 years. During that painful, God-muted time, a great deal happened to Judah. There was the theologically disastrous reign of Manasseh and the reformative rule of Josiah (2 Kings 21:1–23:28). There was the emergence of Babylon as a superpower and the inexplicable death of the good king Josiah (2 Kings 23:29–30). Most of all, there was the destruction of Jerusalem, the razing of the city and the burning of the temple, the termination of the dynasty, and the deportation to Babylon (2 Kings 24:20–25:30). There was a long period of dislocation, during which the exiles voiced their grief and dismay:

> She weeps bitterly in the night,
>   with tears on her cheeks;
> among all her lovers
>   she has *no one to comfort* her.

> [H]er downfall was appalling,
>   with *none to comfort* her.

> Zion stretches out her hands,
>   but there is *no one to comfort* her.

They heard how I was groaning,
with *no one to comfort me.*
(Lam. 1:2, 9, 17, 21)

Judah groaned and cried out, as if to an empty sky. There was "none to comfort," no protector, no one to intervene, no one powerful enough to make a positive difference. For too long Judah in dislocation experienced its life forlorn and bereft of possibility. After 39:5–7, the book of Isaiah requires a long, hopeless wait—until the utterance of chapter 40.

In chapter 40, at long last when all seemed lost, now speaks the Holy One of Israel. This oracle is the voice of Yahweh, who breaks the silence of exile and by utterance transforms the fortunes of Judah. This speech breaks both the despair of Judah and the power of Babylon; it penetrates the emptiness of exile and fills the world of Judaism with possibilities heretofore unanticipated but now available in divine decree.

40:1 **Comfort, O comfort my people,**
       says your God.
  2 **Speak tenderly to Jerusalem,**
       and cry to her
     that she has served her term,
       that her penalty is paid,
     that she has received from the LORD's hand
       double for all her sins.

God speaks an imperative in the midst of the long silence of exile. As is recognized from the familiar words of Handel's *Messiah*, God's utterance is a plural imperative—"comfort ye," that is, "you (plural) comfort." God decrees *comfort* where there had been "none to comfort." We may understand "comfort" as transformative solidarity; that is, not simply an offer of solace, but a powerful intervention that creates new possibilities. Here speaks the God of all comfort, later echoed in Paul's lyrical doxology:

> Blessed be the God and Father of our Lord Jesus Christ, the Father of mercies and the God of all consolation, who consoles us in all our affliction, so that we may be able to console those who are in any affliction with the consolation with which we ourselves are consoled by God (2 Cor. 1:3–4).

It is widely accepted by scholars that the plural of address is spoken to members of the "divine council," the government of Yahweh in heaven that is peopled by angels and messengers. In order to understand this poetic, lyrical vision, it is necessary to conjure a scene of governmental functionaries in attendance on Yahweh, who presides over the government. Whereas in some scenes, that government entourage may engage in probing, informal discussion (as in 1 Kings 22:19–22), here there is no uncertainty, nothing to discuss. Here a decision is made. The head of the government speaks. Policy is determined and needs only to be implemented. The policy is *comfort* for "my people." This is the decisive utterance in the entire book of Isaiah whereby Yahweh's propensity toward punished, exiled Jerusalem is now completely positive.

But we may be more precise about the vision of a heavenly government. It is frequently suggested that the vision of 40:1–11 is deliberately a counterpoint to 6:1–13 in the structure of the book of Isaiah. Chapter 6 is the pivotal authorization for a message of judgment that intends Judah to be obdurate and therefore hopeless. Conversely, this vision is a "second verdict" from God, wherein God now moves to reverse the fortunes of Israel. As 6:1–13 authorizes the *theme of judgment* in chapters 1—39, so 40:1–11 now authorizes the *theme of deliverance* for the remainder of the book.

The rhetorical strategy of the tradition of Isaiah is to ground the future possibility of Judaism in the government of heaven—what Paul Hanson calls "the nerve center of the universe" (*Isaiah 40–66*, 18). That decision then is beyond the despairing weariness of Judah and does not depend upon Judah's resolve. Conversely, the decision is also beyond the arrogant self-aggrandizement of Babylon and does not depend upon imperial cooperation. It is a decision made solely by Yahweh. The depth of resolve that makes the future certain is not unlike the confidence of an earlier utterance in Isaiah concerning another superpower:

> For the LORD of hosts has planned,
> 　　and who will annul it?
> His hand is stretched out,
> 　　and who will turn it back?
> 　　　　　　　　　　(14:27)

Yahweh has planned *comfort* for the exiles, and none can prevent it.

In two verbs, "speak, cry," the members of the government of Yahweh are here instructed to give comfort to Jerusalem. The substance of the world-changing policy is in a threefold statement in verse 2:

> Surely its sentence is full;
> surely its penalty is paid;
> surely it has suffered double.

Jerusalem has suffered enough to satisfy its affront to Yahweh. In the retributive system predominant in Israel, exile is understood as punishment for defiance of Yahweh. That is what the earlier prophets long threatened. Now, says the new decree of the government of God: Enough! Enough sentence, enough penalty, enough payment, enough exile, enough displacement! This is an assertion of forgiveness, but it is not cheap or soft or easy forgiveness. There is, in any case, a limit to the sentence. It can be satisfied and served out. And now it is ended!

40:3 **A voice cries out:**
   "In the wilderness prepare the way of the LORD,
     make straight in the desert a highway for our God.
  ⁴Every valley shall be lifted up,
     and every mountain and hill be made low;
  the uneven ground shall become level,
     and the rough places a plain.
  ⁵Then the glory of the LORD shall be revealed,
     and all people shall see it together,
     and the mouth of the LORD has spoken."

  ⁶A voice says, "Cry out!"
    And I said, "What shall I cry?"
  All people are grass,
    their constancy is like the flower of the field.
  ⁷The grass withers, the flower fades,
    when the breath of the LORD blows upon it;
    surely the people are grass.
  ⁸The grass withers, the flower fades;
    but the word of our God will stand forever.

These verses appear to be a discussion among the members of Yahweh's heavenly government about how best to implement the new decree of *comfort*. First a voice speaks, authorizing a superhighway across the desert between Babylon and Jerusalem for an easy, triumphant, dazzling return home (vv. 3–5). We have already seen in 35:8–10 the image of a highway, a construction project to make the return home dramatic, easy, and speedy. Indeed, highways were built in that ancient world primarily for processional events, when ruler and gods could parade in victory. Now, it is Yahweh and Israel who will parade in victory. Thus the *forgiveness* (vv. 1–2) issues in *homecoming*, a persistent theme in chapters 40—55. Judah can now return home because Yahweh overrides the will of Babylon to keep exiles; Babylon's will for exiles is no match for Yahweh's resolve for homecoming. That homecoming, moreover, will be quite public; onlookers will see the exiles go by and will be able to see that it is Yahweh who makes this joyous return possible. The *return of Judah* amounts to *an exaltation of Yahweh*, who exhibits power and fidelity through the act. Yahweh has "gotten glory" over Egypt in the past (Exod. 14:4, 17); now Yahweh will "get glory" over Babylon.

The image of a highway for return becomes a powerful metaphor for the Christian gospel. In all four Gospel accounts (Matt. 3:3; Mark 1:2–3; Luke 3:4–6; John 1:23), John the Baptist reiterates this image from Isaiah, so that the ministry of Jesus is presented as good news for dislocated people in the ancient world. The ministry of Jesus is a glad and public homecoming for all those alienated and dislocated.

The theme of homecoming, decisive in Isaiah's gospel and prominent in the story of Jesus, is uncommonly pertinent in our current social setting where many sense themselves dislocated as our familiar world vanishes. Commenting on the theme, Frederick Buechner asserts: "No matter how much the world shatters us to pieces, we carry inside us a *vision* of wholeness that we sense is our true home and that beckons us" (*The Longing for Home*, 110). Although Buechner moves well beyond the witness of our text, there is no doubt that the poetry of Isaiah is an enactment among exiles of a vision of wholeness. That wholeness for them meant freedom, peaceableness, and at-homeness in Jerusalem.

But then a second voice speaks, presumably another member of the heavenly government. It speaks an imperative, "Cry out." We do not know to whom the imperative is addressed, except that the "I" of verse 6 answers, "I said." Scholars believe the "I" is the prophet (Second Isaiah, Isaiah in exile, the one who speaks these chapters to the exiles) who is charged with making the new decision from the government of God available on the earth among the displaced Jews. If this identification of the "I" is accepted, then this text is not unlike chapter 6, wherein the prophet of the eighth century is authorized to speak for the government of God. What we have here, scholars suggest, is a "call narrative" paralleling Isaiah 6, a rhetorical strategy for *human utterance* of *divine decree*.

In Isaiah 6:5, the prophet protests the summons of the government of Yahweh by asserting his own ineligibility as "unclean." Here, in parallel, the prophet protests the call by asserting that the "people is grass," that is, transitory, ephemeral, unreliable (vv. 6–7). The rhetoric suggests that the gospel assurance of comfort will be wasted on such a subject; therefore, the utterance of the new decision is not worth performing.

The resistance of the prophet, however, is countered in verse 8 as it is in 6:6–7. Although there is no signal that a new voice speaks in verse 8, it is most likely the case. The speaker in verse 8 is perhaps the one who issued the imperative of verse 6. This insistent speaker acknowledges the point: Yes, the people is grass. But then this speaker refutes the conclusion just drawn from the assessment of transitoriness: "But!" "But the word of our God stands forever." The offer of comfort is not based on the suitability or qualification of the people but upon the resolve of God. The good news of life beginning again for the exiles is rooted solely in Yahweh's decision already given in verses 1–2. The prophet no longer has any ground for refusing the message or its delivery.

> 40:9 **Get you up to a high mountain,**
> **O Zion, herald of good tidings;**
> **lift up your voice with strength,**
> **O Jerusalem, herald of good tidings,**
> **lift it up, do not fear;**
> **say to the cities of Judah,**
> **"Here is your God!"**
> 10 **See, the Lord GOD comes with might,**
> **and his arm rules for him,**
> **his reward is with him,**
> **and his recompense before him.**
> 11 **He will feed his flock like a shepherd;**
> **he will gather the lambs in his arms,**
> **and carry them in his bosom,**
> **and gently lead the mother sheep.**

The same voice as in verse 6a and verse 8 speaks now a more extended message. There is a sequence of imperatives, so that the urgency of the Lord of the divine council is now reflected in the speech from a member of the council: "get up, lift, lift, do not fear, say." These five imperatives echo the lead imperative of verse 6: "Cry out!" "Proclaim." The one addressed, now presumably the prophet who was present in the governmental debate in heaven, is twice addressed as "herald of good tidings." The substance of this address is so crucial because this is the first intentional, self-conscious use of the term *gospel* in the Old Testament. The prophet-herald is to announce "gospel" to the cities of Judah. The "good news" is summarized: "Behold your God." Or we might say, "Look, here is your God." The gospel makes the God of Israel visible and effective in a setting from which Yahweh had seemed to be expelled. Certainly the Babylonians, in their arrogance, construed a world without Yahweh. Equally certain, the exiles in their despair

construed a world without Yahweh. Now both imperial arrogance and exilic despair are countered. Yahweh is present, powerful, active; Yahweh's
presence changes everything. Calvin says of this gospel assertion:

> This expression includes the sum of our happiness, which consists solely in
> the presence of God. It brings along with it an abundance of all blessings;
> and if we are destitute of it, we must be utterly miserable and wretched; and
> although blessings of every kind are richly enjoyed by us, yet if we are es-
> tranged from God, everything must tend to our destruction.

We are able to see why this gospel pronouncement is so prominent in the
utterance of John the Baptist, for John wants to assert that God is decisively present and at work in Jesus, in order to counter both the arrogance
and the despair that shapes a world without Yahweh.

The mandated message of verse 9—which we take to be a summation
of the good news—is explicated in verses 10–11. Verse 10 asserts Yahweh
as a massive, conquering warrior who is seen to be an enactment of resolved power. This is an exhibit of the majesty of Yahweh. But verse 11,
by contrast, portrays Yahweh as a gentle shepherd who exercises maternal
care for those who are vulnerable. This is an exhibition of the mercy of
Yahweh. The two verses together, with the twin images of warrior and
shepherd and the twin accents of majesty and mercy, bespeak all that is
crucial about the good news. Yahweh is strong enough to emancipate, gentle enough to attend to wants and needs. The same juxtaposition of themes
is already given in the first entry into the land:

> The LORD your God, who goes before you, is the one who will fight for you,
> just as he did for you in Egypt before your very eyes, and in the wilderness,
> where you saw how the LORD your God carried you, just as one carries a
> child (Deut. 1:30–31).

Now the exiles make a second entry into the land, again assured of the
majesty of the warrior, the mercy of the shepherd.

The cruciality of this opening poem for the book of Isaiah cannot be
overestimated. It is the decisive decree from Yahweh's own mouth, implemented through Yahweh's own government, uttered in Israel by Yahweh's
own prophet. By the decree, the life of Judah is decisively altered for good.
But that of course is the way of Yahweh's gospel. The good news asserts
that the world is changed by God. It is no longer the way we have long
taken it to be, ordered by an arrogance that required despair. The decree
is, to be sure, only a word; but it is a word enormously durable. On this

word rests the future of the Jews. Writ larger, on this word rests the future of the world, for it is an exile-ending word.

IT IS YAHWEH—INCOMPARABLE!
40:12–31

The initial gospel announcement of 40:9–11 exhibits Yahweh as strong enough to counter Babylonian claims and able enough to override the submissive despair of Jews in Babylon. The core announcement is "See, your God!" (v. 9). In verses 12–31, this God so abruptly voiced is now shown to be stronger than Babylon and attentive to the exiles. On both counts of strength and attentiveness, it is asserted that Yahweh is incomparable. There is no one or no thing to which Yahweh can be compared. Yahweh is without rival or partner or associate or analogue. Yahweh defies all conventional interpretive categories precisely because Yahweh is the original creative agent in the life of the world; it is Yahweh who governs the affairs of the nations and guards the well-being of Israel.

Yahweh without Parallel (40:12–17)

40:12 **Who has measured the waters in the hollow of his hand**
          and marked off the heavens with a span,
      enclosed the dust of the earth in a measure,
          and weighed the mountains in scales
          and the hills in a balance?
    [13] **Who has directed the spirit of the LORD,**
          or as his counselor has instructed him?
    [14] **Whom did he consult for his enlightenment,**
          and who taught him the path of justice?
      Who taught him knowledge,
          and showed him the way of understanding?
    [15] **Even the nations are like a drop from a bucket,**
          and are accounted as dust on the scales;
          see, he takes up the isles like fine dust.
    [16] **Lebanon would not provide fuel enough,**
          nor are its animals enough for a burnt offering.
    [17] **All the nations are as nothing before him;**
          they are accounted by him as less than nothing and emptiness.

These verses, as doxology and as polemic, assert Yahweh to be the one worthy of praise and trust. The first part of the unit consists of a series of rhetorical questions designed to enhance Yahweh in the eyes of Israel (vv. 12–14). The first of these questions concerns the capacity of a creator God to be (1) so massive as to hold the oceans of the earth in the palm of a hand and to measure the heavens as a seamstress might measure cloth from nose to outstretched hand, and (2) so sovereign as to weigh the mountains and hills in a scale as a pharmacist weighs herbs (v. 12). The appeal is to the largeness and wonder of creation, all of which is small when seen in relation to Yahweh. The answer to the rhetorical question is, *Only Yahweh* could do all this. The questions are not unlike the great doxological "putdowns" of Job in Job 38.

The second question implies that *no one* can advise Yahweh (v. 13), and the third question implies that *no one* consulted or taught Yahweh. Thus, although the questions enhance Yahweh, they also dismiss the claims of all other gods. The dismissal in context is not generic but concerns the gods of Babylon who had too long impressed and intimidated the exiles. The subtext is that there is no ground for being intimated by the Babylonian gods.

The second part of the unit turns from *dismissed gods* to the *minimization of the nations* (vv. 15–17). These verses begin (v. 15) and end (v. 17) with reference to all the nations; in between Lebanon, known for its forests, is cited as a case in point (v. 16). All the nations and any of the nations are as nothing. They are small and trivial and unimportant. James Muilenburg notes: "The nations are no threat; they have no power of their own; their pretensions have no weight with God." Moreover, if verses 12–14 have dismissed Babylonian gods, then these verses in parallel fashion dismiss the reality of Babylonian politics. If taken alone, the empire of Babylon might be formidable. Seen in the purview of Yahweh, however, Babylon is emptiness (*tôhû*, v. 17), not in any way important or substantive.

Like Gods, Like Nations (40:18–24)

40:18 **To whom then will you liken God,**
      or what likeness compare with him?
   19 **An idol? —A workman casts it,**
      and a goldsmith overlays it with gold,
      and casts for it silver chains.
   20 **As a gift one chooses mulberry wood**
      —wood that will not rot—
    then seeks out a skilled artisan
      to set up an image that will not topple.

²¹ Have you not known? Have you not heard?
    Has it not been told you from the beginning?
    Have you not understood from the foundations of the earth?
²² It is he who sits above the circle of the earth,
    and its inhabitants are like grasshoppers;
  who stretches out the heavens like a curtain,
    and spreads them like a tent to live in;
²³ who brings princes to naught,
    and makes the rulers of the earth as nothing.

²⁴ Scarcely are they planted, scarcely sown,
    scarcely has their stem taken root in the earth,
  when he blows upon them, and they wither,
    and the tempest carries them off like stubble.

The twin accents of a doxology that enhances Yahweh and a polemic that dismisses alternatives are reiterated. The question of comparability is raised in verse 18. The poet theoretically invites nominations for comparable gods. But then, perhaps without waiting, the poet offers the nomination that must have been on everyone's horizon. The listeners might have nominated Marduk or one of the other Babylonian gods who have seemed quite formidable. But before such a nomination can be made as a credible alternative to Yahweh, the poet preempts the chance by labeling the other gods—including the powerful gods of the empire—in debunking ways. The poet permits them no noble title or adjective, but labels them polemically "idol." The utterance intends to invite ridicule, a good laugh at the gods of the oppressor state. The theological passion of the poet is enormous. As a result, he perhaps deliberately misconstrues, for imperial religion surely assumed that its gods were imbued with real power. The success of the empire, moreover, seemed to indicate as much. In a rhetorical fight that is scarcely fair, however, the poet allows for nothing of imperial claims. In a recurring motif, rival gods are dismissed as "man made" and "man adorned," having no intrinsic power of their own.

The dismissal of the other gods is matched in verses 21–23 with a doxology toward Yahweh. The lyric begins with rhetorical questions, chiding the Israelites for not having recognized who Yahweh is (v. 21). Appeal is made, in parallel with the whirlwind speeches of Job, to Yahweh as creator. Yahweh is the ground of "the beginning, the foundations." Yahweh is the source of all that is in the world. Yahweh is the subject of the great verbs of creation: "who sits, who stretches, who spreads, who brings, who makes." Everything else is an object of Yahweh's verbs. When the verbs are positive, the object is a feature of creation. When the verbs are acts of negation, the object is nullified. Everything submits to Yahweh's power. In these verses, the move is from earth and its inhabitants and the heavens to princes and rulers. But whereas earth and heavens are established by the power of Yahweh, princes and rulers are negated. Indeed, they become "nothing" (*tôhû*), like the gods they serve (v. 23; cf. v. 17). The poet echoes the old song of mother Hannah:

> The LORD makes poor and makes rich;
>   he brings low, he also exalts.
> He raises up the poor from the dust;
>   he lifts the needy from the ash heap,
> to make them sit with princes
>   and inherit a seat of honor.
>   (1 Sam. 2:7–8)

And in like manner, the poet anticipates Paul: "God chose what is low and despised in the world, things that are not, to reduce to nothing things that are" (1 Cor. 1:28).

Verse 24 introduces a different metaphor, but the pronoun "they" in verse 24 has "princes and rulers" in verse 23 as its antecedent. Earthly governments are as fragile as newly planted growth. They are exceedingly vulnerable. When assaulted by Yahweh, one gust of Yahweh's hot air makes the nations wither. Yahweh's power is commensurate with the fragility and transitoriness of all else in the world. (Notice the same theme in 40:6–8.) The story line of this poetry is simple and rather one-dimensional, and the main argument is clear. What warrants more attention is the remarkable richness of articulation whereby the case is imaginatively made. The poet intends that listening exiles, upon hearing, should have the emotional experience of having their established "plausibility structures" diminished and nullified. There is no alternative source of life in the world except Yahweh. Any other reliance is foolishness that is sure to fail.

The Incomparable Creator (40:25–26)

40:25 To whom then will you compare me,
**   or who is my equal? says the Holy One.**
**   26 Lift up your eyes on high and see:**
**   Who created these?**
**   He who brings out their host and numbers them,**
**   calling them all by name;**

> because he is great in strength,
>   mighty in power,
>   not one is missing.

In something like a coda, the poet again raises the issue of Yahweh's incomparability (v. 25; see v. 18). The response to the question of incomparability, however, is here somewhat different. Whereas verses 19–20 answered the question of verse 18 by a dismissal of the idols, here the question of verse 15 is answered by the naming of the stars (the "host"). No one can deny that the stars are impressive, especially in a society where astronomy was advanced and astral worship was prominent. But, insists the poet, the stars are not rivals to Yahweh. Rather, they are witnesses to the power of Yahweh; it is Yahweh who created them, who numbers them to be sure they are in the right place, who calls them by name, and who keeps them all present, available, and functioning (see Psalm 143:3–4). No other god, no Babylonian god, no idol can make any comparable claim.

The Creator as the Tireless God of Israel (40:27–31)

40:27 **Why do you say, O Jacob,**
   and speak, O Israel,
 "My way is hidden from the LORD,
   and my right is disregarded by my God"?
 [28] **Have you not known? Have you not heard?**
 The LORD is the everlasting God,
   the Creator of the ends of the earth.
 He does not faint or grow weary;
   his understanding is unsearchable.
 [29] **He gives power to the faint,**
   and strengthens the powerless.
 [30] **Even youths will faint and be weary,**
   and the young will fall exhausted;
 [31] **but those who wait for the LORD shall renew their strength,**
   they shall mount up with wings like eagles,
 they shall run and not be weary,
   they shall walk and not faint.

The doxology and polemic of this chapter have thus far remained more or less general. Now, in these final verses, the argument becomes specific. For the first time in this extended doxological unit, the people of Judah are mentioned. The climax of this lyric concerns "Jacob, Israel." Creation faith comes down to the crisis of God's people in exile. The statement of verse 27 is a question. The poet apparently reiterates a complaint Judah voiced in exile, perhaps a complaint given stylized, liturgical expression. Thus the statement may echo something like Psalm 44:24: "Why do you hide your face?/Why do you forget our affliction and oppression?" The question of Israel, deep in crisis, awaits an answer from Yahweh; but the wait is long and the answer is not forthcoming. The dread complaint lingers in alienation between suffering Israel and silent Yahweh. The judgment of Israel against Yahweh implied in the complaint was not a remote conclusion for the exiles. They judged that Yahweh did not care or did not notice or was not able.

But the quotation of a complaint is only a launching pad for the gospel assertion that now follows. The poet, as we will subsequently see, delights to state a complaint in order to provide an overwhelming answer. The answer in verses 28–31 is introduced, as in verse 21, with questions that imply a reprimand for not understanding Yahweh better. Israel should have known!

The answer to the alleged complaint of Israel begins in sweeping monotheistic faith. Indeed, the poet of the exile provides the most extreme claim for the incomparability and singularity of Yahweh as creator. But Yahweh's work as creator is not a one-time deal. It is continuing work that entails Yahweh's endless, energetic attentiveness to creation. Yahweh is not worn out, not exhausted. Yahweh the creator God is directly attentive to the faint and powerless, to those who have no energy of their own. The creator God sustains and gives life to creatures who have no intrinsic power for life of their own. In context, of course, it is precisely the exiles who are resourceless, faint, and powerless. It is precisely for them that Yahweh is decisive.

The concluding verses state a drastic, Yahwistic either/or. *Either* folk will be faint, weary, and exhausted—indeed, even youths, even high-energy young people with seemingly inexhaustible supplies of energy! *Or* those who hope and wait and expect Yahweh will have strength to fly, to run, to walk—with no weariness or fainting (v. 31). Yahweh is the single variable—either weakness or Yahweh. There is no third alternative, no chance for strength apart from Yahweh—not from the gods who are nothing, not from the princes and rulers who are nothing, and certainly not from the exiles themselves.

Taken at face value, this long doxology is designed to enhance Yahweh. It is a piece of eloquent theology. But taken in context, its function is pastoral and political. Pastorally, it asserts that the seemingly abandoned

exiles are not alone but have available a source of energy and power. Po-
litically, the poetry is an invitation for exilic Jews to conjure their life Yahwistically, outside the bounds of Babylonian possibility. Indeed, the double
"nothing" of verses 17 and 23 intends precisely to debunk imperial gods
and imperial rules. Israel, in territory governed by Yahweh, may take up a
life of new possibility.

We need not be so enthralled by the eloquent poetry that we miss the
sharp bite of faith given here. In our own time, it is not very difficult to
identify as Babylon the global system of consumer capitalism that seems to
sweep all before it, so that it has the power through its relentless "liturgy"
(that is, advertising) to tell us what is possible. The struggle for women and
men of faith now, as always, is to be able to imagine our life out beyond *the
system* that seems totally comprehensive and encompassing. It is an act of
remarkable courage to utter such a doxological claim that always includes
a polemic against alternative claims.

It is also an act of boldness, then or now or any time, to engage in
reimagining and reconstruing life in terms of Yahweh, the creator who
brings to nought both the wonders of creation and the pretenders of politics. It is easy for people of faith to conclude that the creator God is an irrelevance in a contemporary system that seems to be set in stone.

The poet, however, will not permit such a verdict. The very God taken
to be obsolete is the one who governs and gives strength, who makes it possible for life to be taken up again without the force of empire. The claim
made by the poet is remarkable, against all the evidence of the empire. It
must have seemed outrageous then, as it does now. But there must have
been enough listening and treasuring to conclude that this One who speaks
can override the nothingness offered by imperial task masters. It is this incomparable, tireless God who is exhibited in the gospel assertion "See,
your God!" (40:9).

YAHWEH, POWERFUL AND MERCIFUL
41:1–29

The intent of Second Isaiah is to reconstrue the life and history and destiny of exilic Israel by placing Yahweh at the center of its existence and discernment. Babylonian ideology had eliminated Yahweh from the horizon
of Israel's historical possibility, and now the poet counters the effectiveness and persuasiveness of Babylonian propaganda. That is, the poet sets
forth the gospel claim "See, your God!" (40:9). The work of the poet is to

employ a heightened rhetoric in order to exhibit Yahweh in the most compelling ways possible so that Babylonian definitions of reality may be seen as fraudulent and unreliable.

In this long chapter, the poet uses two characteristic rhetorical strategies to exhibit Yahweh as the decisive actor in Israel's life. At the beginning and end of the chapter, the poet utters *a speech of disputation*, presenting the claims of Yahweh in conflict with the ideological claims of Babylon (vv. 1–7, 21–29). To do this, the poet imagines, and invites listeners to imagine with him, a courtroom trial in which different witnesses bring evidence about the identity of the true God. Powerful evidence is offered for Yahweh, whereas no compelling evidence is offered for Babylonian gods, leading to the (inevitable?) poetic verdict of the truth of Yahweh as the real God.

Between these two speeches of disputation, the second rhetorical strategy of this poetry is a series of *salvation oracles* that offer the assurance of Yahweh's caring, attentive presence in the midst of the exiles (vv. 8–13, 14–16, 17–20). This mode of speech, in contrast to the speeches of disputation, is completely focused on Israel's needs and the prospects made possible by Yahweh's promise and intention; it completely ignores the other nations and the other gods who are the subject of the speeches of disputation.

These twin modes of *speech of disputation* and *oracle of salvation* are quite distinct and move in opposite directions. But they need to be seen in relation to each other, for together they permit the exilic community to "see Yahweh" (40:9), who makes a decisive difference in its life. The speech of disputation concerns the external world of the empire that threatens exilic Israel, whereas the oracle of salvation focuses upon the internal life of Israel with Yahweh. The speech of disputation asserts the massive power of Yahweh, power sufficient to override the rival claims of the empire, whereas the oracle of salvation exhibits the pastoral attentiveness and care of Yahweh toward needy Israel. Taken together, the two rhetorical practices situate the majesty and mercy of Yahweh in the midst of exilic Israel, making it possible for Israel to reconstrue its own life outside the defining and crushing claims of Babylon.

Yahweh First and Last (41:1–7)

41:1 **Listen to me in silence, O coastlands;**
      let the peoples renew their strength;
    let them approach, then let them speak;
      let us together draw near for judgment.

2 Who has roused a victor from the east,
  summoned him to his service?
He delivers up nations to him,
  and tramples kings under foot;
he makes them like dust with his sword,
  like driven stubble with his bow.
3 He pursues them and passes on safely,
  scarcely touching the path with his feet.
4 Who has performed and done this,
  calling the generations from the beginning?
I, the LORD, am first,
  and will be with the last.
5 The coastlands have seen and are afraid,
  the ends of the earth tremble;
  they have drawn near and come.
6 Each one helps the other,
  saying to one another, "Take courage!"
7 The artisan encourages the goldsmith,
  and the one who smooths with the hammer encourages the one who
    strikes the anvil,
saying of the soldering, "It is good";
  and they fasten it with nails so that it cannot be moved.

This speech of disputation conducts an imagined courtroom trial in which listening exilic Israel observes while the claims of rival gods are adjudicated. The speech begins with a summons to court (vv. 1–2), not unlike the opening summons of 1:2–3. However, in 1:2–3 the issue of the court is between Yahweh and Israel, whereas here it is between Yahweh and the nations with their gods. This summons is not unlike a court summons requiring one to appear in court, or even the cry of the bailiff, "Hear ye, hear ye." The most freighted term in the summons is "judgment"; that is, the resolve to render a "right verdict," to make a decision about the truth of rival claims of sovereignty. Although the rhetoric is imaginative and dramatic, it surely touches a genuine concern of disappointed Israel: "Is our God really reliable in such a circumstance as exile?"

First in this presentation of an imagined trial, Yahweh gives evidence to establish Yahweh's own claim for allegiance (vv. 2–4). The evidence offered by and for Yahweh is arranged in two questions, each of which asks, "Who?" (vv. 2, 4). The first "who" question concerns one verb: "Who roused?" Who initiated? James Muilenburg asserts: "The answer to the *Who* of world history is proclaimed by God with a mighty word of self-revelation reminiscent of the supreme revelation at Sinai (Exod. 20:2)."

The object of divine arousal is a "victor from the east" (v. 2). The term "victor" refers to *one* who will transform historical reality and correct it. In context, the reference is to Cyrus, the rising Persian king, who in this moment of history emerges as a dominant force about to become a superpower as the founder of the mighty Persian dynasty (see 44:28; 45:1).

The Persian Empire is to the east of Babylon in what is now Iran; Babylon occupies what is now Iraq. Cyrus and his successors dominated the region for over two hundred years, until the rise of Alexander the Great in Macedonia. Thus the prophetic utterance anticipates the coming west of Cyrus to threaten and subjugate Babylon; but the point is that Yahweh—and no other god—has initiated and is responsible for the rise of Cyrus. It is because of Yahweh's resolve to threaten and undo Babylon that Cyrus and Persian power appear in world history. The remainder of verses 2–3 characterizes the massive military power that Cyrus will implement, before which all powers, including Babylon, will be helpless.

The second "who" of verse 4 reiterates the question about this stirring of world power and provides the "right answer" to the question of "who?" It is Yahweh, first and last, beginning and end, alpha and omega, who does this. This is a sweeping, nervy theological claim, characteristic of prophetic faith in Israel. To be sure, the rise of Cyrus and Persia could be explained in other ways with reference to many complex geopolitical factors. In the imagination of Israel, however, it is all Yahweh. This assertion, this claim for Yahweh, in effect answers the implied question of verses 1–2. The only credible verdict that can come out of the trial is to decide for Yahweh as the true God.

After Yahweh's overwhelming self-assertion, the court waits for the Babylonians to counter Yahweh's testimony with testimony on behalf of their gods, who are rivals to Yahweh. It is, however, the deliberate poetic strategy of the text to make the response of Babylon (in court) as feeble and unpersuasive as possible (vv. 5–7). What comes next is not a vigorous counterclaim, as we might expect, but a response of fear and confusion. Babylon and to the west as far as the Greek isles—that is, the entire world of poetic horizon—are all terrified at the threat of Cyrus, tool of Yahweh. They tremble in impotence and weakness. They know, it is implied, no counterpower and can appeal to no countergod. As Cyrus cannot be resisted, so Yahweh cannot be opposed.

Indeed, the response in fear is one of self-deluding panic. They try to embolden each other: "Take courage!" One can translate the Hebrew as "Be strong!" or, more likely, "Get a grip!" But the assurance is baseless. There is in Babylon no ground for courage because there is nothing that can resist Cyrus-sent-by-Yahweh. The second response of panic is to *make* some gods who will counter Yahweh. The scene, of course, is ludicrous and is meant by the poet to be ludicrous. Obviously, "homemade" gods have no power, cannot resist Cyrus, and surely cannot challenge Yahweh. These gods have to be nailed down so that they will not fall over, and if nailed down, they have no power, force, or mobility and so are irrelevant (cf. Psalm 115:4–8).

The purpose of the poetry is to communicate to the exiles how absurd it is to trust or fear or obey Babylonian gods. The exiles are invited to count on Cyrus and to anticipate a new historical possibility, precisely because they count upon Yahweh. The large claim is that although Babylon appears to control history, the real ruler is Yahweh. And Cyrus is Yahweh's exhibit number one in the courtroom.

Israel beyond Fear (41:8–13)

41:8 **But you, Israel, my servant,**
    Jacob, whom I have chosen,
    the offspring of Abraham, my friend;
   9 **you whom I took from the ends of the earth,**
    and called from its farthest corners,
   saying to you, "You are my servant,
    I have chosen you and not cast you off";
  10 **do not fear, for I am with you,**
    do not be afraid, for I am your God;
   I will strengthen you, I will help you,
    I will uphold you with my victorious right hand.

  11 **Yes, all who are incensed against you**
    shall be ashamed and disgraced;
   those who strive against you
    shall be as nothing and shall perish.
  12 **You shall seek those who contend with you,**
    but you shall not find them;
   those who war against you
    shall be as nothing at all.
  13 **For I, the LORD your God,**
    hold your right hand;
   it is I who say to you, "Do not fear,
    I will help you."

The impressive court scene of verses 1–7 offers assurance, but it does not mention Israel. The agenda of verses 1–7 is too large and contentious to mention Israel. But immediately, in verse 8, the poetry shifts into a new genre that is now completely preoccupied with the exilic community: "But you!"

This unit is a characteristic *salvation oracle*, a genre recurring in exilic Isaiah. The oracle begins with an address to Israel, so that it is completely clear that Yahweh as speaker is fully and unreservedly focused on the needs of Israel (vv. 8–9). The address is full and reassuring, mobilizing the entire past through which Yahweh has established a peculiar relation with Israel. Connection is made to the ancestral, promissory stories of Genesis, with reference to both Jacob and Abraham. And the final assertion of verse 9, governed by the positive "chosen" and the negative "not cast off" refers to Israel's memory of Moses and more especially the tradition of Deuteronomy. That is, the entire memory of Israel is mobilized in this moment in order to assure the exiles that this guaranteed relationship still operates and is decisive for the present and for the future.

In verse 10, the oracle turns from a review of memory to present-tense crisis. Yahweh speaks the most characteristic phrase of the salvation oracle, "Do not fear." These words are the decisive gospel message God has for exiles. The enduring threat of Babylon invited Israel to live always in the face of intimidation, completely unsure about survival or well-being. And now speaks the magisterial Lord, the one who roused Cyrus, with an utterance designed to change the perceived world of the exiles and to re-situate the exilic community positively. This same "Do not fear," a saving, world-changing utterance, is spoken at the decisive turns in the appearance of Jesus in the world, at birth (Luke 2:10) and at Easter (Matt. 28:5).

The speech provides the basis for a move beyond fear, dominated by a fourfold "I" of Yahweh (v. 10). Yahweh is the subject of decisive verbs in a way that the homemade gods of Babylon can never be. Thus Yahweh asserts: "I am your God, I strengthen, I help, I uphold!" Israel is not alone in the world of Babylon. Israel has not been abandoned but now is accompanied and guaranteed by the power of Yahweh that Babylon cannot resist.

Verses 11–13 are a reflection on the consequence of this massive intervention of Yahweh. The unit is introduced by "Yes," "behold" (v. 11); that is, take notice! If you look, what you will see is that those who stood against Yahweh will be "as nothing," completely nullified in the historical process. The concluding "as nothing" in verse 11 is reiterated in verse 12. Who would have thought that the "enduring nation" (Babylon) anticipated by Jeremiah (5:15), which seemed to perpetuity, would simply evaporate! The "as nothing" is reminiscent of Exodus 14:30–31, wherein the Egyptians became "as nothing":

Thus the LORD saved Israel that day from the Egyptians; and Israel saw the Egyptians dead on the seashore. Israel saw the great work that the LORD did against the Egyptians.

Theologically, that is how the poetry imagines the world of Yahweh. And historically, that is how it turned out. In a flash, Babylon disappeared from the map. The most recent parallel is perhaps the Soviet Union, which became "as nothing"; however, history is everywhere filled with examples of powers that evaporate when they run amuck of Yahweh's intention for well-being in the world. The practical reason the exiles shall "not fear" is that Babylon is soon to be "as nothing."

Such a reversal of the course of human events, however, is not a happenstance of "progressive history." It is rather the stunning doing of Yahweh (v. 13), who has "performed and done this" (v. 4). It is Yahweh who stands by and for Israel. It is Yahweh who sounds the salvation oracle (v. 13). The merciful inclination to say "do not fear," however, is groundless if the merciful one is not also the powerful one. Israel's assurance arises from Yahweh's capacity to reorder the public processes of world power, a most remarkable claim.

News for the Worm (41:14–16)

41:14 **Do not fear, you worm Jacob,**
     you insect Israel!
   I will help you, says the LORD;
     your Redeemer is the Holy One of Israel.
 [15] **Now, I will make of you a threshing sledge,**
     sharp, new, and having teeth;
   you shall thresh the mountains and crush them,
     and you shall make the hills like chaff.
 [16] **You shall winnow them and the wind shall carry them away,**
     and the tempest shall scatter them.
   Then you shall rejoice in the LORD;
     in the Holy One of Israel you shall glory.

This unit of poetry reiterates, in a slightly variant form, the salvation oracle of verses 8–13. It begins abruptly, with "Do not fear," the characteristic sign of the salvation oracle, here surely as an echo of the concluding "Do not fear" of verse 13. Whereas the address of verses 8–9 is fulsome and positive, here the address is to "worm-insect" Israel. Perhaps these derogatory terms reflect Israel's expressed self-evaluation as unimportant and hopeless (see Psalm 22:6). If this is correct, then the salvation oracle takes Israel as it is and as it perceives itself—lowly, ignoble, without hope. All of that, however, is immediately countered by the speech and promised intervention of Yahweh. Here Yahweh's self-reference is to "your Redeemer, the Holy One of Israel." That is, the rhetoric employs a formidable title for Yahweh, asserting Yahweh's massive commitment to Israel. The term "redeemer," moreover, is a metaphor that carries with it an old familial reference. Yahweh is next-of-kin to exilic Israel and will act for the honor and well-being of an abused kinsperson.

The action of Yahweh is for Israel as it is for Cyrus in verses 2–4. There Yahweh had only two verbs ("rouse" and "summons") and Cyrus did all the rest ("deliver, trample, pursue, pass"). Here Yahweh has only one verb, "I will make," and Israel has all the other verbs: "thresh, crush, winnow." Yahweh energizes, authorizes, and empowers; Israel now does all the rest, able to take initiative and responsibility for its own life in the world through forceful activity. The metaphor is of a farm implement with sharp teeth (threshing sledge) that is dragged over the land to smooth the soil, forcibly crushing and breaking and refining what is not yet amenable to planting. This is exceedingly vigorous language whereby Israel is imagined to become a force and an agent who can "rough up" even Babylon. Thus the speech imagines a complete role reversal between powerful Babylon and pitiful, wormlike Israel, whereby Israel becomes threshing sledge and Babylon is left to be leveled, abused soil.

This reversal is no accidental happening (v. 16b)! As the anticipated success of Cyrus must be referred back to Yahweh, the first and the last, so the anticipated vigor of Israel is to be referred to Yahweh. When Israel enacts its new initiative-taking power, it will not move to self-exaltation and self-congratulations. Rather, the "now" of triumph (v. 15) will lead to joy and praise given to Yahweh. It is Yahweh, not Israel, who does this and whom Israel gladly acknowledges. The focus of history—as for Cyrus, so for Israel—is Yahweh, the Holy One of Israel. Yahweh is the ground of "do not fear," the basis for new life even in the empire.

Yahweh's Transformed Landscape (41:17–20)

41:17 **When the poor and needy seek water,**
      and there is none,
      and their tongue is parched with thirst,
   I the LORD will answer them,

> I the God of Israel will not forsake them.
> ¹⁸ I will open rivers on the bare heights,
>   and fountains in the midst of the valleys;
> I will make the wilderness a pool of water,
>   and the dry land springs of water.
> ¹⁹ I will put in the wilderness the cedar,
>   the acacia, the myrtle, and the olive;
> I will set in the desert the cypress,
>   the plane and the pine together,
> ²⁰ so that all may see and know,
>   all may consider and understand,
> that the hand of the LORD has done this,
>   the Holy One of Israel has created it.

This unit of poetry is congruent with the salvation oracles of verses 8–13, 14–16 and may be roughly grouped with them. However, it moves in a somewhat different direction. It does not focus so singularly upon Israel but anticipates the transformation of creation (as distinct from the liberation of Israel), and it lacks the tag phrase "do not fear." Nonetheless, as a "portrayal" of the new age of well-being, it is like the salvation oracle in that it anticipates a radical intervention of Yahweh whereby those addressed will be resituated in a context of wondrous well-being. Although the rhetoric is somewhat different, it is clear that this unit serves the same purpose as the preceding—to invite Israel to new possibility beyond empire-conjured despair.

The more expansive imagery of this unit is tied to the preceding by reference to "the God of Israel" (v. 17) and "the Holy One of Israel" (v. 20), the latter a title we have also seen in verses 14 and 16. The subject of verse 17, "poor and needy," is not so precise as the fulsome address of verses 8–9 or the pastoral address of verse 14. And although "poor and needy" may be a more general address, in context there can be no doubt that the poetry concerns exilic Israel as "poor and needy," bereft of resources. It may be, given the dominant imagery here, that these verses already envision Israel headed home to Jerusalem across the desert, for the verses anticipate the transformation of the desert.

The central problem of the desert, of course, is water. This crisis is already anticipated in the vision of homecoming in 35:6b–7:

> For waters shall break forth in the wilderness,
>   and streams in the desert;
> the burning sand shall become a pool,

and the thirsty ground springs of water;
the haunt of jackals shall become a swamp,
the grass shall become reeds and rushes.

Yahweh has the will and capacity to invert the condition of creation just as Yahweh has the will and capacity to transform the circumstance of imperial history. But Israel has long known this, since the needy days of Moses and the Exodus: "But the people thirsted there for water; and the people complained against Moses. . . . [Yahweh said to Moses,] 'Strike the rock, and water will come out of it, so that the people may drink.' Moses did so" (Exod. 17:3, 6).

Our poetic unit begins in radical need (v. 17a). The need may be matched by complaint and petition, as it characteristically is in Israel, though that is not explicit here. In any case, Yahweh answers Israel—either answers the material need for water or answers the implied petition, or both. Yahweh is present and active and will not leave "the poor and needy" to their own resources, for without Yahweh they will perish.

The answer of Yahweh promised in verse 17b is given in the lyrical assertion of verses 18–19. Yahweh announces, concerning "the poor and needy," what Yahweh will do. The resolve of Yahweh is a series of first-person verbs: "open, make, put, set." The action concerns rivers, pools, and springs from which will come a wondrous abundance of trees, precisely in arid places where there had been no growth or vegetation and where life did not seem possible. Here speaks the creator God, who has available all the resources of heaven and earth to work newness in the historical process. Here speaks the powerful One who overturns empires, who defeats rival gods, who summons new superpowers and makes new life possible for Israel. The rhetoric of this resolve is surely extreme, but then an extreme claim is made for Yahweh. As Israel receives new life from Yahweh, so the world is made new.

The purpose of this astonishing transformation is voiced in verse 20. It is not simply so that the "poor and needy" (ostensibly Israel) may have life. It is not just so that the world may prosper with abundant water. It is so that Yahweh may be enhanced. The miracle of creation points to the creator. Although the poetry of these verses is most compatible with the salvation oracles of verses 8–13, 14–16, the appeal of the verses may be to the "coastlands and peoples" of verse 1. This is the decisive evidence on behalf of the sovereign power of Yahweh. The world is watching; the nations will now see the hand (= power) of Yahweh. The same hand "stretched out" against Pharaoh (Exod. 3:20) is now stretched out against Babylon and is now stretched out against the powers of chaos here embodied as dryness. Every-one will see. Everyone will know (acknowledge). Everyone will understand. The God committed to Israel is the one who acts powerfully over the larger domain of creation. How could the exiles not believe that from this same hand a new future is possible!

More Adjudication (41:21–29)

41:21 Set forth your case, says the LORD;
      bring your proofs, says the King of Jacob.
  22 Let them bring them, and tell us
      what is to happen.
  Tell us the former things, what they are,
      so that we may consider them,
  and that we may know their outcome;
      or declare to us the things to come.
  23 Tell us what is to come hereafter,
      that we may know that you are gods;
  do good, or do harm,
      that we may be afraid and terrified.
  24 You, indeed, are nothing
      and your work is nothing at all;
      whoever chooses you is an abomination.

  25 I stirred up one from the north, and he has come,
      from the rising of the sun he was summoned by name.
  He shall trample on rulers as on mortar,
      as the potter treads clay.
  26 Who declared it from the beginning, so that we might know,
      and beforehand, so that we might say, "He is right"?
  There was no one who declared it, none who proclaimed,
      none who heard your words.
  27 I first have declared it to Zion,
      and I give to Jerusalem a herald of good tidings.
  28 But when I look there is no one;
      among these there is no counselor
      who, when I ask, gives an answer.
  29 No, they are all a delusion;
      their works are nothing;
      their images are empty wind.

After the wondrous assurances of verses 8–13, 14–16, and 17–20, the poetry now returns to the rhetorical pattern of verses 1–7 and offers a concluding speech of disputation. The summons of verse 21, expressed in two verbs using judicial language, is combined with a challenge to Babylon (vv. 21–24). Whereas Yahweh testified first in verses 2–4 before the pitiful testimony of Babylon in verses 5–7, here the process is reversed. Now Babylon goes first. The rivals to Yahweh and their adherents are now on the witness stand and are given their day in court. They are asked hard questions. But because the questions receive no answer, in fact the questions function as dismissive ridicule. The question put to Babylon is in a series of imperatives: "Tell the court"—"bring, tell, tell, declare, tell, do, do." The court wants to know: "that we may consider, . . . that we may know, . . . that we may know, . . . that we may be afraid and terrified."

The final invitation is to see if the Babylonian gods can scare people in the courtroom. The court wants to know if these gods can say something about the past, the present, or the future—if a statement can be offered that will inform, impress, illuminate, or intimidate. The questions taunt and dare, clearly becoming abusive to the supposed Babylonian witness.

The poetry is set up to make a negative point. There is no answer! There is silence! The gods do not speak. Their witnesses can make no statement. The silence is because the gods are unable to speak:

> Their idols are silver and gold,
> the work of human hands.
> They have mouths, but do not speak;
> eyes, but do not see.
> They have ears, but do not hear;
> noses, but do not smell.
> They have hands, but do not feel;
> feet, but do not walk;
> they make no sound in their throats.
> Those who make them are like them,
> so are all who trust in them.
> (Psalm 115:4–8)

But more important, they do not speak because they have nothing to say. They know nothing, have caused nothing, can claim nothing. They are, as indicated already in verses 11–12, "as nothing." The poetry intends a long pause, a long embarrassed wait in the courtroom "until hell freezes over."

And then finally, the inevitable, dismissive verdict (v. 24): "You, indeed, are nothing." The word is the same as in verses 11–12. Not only are the gods nothing. Their deeds are nothing, apparently the same word as in

40:17, though the Hebrew is suspect. The adherents of these gods, more-over, are condemned and rejected. The poetry moves, predictably, from a lack of positive evidence to a negative verdict. The rhetorical gain is that the listening exilic community sees that their threatening overlords, through ostensible "due process," are rendered null and void. The Baby-lonian gods are legally declared to be an irrelevance who can no longer dic-tate Israel's life.

With such a verdict, the way is now clear for Yahweh to testify; Yahweh offers a very different testimony (vv. 25–29). Echoing the claim of verse 2, the testimony of Yahweh again begins with a first-person claim, "I." The verb "stir up" translates the same Hebrew term as does "rouse" in verse 2. (For this verb, see 13:17; 45:13; Jer. 50:9; 51:1, 11.) Yahweh is the initiat-ing agent. The claim is again made for Cyrus, now "from the north." Verse 26 echoes verse 4 with the interrogative "who," which can have only one answer. It is Yahweh and only Yahweh who initiated the decisive turn in history. The positive claim for Yahweh is reasserted in verse 27: Yahweh will dispatch a messenger to Zion, asserting the turn of history that Yah-weh has initiated. The term "gospel messenger" ("herald of good tidings") here echoes 40:9. It is only Yahweh who has gospel messengers because only Yahweh can work a genuine newness. But then these verses are dom-inated by the negative dismissal of rivals or aides. There is "no one, none, none, no one, no counselor." The Babylonian gods, whom the exiles so much fear, simply are not players. They have nothing to do with the turn of history.

The dismissal of rivals or aides leads inescapably to the resounding neg-ative verdict of verse 29 that echoes verses 11–12, 24. The gods, their ac-complishments, and their images are all nothingness. The final term of dismissal is again *tôhû* ("nothingness"), as in 40:17, 23. Indeed, unlike Yah-weh, they have no "works." They are able to do nothing, and nothing good or ill should be expected of them.

The twin themes of Yahweh's attentive power and the nullification of rivals run through the chapter. The arrangement of the chapter with *speech of disputation—salvation oracle—salvation oracle—salvation oracle—speech of disputation* holds together large claims of power and intimate promises of well-being. The immediate intent of the chapter is to persuade exilic lis-teners that their future is to be received outside the claims, promises, and intimidations of Babylon, for it is an empire void of any future. Subsequent listeners (including us) are invited to the claim that our life as well is vested outside the pretended claims of every system of domination, systems that cannot keep their promises. For all listeners to this text, primary as well as subsequent, it is evident that the tone is one of persuasion. To look outside the dominant system for future prospects is not an easy or obvious thing to do. The poet seeks to make the option credible and compelling.

A SERVANT, A WARRIOR, A DISPUTE
42:1–25

This chapter moves boldly and imaginatively in several directions with powerful imagery and daring transactions. In a most general way, the chapter may be understood as an attempt to come to terms with the demanding, overwhelming gospel announcement of chapters 40—41. This chapter begins with a summons to "my servant" (vv. 1–9), celebrates Yahweh's coming powerful intervention in behalf of Israel (vv. 10–17), and surprisingly culminates in a dispute between Yahweh and Yahweh's people (vv. 18–25).

A Called Agent (42:1–9)

These verses concern "my servant," who is assigned decisive work on behalf of Yahweh in the world. Chapters 40—41 have been vigorously theocentric, attending to Yahweh's resolve and direct action in behalf of Israel in the midst of Babylonian power. The focus upon Yahweh's own work is interrupted, heretofore, only by mention of the "herald of good tidings" (40:9; 41:27). Consistently, the turn of history is God's own work. Now, in a way characteristic for Israel's faith, it is affirmed that God's work in the world is to be enacted by *human agency*. These verses deal with two units of poetry on the theme of human agency that are intimately linked to each other (vv. 1–4, 5–9).

42:1 **Here is my servant, whom I uphold,**
my chosen, in whom my soul delights;
I have put my spirit upon him;
he will bring forth justice to the nations.
² **He will not cry or lift up his voice,**
or make it heard in the street;
³ **a bruised reed he will not break,**
and a dimly burning wick he will not quench;
he will faithfully bring forth justice.
⁴ **He will not grow faint or be crushed**
until he has established justice in the earth;
and the coastlands wait for his teaching.

This section begins with the first mention of "my servant" in Isaiah of exile, a theme that recurs in the subsequent poetry. The theme of "the servant" is notoriously difficult in Isaiah studies and has greatly occupied scholarship. There is no agreement about the identity of the servant, the issue being especially problematic when conventional Christian interpreters seek to identify the servant with the anticipated Jesus as messiah. Here it is enough to assume, as is generally the case, that "my servant" is the people Israel. That appellation draws upon the entire memory of ancient Israel that affirms that Israel is related to Yahweh as servant to master (king) and that the life of Israel consists in obedience to the will and command and purpose of the king. Already at Mount Sinai, Yahweh addresses Israel by royal decree that becomes torah commandment (Exod. 20:1–17). It is not to be thought, however, that the relationship is one of abrasion, coercion, or resistance. Characteristically, Yahweh assumes a gladly obedient Israel and therefore "delights in" and gladly sustains the servant (see v. 1).

Although the designation "servant" is traditional, it is anything but "natural" in the midst of exilic despair. It is a remarkable theme in exile that Israel is freshly reminded of its relation to Yahweh and its consequent role with duties to perform and obligations to fulfill. In exile, Israel tended to be more self-preoccupied and self-absorbed with its own destiny. In this utterance, however, Yahweh changes the subject and summons grieving Israel out beyond its own self-preoccupation to other work.

There is work to be done, and Israel is to do it! In these verses, the term "justice" is sounded three times (vv. 1, 3, 4). The characteristic notion of justice, rooted in Mosaic tradition and explicated in prophetic utterance, is the reordering of social life and social power so that the weak (widows and orphans) may live a life of dignity, security, and well-being. If we assume such a substantive notion of justice (well explicated by Paul Hanson), then the exilic community as servant is dispatched by Yahweh to reorder social relations for the sake of the vulnerable. Indeed, the mode of work proposed in verses 2–3 suggests such a content for servanthood. Israel itself is to practice vulnerability and to be attentive to others who are vulnerable, "bruised reeds and dim wicks." Israel's way of relationship is thus drastically contrasted with the way of Babylon (or any other worldly power), which is to break such reeds and snuff out such wicks. Israel is to pursue a different way in the world—to refuse the modes of power mostly taken for granted.

It is a difficult question about how to interpret the "universal outreach" of this imagery. It is asserted in verse 4 that the "coastlands" wait for the new ordering of social reality to be accomplished by the servant. It is a characteristic propensity of Christian interpretation, voiced by Hanson, that Israel's work is to transform the Gentile world and to make a welcoming place for the vulnerable. Such a reading, however, must be done with extreme caution. It is equally possible (probable?) that this scenario concerns *Jewish* people scattered around the Mediterranean basin who wait for Jewish rehabilitation. Even if that be accepted as a proper reading, however, there is no doubt that these texts have subsequently, and especially in Christian interpretation, yielded a much wider "missional" reading. This is perhaps a "second reading" that needs to be done with some tentativeness. In any case, what is not reversible is that a *servant* for *justice* is now at the center of imagination in the exilic community.

42:5 **Thus says God, the LORD,**
     who created the heavens and stretched them out,
     who spread out the earth and what comes from it,
   who gives breath to the people upon it
     and spirit to those who walk in it:
     ⁶I am the LORD, I have called you in righteousness,
     I have taken you by the hand and kept you;
   I have given you as a covenant to the people,
     a light to the nations,
       ⁷to open the eyes that are blind,
     to bring out the prisoners from the dungeon,
       from the prison those who sit in darkness.
     ⁸I am the LORD, that is my name;
       my glory I give to no other,
       nor my praise to idols.
     ⁹See, the former things have come to pass,
       and new things I now declare;
     before they spring forth,
       I tell you of them.

The second articulation of servanthood is more lyrically put. At the center of this unit, the servant is called (vv. 6–7). Again all the problems persist concerning the identity of the servant and the issue of the scope of the enterprise. Although the scope is uncertain (that is, Gentile or Jewish), the task is concrete, whether to be enacted for Gentiles or for Jews. The servant (Israel) is "called, taken, kept, given" by Yahweh. That is, the servant is well protected as well as irresistibly energized. This is indeed the work of Yahweh now to be done by the servant.

The mandate of the servant is first voiced in two large phrases, "covenant to the people" and "light to the nations." The phrases are rich and suggestive, but their precise intent is not at all clear. The text juxtaposes "covenant" and "people" without any sign or clue about the relation of the words. The phrase is commonly taken to mean that Israel is to live so as to bring others to a defining relationship with Yahweh or, alternatively, to transform social relationships in order to make them neighborly. The poetry seems to entertain the thought that social relationships in the world can be radically reordered, and the servant is to effect that reordering. The second large phrase, "light to the nations," also offers a general notion of rehabilitation.

Whatever may have been the original intent, subsequent Christian reading has found here a sweeping mandate for a worldwide mission for a renovation of the relation the world has to Yahweh and the relation people have to each other. Israel's servanthood makes a new day possible in the world, a theme already anticipated by the programmatic statement of Genesis 12:3: "In you all the families of the earth shall be blessed." (See also Gal. 3:8.)

The mandate of the servant is more specific in verse 7, with particular reference to prisoners. Because it is plausible that in the ancient world (as in the contemporary world) imprisonment is primarily an economic function so that the *poor* are the *imprisoned*, this authorization perhaps suggests something like the ancient Israelite practice of debt cancellation, whereby the poor may be released from prison because they are released from debt (see Deut. 15:1–11). It seems clear that the work of the servant is indeed linked to the most elemental of human transactions, including those of an economic variety.

The mandate to the servant (vv. 6b–7) is powerfully framed by self-uttered doxologies of Yahweh (vv. 5–6a, 8–9). In verse 5, it is the creator who speaks, and in verses 8–9, it is Yahweh who speaks and who shares nothing of divine splendor with any other. It is all Yahweh and only Yahweh. Thus the call of the servant is sandwiched to make clear that it is the will of the creator that is to be enacted by the servant. The reason the servant can traffic in covenant is that Yahweh wills covenant; the reason the servant can bring light is that Yahweh is against the darkness. The reason debts are cancelled and the poor are liberated is that Yahweh is attentive to the vulnerable and wills none to live in hock.

One other comment on verse 9 is required. The book of Isaiah often refers to "former things" and "new things" (see 9:1; 41:22). It is plausible that the phrase "former things" refers to the work of judgment that has dominated chapters 1—39 of Isaiah, and that the phrase "new things" concerns the restoration of Israel after the Exile, a theme prominent in later Isaiah. If so, we may suggest that the *work of the servant*, specified in verses 6–7, is the work of "new things" whereby Israel is brought to a new place, or that "the nations" are brought to a way of life intended by the creator. The people Israel now figures decisively in God's newness in the world.

A New Song for a New World (42:10–17)

Now the servant is for the moment disregarded. Now it is all Yahweh, no proximate agents. The whole earth and all its creatures are invited to sing along with Israel in exuberant praise of Yahweh. The language is the rhetoric of theophany (an appearance of God) that anticipates the radical coming of Yahweh to work a newness. The praise of verses 12–13 is in anticipation of the coming of verses 14–17, when all things will be inverted for the good of Israel.

42:10 **Sing to the LORD a new song,**
  his praise from the end of the earth!
 Let the sea roar and all that fills it,
  the coastlands and their inhabitants.
 [11] **Let the desert and its towns lift up their voice,**
  the villages that Kedar inhabits;
 let the inhabitants of Sela sing for joy,
  let them shout from the tops of the mountains.
 [12] **Let them give glory to the LORD,**
  and declare his praise in the coastlands.
 [13] **The LORD goes forth like a soldier,**
  like a warrior he stirs up his fury;
 he cries out, he shouts aloud,
  he shows himself mighty against his foes.

Verses 10–13 are a characteristic hymn in Israel. They begin with a rich summons to praise in which the several members of the choir are identified (vv. 10–12). The singers include all the creatures, the sea, the coastlands, the desert, the villagers. All are to sing in joy. Indeed, they are to sing a "new song." The phrase "new song" has become a cliché for any great exuberant anthem. It probably originated when a new anthem was commissioned for a special liturgical occasion. The phrase functions liturgically so that a new song matches a new action of Yahweh. Our verse corresponds closely to Psalm 96, thus appropriating what was likely an old liturgy in the temple now used for homecoming among exiles. In Psalm

96, the "new song" (v. 1) is to celebrate the newly established rule of Yahweh that causes all creatures (especially endangered species!) to welcome the new governance. In our text as well, the celebration concerns the newly established governance of Yahweh, a rule now to displace harsh Babylonian rule. The several creatures have ample reason to exult, for the old governance had been stultifying and life-threatening. Military powers like Babylon are not only exploitative of human habitation; they abuse the environment as well. No wonder all the creatures welcome the new governance, a welcome echoed in Revelation 5:9, where the ultimate rule of Yahweh evokes "a new song."

In Israel's characteristic hymn, after the summons to praise (here vv. 10–12) there follows the reason (v. 13). Here the reason is that Yahweh—a man of war—is about to mobilize for action. Since the days of the Exodus, Yahweh has been a "man of war" capable of terrible and powerful activity (see Exod. 15:3). Although the imagery may be offensive to us in its savage potential, it is the capacity of Yahweh to work Yahweh's own powerful will that is the basis of Israel's life and hope in the world. Now Yahweh, the powerful, is about to act. Yahweh "stirs up" (the same term we have seen in 41:2, 25) and, like a wildly exuberant army, begins to move with noise and boisterousness, perhaps designed to intimidate. Yahweh is on the way! Things are going to change!

42:14 **For a long time I have held my peace,**
  I have kept still and restrained myself;
  now I will cry out like a woman in labor,
  I will gasp and pant.
 15 **I will lay waste mountains and hills,**
  and dry up all their herbage;
  I will turn the rivers into islands,
  and dry up the pools.
 16 **I will lead the blind**
  by a road they do not know,
  by paths they have not known
  I will guide them.
  I will turn the darkness before them into light,
  the rough places into level ground.
  These are the things I will do,
  and I will not forsake them.
 17 **They shall be turned back and utterly put to shame—**
  those who trust in carved images,
  who say to cast images,
  "You are our gods."

Although the thought of Yahweh's coming continues in this new unit, the terms change. Now Yahweh speaks in the first person. In the first two lines of this unit, the God of Israel reflects on times past. Yahweh has been dormant, silent, quiet, passive for a long time—too long! Indeed, that is how things have gotten so bad for Israel. The hint is that the only reason Babylon has flourished at the expense of Israel is that Yahweh has been a nonparticipant. Babylon has prevailed by default. But now, the warrior is about to act. No wonder a new song is required! It is the kind of new song always required—as in Advent and Easter—when the people of God anticipate or recognize Yahweh's mobilization. For when God acts, everything is changed.

In this utterance, however, all that time of inactivity is passed. Yahweh is roused (v. 13). Yahweh is about to move. And when Yahweh breaks the silence, the effect is not quiet or discreet or private. The new activity is restless and noisy, like the noise and activity of a woman in childbirth. The poet is daringly inventive and does not hesitate to juxtapose a woman in labor pains and a warrior now bestirred. It is not likely, in my judgment, that this is any argument for the femininity or maternity of Yahweh. But the usage does attest that there is no limit to the imagery that can and must be exhibited in order to make Yahweh available and compelling to those who despair. And because a metaphor always makes substantive even if elusive claim, the imagery of God panting in labor is a fresh datum for Israel's faith. Something is about to be birthed; Israel has cause for exuberance.

The poetry moves quickly beyond the imagery of birth in verse 14 back to the motif of warrior in verse 13 (vv. 15–16). These verses are laden with first-person verbs in which Yahweh advances "like a mighty army," working devastation in the land like Sherman through Georgia. Everything will be changed because nothing lies beyond the reach of Yahweh or Yahweh's capacity to interfere. The vegetation of the landscape will be devastated. Yahweh will transform the water supply. But most poignantly, this marauding general—seemingly out of control—will attend to the blind and will lead them home safely, carefully, patiently on a safe road. The powerful acts of verse 15 are in the service of the rescue of verse 16. The "blind" are surely the helpless Israelite victims of Babylonian power. This foray of the warrior is like the rescue mission at Entebbe. God will with power (and at great risk?) seize the blind Israelites too long held hostage by Babylon.

The proposed action is summarized in the victorious statement of verse 16, perhaps uttered in the same triumphant tone of Jesus' assertion on the cross: "It is finished!" (John 19:30): "I will do it." The phrase is a claim of power. But the power of the first line is matched in the second line by an assertion of *fidelity*. Israel in exile has the sense that Yahweh has abandoned them. And so it has seemed, momentarily (see Isa. 54:7–8). Here is a resolve of the powerful God of Israel. No member of the covenant community is forgotten. All will be rescued (see the parallel insistence of Moses (Exod. 10:9, 25–26). Nobody can keep the Israelites in captivity when Yahweh moves to rescue. Yahweh is completely resolved.

The negative counterpoint is the disastrous future of Israel's adversaries (v. 17). They—presumably the recently arrogant Babylonians—will be left defeated and in shame. They will have failed because they relied on failed, phony gods. The action is concrete, political, military, historical. It is undertaken for concrete Israel. The poet, however, cannot resist the theological point. It is a God-question and Yahweh has won. But the God-question is never in a vacuum, any more than the historical point is in isolation. The two are always joined. This joining of *God to life* is the nature of Yahweh, the destiny of Israel, and the truth of Israel's faith. Ancient Babylon, like contemporary powers, seeks to impose a way on history without taking Yahweh into account. It cannot be done! Such an effort causes Yahweh to "stir up his fury." And when that happens, nothing stays safe.

A Rebuke from the Rescuing God (42:18–25)

42:18 **Listen, you that are deaf;**
> **and you that are blind, look up and see!**
> 19 **Who is blind but my servant,**
> > **or deaf like my messenger whom I send?**
> **Who is blind like my dedicated one,**
> > **or blind like the servant of the LORD?**
> 20 **He sees many things, but does not observe them;**
> > **his ears are open, but he does not hear.**

Up until this point in this chapter, everything is positive. Yahweh is active and to be praised. The servant is commissioned to do Yahweh's work. In verse 18, however, there arises a major abrasion between Yahweh and Israel. Perhaps this is a completely new literary unit. Or perhaps it is the case that Israel—the commissioned servant of Yahweh—is so preoccupied with its own sorry state in exile that it cannot get its mind off itself to attend to the mission of Yahweh. In verses 18–20, it is Yahweh who speaks, who refers to "my servant . . . my messenger." Yahweh's tough talk here is in response to a statement of Israel that is here assumed but not quoted. That statement on the part of Israel is, apparently, a complaint against Yahweh for the present hopeless condition of Israel. Perhaps the complaint is parallel to 40:27: "'My way is hidden from the LORD,/and my right is disregarded by my God.'" Indeed, a fuller articulation of the same assertive accusation is in the liturgical expression of Psalm 44:9–12:

> Yet you have rejected us and abased us,
>   and have not gone out with our armies.
> You made us turn back from the foe,
>   and our enemies have gotten spoil.
> You have made us like sheep for slaughter,
>   and have scattered us among the nations.
> You have sold your people for a trifle,
>   demanding no high price for them.

Yahweh, in such speech that recurs in Israel, is blamed for inattentiveness whereby Israel suffers. It is cogent to imagine that Yahweh was accused of blindness and deafness, of being unable to see Israel's plight or hear Israel's cry for help.

Assuming such a complaint, now in Yahweh's response the tables are turned. It is not Yahweh who is blind and deaf. It is Israel who is blind and deaf—blind servant, deaf messenger. Verses 18–19 use the term "deaf" twice and "blind" four times. It is Israel who is inattentive, unable and unwilling to notice or attend to Yahweh. The imperative of Yahweh bids Israel to new behavior, to see and hear, to listen and look up, to notice, to receive what Yahweh is doing. But alas, Israel does not see, does not notice, and so consigns itself to a continuing hopelessness.

Appeal to the organs of attentiveness (ears, eyes) may be usefully connected to two other uses. First, the entire Exodus tradition of treasured memory is premised on Yahweh's attentiveness: "God heard their groaning, and God remembered his covenant with Abraham, Isaac, and Jacob. God looked upon the Israelites, and God took notice of them" (Exod. 2:24–25). There can be no doubt in Israel that Yahweh is attentive. And there can be no doubt that in response to Yahweh, Israel in that ancient miracle was able to see and regard Yahweh's deliverance: "Israel saw the great work that the LORD did against the Egyptians. So the people feared the LORD and believed in the LORD and in his servant Moses" (Exod. 14:31). Thus, compared with the generation of the Exodus, the generation of the Exile is obtuse and unresponsive. They just don't get it.

Second and more immediately pertinent, the announcement of God in the divine council in the stunning disclosure of Isaiah 6:9–10 had fated Israel to obtuseness:

> " 'Keep listening, but do not comprehend;
> keep looking, but do not understand.'
> Make the mind of this people dull,
>   and stop their ears,
>   and shut their eyes,
> so that they may not look with their eyes,
>   and listen with their ears,
> and comprehend with their minds,
>   and turn and be healed."

Thus the judgment of Israel in the book of Isaiah is propelled by the conviction that Israel has been made by Yahweh unable to respond or notice or receive. In our verses, then, the ominous sentence of chapter 6 seems still to be in force. Israel still has dull mind, stopped ears, and shut eyes, unable to discern what Yahweh is doing—consequently, unable to turn and be healed.

42:21 **The LORD was pleased, for the sake of his righteousness,**
> **to magnify his teaching and make it glorious.**
> 22 **But this is a people robbed and plundered,**
> **all of them are trapped in holes**
> **and hidden in prisons;**
> **they have become a prey with no one to rescue,**
> **a spoil with no one to say, "Restore!"**
> 23 **Who among you will give heed to this,**
> **who will attend and listen for the time to come?**
> 24 **Who gave up Jacob to the spoiler,**
> **and Israel to the robbers?**
> **Was it not the LORD, against whom we have sinned,**
> **in whose ways they would not walk,**
> **and whose law they would not obey?**
> 25 **So he poured upon him the heat of his anger**
> **and the fury of war;**
> **it set him on fire all around, but he did not understand;**
> **it burned him, but he did not take it to heart.**

Whereas Yahweh speaks directly in verses 18–20, Yahweh is spoken about in verses 21–25 in language that is typically Deuteronomic: (a) Yahweh has given wondrous torah instruction to Israel. Yahweh's purpose and will is available and abundantly clear in Israel (v. 21; see Deut. 30:11–14). The purpose of torah is to generate righteousness in the earth. (b) But Israel is now in a state of misery, confusion, and suffering (v. 22). Indeed, the poet accentuates the rhetoric of suffering in a way not unlike Israel's own inclination to exaggeration in its complaints against Yahweh. It was, moreover, Yahweh who caused the suffering (v. 24). The suffering of exile is not happenstance, and it is not caused by Babylonian brutality. The poet insists that Yahweh's covenantal governance is total and comprehensive. The suffering happens precisely because Yahweh intends it to happen (see Jer. 30:14–15). (c) The suffering of exile is not capricious on the part of Yahweh; it is well-deserved punishment. Thus verse 24 concludes with a threefold confession of sin: "We have sinned, . . . they would not walk, . . . they would not obey." (d) In verse 25, the point on punishment and consequent misery is given a reprise. It is as though the confession (and accusation) of sin in verse 24 triggers a rhetorical escalation in verse 25. Yahweh is filled with rage, even if deserved rage. The dominant image is fire, perhaps alluding to the burning of Jerusalem. The final lines of verse 25 suggest, as in Amos 4:6–11, that the punishment was to produce repentance on the part of Israel. But it did not work! Israel is completely obdurate and recalcitrant: "He did not understand; . . . he did not take it to heart."

These verses are peculiar in this context and sound more like the accents of judgment in chapters 1—39. They are a neat articulation of the full theology of retribution so prominent in the Old Testament and best known in the tradition of Deuteronomy. This theology asserts that Yahweh's governance of history has moral symmetry, and therefore the suffering of Israel in exile is merited. The final indictment of verse 25 relates to the heavy theme of verses 18–20. Israel does not get it. Israel did not get it at the moment of the destruction of Jerusalem, but Israel still does not get it two generations later. Israel is unable to see that Yahweh's covenant is demanding and in the end costly.

It is suggested by some scholars that the first seven verses of chapter 43 are placed as a positive counterpoint to 42:18–25. In and of themselves, nonetheless, the harshness of these verses is unmitigated. The only relief from misery is hearing and seeing, of attending to Yahweh's wondrous Torah. The juxtaposition of this harshness with the wondrous praise of verses 10–12 and the enormous expectation of verses 15–16 is stunning indeed.

THE CREATOR WHO REDEEMS, FORGIVES, AND PROFANES
43:1–28

In this long chapter, with its abrupt rhetorical reversals, the poet sounds the primary themes of Israel's faith: Yahweh is *deeply devoted* to Israel and will act to liberate Israel from exile. Yahweh is *uncompromisingly sovereign* and will deal harshly with Israel when Israel is disobedient and unresponsive. The positive affirmation of *Yahweh toward Israel* includes the salvation oracles of verses 1–7, 14–21, and the astonishing verse 25. Conversely, the threat of *Yahweh against Israel* is sternly voiced in verses 22–24, 26–28. A third motif is *Yahweh's summons to Israel* to testify on behalf of Yahweh in a contested context of trial.

It is convenient for us to treat the chapter as a literary entity. However, it is by no means clear that the chapter can be set apart from its surrounding context. Thus it may well be that the salvation oracle of verses 1–7 is deliberately designed and placed as a counterpoint to the shrill assertion of 42:21–25. In parallel fashion, it may be that the harsh closure of verses 22–28 is deliberately answered by 44:1–8. Tactically, it is useful to treat the text in smaller units. But the smaller units can be seen in close and intentional relationship to each other. The series of rhetorical disjunctions that characterize this chapter make clear that Israel's life with Yahweh is a live and engaged one that arrives at no abiding equilibrium. The gifts and requirements of Yahweh assure that the relationship will remain a dynamic, surprising, and sometimes costly one.

Yahweh's Decisive Love for Israel (43:1–7)

This unit articulates, as forcefully and compellingly as anywhere in the Bible, Yahweh's defining and uncompromising love for Israel, a commitment and devotion that completely repositions Israel's life in the world. The initial "But now" likely contrasts this affirmation with the abrasiveness of 42:21–25. Now, in this present hour, Israel in exile is made freshly aware of Yahweh's profound commitment to Israel, a commitment that persists through and is undisturbed by any circumstance. The oracle is sounded around the double "Do not fear" of verses 1 and 5, an assurance designed to overcome Israel's exilic sense of abandonment.

43:1 **But now thus says the LORD,**
> **he who created you, O Jacob,**
> **he who formed you, O Israel:**
> **Do not fear, for I have redeemed you;**
> > **I have called you by name, you are mine.**
> > 2 **When you pass through the waters, I will be with you;**
> > > **and through the rivers, they shall not overwhelm you;**
> > **when you walk through fire you shall not be burned,**

and the flame shall not consume you.
³ For I am the LORD your God,
   the Holy One of Israel, your Savior.
 I give Egypt as your ransom,
   Ethiopia and Seba in exchange for you.
⁴ Because you are precious in my sight,
   and honored, and I love you,
 I give people in return for you,
   nations in exchange for your life.

In the first "Do not fear" of verse 1, the speaker is the creator and former of Israel who is also the creator of the world. The ground for the imperative to "not fear," introduced by "for," is that Yahweh has "redeemed" Israel. The verb refers to family intervention and solidarity whereby a stronger member of the family intervenes to assure the well-being of a weaker member. The second assurance, "I have called you by name," is perhaps an adoption formula. Israel now is fully identified with, belongs to, and is cherished by Yahweh (v. 1). Calvin observes: "God refuses to be deprived of his rightful possession" (*Isaiah* III, 319). This intimate and nonnegotiable relationship is a present help in every danger (v. 2). The poet imagines the threat of flood waters and fires, realities that may jeopardize Israel. These two threats are probably metaphorical and may refer, through the use of an allusion to the waters of the Exodus, to the long trek out of exile. Or they may allude to an ancient practice of "ordeal" whereby accused persons are submitted to the testing dangers of water and fire. Christians will readily take the references to *water* and *name* as welcome illuminations of baptism, a sacrament of relationship whereby we are inducted into the protective and sure care of Yahweh.

In verses 3–4, the imagery shifts abruptly. The rhetoric features "the Holy One of Israel," who engages in bartering in order to secure the release and homecoming of members of the community held in bondage by other powers and authorities. The imagery suggests something like an exchange of prisoners or perhaps even an exchange of slaves. Because the scattered Jews are "precious in my sight," Yahweh is prepared to trade citizens of other countries for the emancipation and rehabilitation of Jews. Such an image may sound crass and materialistic to us, and we may, at our distance, wonder about "the others" who are readily shipped off by Yahweh to subservience elsewhere. But the imagination of Israel does not shrink from such crassness; it is willing to accuse Yahweh elsewhere: "You have sold your people for a trifle,/demanding no high price for them" (Psalm 44:12). The insistence here is not that practice of barter for persons is wrong, but only that Yahweh sold too cheap. That is, Yahweh is willing to set a price on other peoples because Yahweh values Yahweh's own needy people. The reality is that the entire evangelical rhetoric of "ransom" is shot through with high-priced negotiation. Peter Stuhlmacher suggests that this use of "ransom" in verse 3 is the direct source of "ransom" mentioned in Mark 10:45 as concerns the work of Jesus (*Reconciliation*, 16–29). It is clear that we are not intended to follow the metaphor to its extreme and logical conclusion, but to take it only for the single feature of *treasuring Israel* in an extreme way. Claus Westermann comments on this remarkable imagery:

> A tiny, miserable and insignificant band of uprooted men and women are assured that they—precisely they—are the people to whom God has turned in love; they, just as they are, are dear and precious in his sight. And think who says this—the lord of all powers and authorities, of the whole of history and of all creation! (*Isaiah 40–66*, 118)

43:5 **Do not fear, for I am with you;**
  I will bring your offspring from the east,
    and from the west I will gather you;
   ⁶**I will say to the north, "Give them up,"**
    and to the south, "Do not withhold;
  bring my sons from far away
    and my daughters from the end of the earth—
   ⁷**everyone who is called by my name,**
    whom I created for my glory,
    whom I formed and made."

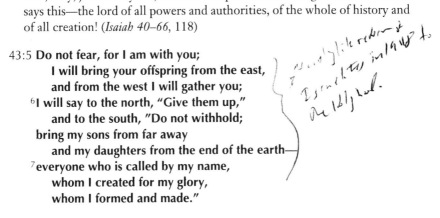

The tag phrase "do not fear" is reiterated in verse 5, and the intentional gathering of the scattered from all corners of the earth is here imagined. As verse 2 well reminds Christians of the cadences of baptism, so the ingathering of peoples in verse 6 will call to mind the large vision of the Eucharist: "People will come from east and west, from north and south . . ." (see Luke 13:29). The Eucharist is the church's dramatic enactment of the great ingathering of God's beloved from all of God's creation.

There is no doubt that the ingathering, or exchange of persons, initially referred to Jews who had been forcibly removed from their homeland and made subservient to other powers. Thus the poetry envisions a dramatic deployment of new power in the sixth century (Cyrus dispatched by Yahweh), whereby the homecoming of Jews from many places of scattering is implemented. But as surely as the initial articulation refers to Jews, it is equally sure that this poetry in other contexts has in purview other treasured peoples of Yahweh. In conventional Christian imagery, the words are heard as the ingathering of the church as the beloved of God. Or in a liberation hermeneutic, these words point to "God's preferential option for the poor," whereby the God of homecoming intends none of the poor to be finally displaced. Although these subsequent readings are treasured and I think valid, they never eliminate the primary claim of Jews. Indeed, Yahweh's treasuring love for Jews is an epitome of God's powerful capacity for homecoming that is operative in many places for many peoples.

Thus the salvation oracle enacts a great scenario of homecoming. It is for the benefit of the displaced who are the beloved; but that homecoming is rooted solely in Yahweh's profound passion for this people. In the end, the entire transformative intervention is rooted in Yahweh's own resolve, and it culminates in "my glory." The enhancement of Yahweh is accomplished through these wondrous acts of deliverance and homecoming, whereby the true and peculiar character of Yahweh is exhibited in the eyes of the watching nations. A "universalizing" propensity in theology may be affronted by this radical assertion that Yahweh takes sides and values some at the expense of others. The poet, however, does not flinch from the affirmation. Indeed, this conviction and passion are the ground of hope for the exilic community. It is, moreover, a hope to which any subsequent displaced and despised peoples (and there are many) cling desperately but firmly.

Testimony to the Holy, True God (43:8–13)

43:8 **Bring forth the people who are blind, yet have eyes,**
        who are deaf, yet have ears!
    ⁹**Let all the nations gather together,**
        and let the peoples assemble.
    Who among them declared this,
        and foretold to us the former things?
    Let them bring their witnesses to justify them,
        and let them hear and say, "It is true."
    ¹⁰**You are my witnesses, says the LORD,**
        and my servant whom I have chosen,
    so that you may know and believe me
        and understand that I am he.
    Before me no god was formed,
        nor shall there be any after me.
    ¹¹**I, I am the LORD,**
        and besides me there is no savior.
    ¹²**I declared and saved and proclaimed,**
        when there was no strange god among you;

> and you are my witnesses, says the LORD.
> ¹³ I am God, and also henceforth I am He;
>   there is no one who can deliver from my hand;
>   I work and who can hinder it?

These verses again take us to trial rhetoric we have already seen in 41:1–7, 21–29. Yahweh again enters into a formal dispute with the other gods in order to determine who is the true God and who is the proper subject of worship, fear, and obedience. The summons to the nations to come to trial with their gods is again issued in verse 9. There is here, however, a new feature we have not encountered in previous speeches of disputation. Here "blind, deaf" Israel is summoned to be Yahweh's witness, to give evidence, to tell the truth on Yahweh's behalf (v. 8).

The summons to the witnesses in verse 8 identifies them as blind and deaf; they are not identified as witnesses for Yahweh until verse 10. The characterization of Israel as witness is remarkable. We are aware that in 6:9–10 Israel is fated by Yahweh to blindness and deafness, and in 42:19, that sentence has not been overcome, for Israel is still identified with these disabilities as in our verse. Nonetheless, it is these very same Israelites, disability and all, who are now to come to court as witnesses, to give eyewitness evidence that Yahweh is qualified to be the true God. Even in its disability, Israel is reckoned to be an adequate and the only qualified witness to give such testimony.

The counterpoint to verses 8 and 10 is given in verse 9. The nations are to come to trial as advocates for their gods, and they also are to offer testimony. Thus the trial is not only god versus god; it is also witness versus witness and truth versus truth. Israel is placed by the poet in a context of contested truth, where it is not known ahead of time which truth will be vindicated and accepted by the court. The dispute about truth concerns theological claim about God, but it also concerns historical possibility; that is, whether Israel will be emancipated for homecoming. There is a great deal at stake in this judgment for Israel, as there is for Yahweh. This dispute about contested truth runs through the Bible; that is, wherever Yahweh's claim is in conflict with counterclaims. It is the question succinctly put to Jesus by Pilate: "What is truth?" (John 18:38). The question is endlessly posed and rings in the ears of the faithful. In our text, Israel must now give answer and tell the truth, a truth Israel has doubted in exile and the empire has rejected. It is a truth the empire can hardly bear; it is a truth the exiles can hardly entertain. But it is about to be said, clearly and without compromise.

The witnesses for the other gods are first invited to give evidence to the court (v. 9), with echoes of 41:21–24, 29. But they are "false witnesses." They are not false because they lie, but because that to which they testify is fraudulent and unreliable. We are waiting, says the poet, to be persuaded by their evidence, but of course we will not be. The poem does not linger long over their nonevidence.

But now comes Israel to testify. Even if blind and deaf, Israel is to give evidence, in the presence of the watching nations, that Yahweh is indeed the true and reliable God. In the midst of the summons to testify, Yahweh instructs the witness. It is as though the attorney briefs the witness on the right answers to the questions about to be asked in court. The evidence is that Yahweh is the only savior, that Yahweh is the only one who can deliver, that Yahweh will not be impeded by any counterforce—including Babylonian gods, Babylonian ideology, or Babylonian power. The evidence is ostensibly to persuade the watching nations. In effect, the text is addressed to Israel, "so that you may know and believe me/and understand that I am he" (v. 10b). The linkage between *the theological claim of Yahweh* and *the witness of Israel* is of primal importance. Indeed, Yahweh will not matter in the turn of history unless Israel gives evidence. Israel is instructed and empowered and authorized, and is able to "retell the world" in a Yahwistic version, its blindness and deafness notwithstanding. Because Israel knows and believes and understands, the world may be narrated differently, even in the face of the empire.

A Newness from Yahweh (43:14–21)

Because the disputation of verses 8–13 is ostensibly addressed to the nations but actually addressed to Israel, the move in verse 14 to a fresh salvation oracle is not surprising. The witness of verses 10 and 12 runs risks for the truth of Yahweh, so now follows a massive assurance to the exiles. The speech is introduced by a twofold "Thus says the Lord."

43:14 **Thus says the LORD,**
       your Redeemer, the Holy One of Israel:
     For your sake I will send to Babylon
       and break down all the bars,
       and the shouting of the Chaldeans will be turned to lamentation.
    15 **I am the LORD, your Holy One,**
       the Creator of Israel, your King.

In this first unit, "your Redeemer" promises to "send" to overthrow Babylon

(vv. 14–15). The lines echo 41:2–3 and refer to Cyrus, who will nullify Babylonian power. The historical specificity of the assurance, the most important assurance the exiles could hope to hear, is framed by two defining claims. First, the "sending" of verse 14 is framed by a cluster of names for Yahweh in verses 14a and 15. It is the Holy One, the king of Israel, the Redeemer, the Creator who acts. Second, it is "for your sake." That is, the turn of world history about to occur is because of Yahweh's peculiar attentiveness to the exilic community of Israel. The poetry of exilic Isaiah is insistent on this claim of the relationship between large-scale geopolitics and the core theological passion Yahweh has for Israel: "I love you" (v. 4).

> 43:16 **Thus says the LORD,**
>   **who makes a way in the sea,**
>   **a path in the mighty waters,**
>   [17] **who brings out chariot and horse,**
>   **army and warrior;**
>   **they lie down, they cannot rise,**
>   **they are extinguished, quenched like a wick:**
>   [18] **Do not remember the former things,**
>   **or consider the things of old.**
>   [19] **I am about to do a new thing;**
>   **now it springs forth, do you not perceive it?**
>   **I will make a way in the wilderness**
>   **and rivers in the desert.**
>   [20] **The wild animals will honor me,**
>   **the jackals and the ostriches;**
>   **for I give water in the wilderness,**
>   **rivers in the desert,**
>   **to give drink to my chosen people,**
>   [21]   **the people whom I formed for myself**
>   **so that they might declare my praise.**

The second introductory formula of verse 16 leads to one of the most daring and spectacular assertions of Isaiah. Israel is deeply grounded in the ancient memory of Yahweh. The "former things" likely refers here to the Exodus event, though it is not impossible that it also refers to the creation when Yahweh subdued the waters of chaos. Either way, Israel's faith is rooted in a recital of ancient miracles that affirm the reality and force of Yahweh as the definitive player in its life.

We may also mention an alternative interpretation that is now offered. It could be that the "former things" refers to the harsh judgment on Jerusalem announced repeatedly as the primary theme of Isaiah 1—39. Thus Brevard Childs, in his *Introduction to the Old Testament as Scripture* (p. 329), concludes: "The 'former things' can only now refer to the prophecies of First Isaiah. The point of Second Isaiah's message is that this prophetic word has been confirmed." This reading is a fresh proposal that has not yet been widely accepted in scholarship, but it remains as a live alternative that needs to be taken seriously.

In any case, now Yahweh is doing a "new thing." The new thing is perhaps not unlike the old thing, if we take the old thing to be Exodus or creation. The new thing is a massive miracle that transforms all of life. On this reading, the new thing, with reference to verses 16–17, is a new Exodus, an emancipation from Babylon not unlike the ancient emancipation from Egypt. The new thing, however, is not a thin, isolated historical event. It is rather a cosmic transformation whereby an arid landscape is transposed into a fountain of water that will make new life possible. The rhetoric here recalls the lyric of 35:5–7 and 41:17–20. The creator God will renovate and restore all of creation. Many creatures will benefit, including jackals and ostriches. But the focal point, characteristically, is "my chosen people," the ones seemingly shamed and abandoned in exile (v. 20).

If, on the other hand, Childs is followed in his reading, then the "new thing" here announced is forgiveness that will terminate and overcome the judgment that is the governing theme of chapters 1—39. In this way, Childs suggests that "former thing" and "new thing" refer to the structure of the book of Isaiah that reflects the pivotal turn from judgment to rescue in the life of Israel.

On either reading, the most interesting and delicate issue is the relation between old thing and new thing. Claus Westermann says of the new things:

> Israel requires to be shaken out of a faith that has nothing to learn about God's activity, and therefore nothing to learn about what is possible with him, the great danger which threatens any faith that is hidebound in dogmatism, faith that has ceased to be able to expect anything really new from him.

Scholars variously give nuance to that relationship of old and new, with varying accents of continuity and discontinuity. There is no doubt that the new thing cannot be understood apart from reference to the old thing that gives categories for discernment. But it is equally the case that Israel is here urged to get its mind off old things to focus totally on the new—because it pertains to present reality and not to an ancient memory, and because the new is more dazzling, more overwhelming, more massive than any old memory. Israel never escapes from or transcends its primal memory. But it is true nonetheless that biblical faith is geared to the future. It moves always to God's coming miracle that pushes past old treasured miracles and old suffered judgments.

In *The Old Testament of the Old Testament: Patriarchal Narratives and Mosaic Yahwism*, Walter Moberly has carefully explored the relationship between the old and the new in biblical faith, and has shown (among other things) how this delicate issue is demanding and tricky for Christians who want to affirm that Jesus is a radical newness from God, and yet is situated in and cannot be known apart from all that is old, remembered, and treasured. I suspect that the poet wants Israel to resist a "thin past." Faith requires a "thick memory" that is always letting ancient miracles be reenacted in always fresh and daring ways. It remains for the deaf, blind witnesses to *see and know*, in order that they rightly understand their true, Yahwistic situation. Israel cannot slough off what is old; but Israel cannot stay there either, for Yahweh is moving on to a fresh present tense that is indeed different from what was.

A Wearying People (43:22–28)

Again in verse 22, we are treated to a deep rhetorical disjunction. The God who has spoken to Israel so reassuringly (vv. 1–7), so emphatically (vv. 8–13), and so freshly (vv. 14–21) now reverses field. These verses are a prophetic dispute with Israel not unlike the great prophetic oracles of an earlier time. We are ill-prepared for such rhetoric. And yet we are already on notice in 42:18–25 that everything is not "sweetness and light" with Yahweh's people in exile.

43:22 **Yet you did not call upon me, O Jacob;**
       but you have been weary of me, O Israel!
   23 **You have not brought me your sheep for burnt offerings,**
       or honored me with your sacrifices.
   I have not burdened you with offerings,
       or wearied you with frankincense.
   24 **You have not bought me sweet cane with money,**
       or satisfied me with the fat of your sacrifices.
   But you have burdened me with your sins;
       you have wearied me with your iniquities.

The initial onslaught of these verses is a rebuke to Israel (vv. 22–24). Yahweh expected to be worshiped. Yahweh expected to be called upon and counted upon, and to be served with visible, material, generous gifts. But Israel has been too "worn out" to fulfill its liturgical obligations.

This particular indictment of Israel may come to us as a surprise. In 1:12–15 the ancient prophet Isaiah had God reject all the dramatic offers of Israel's worship. However, that dismissive pronouncement did not say that Yahweh did not want and welcome such offerings. Rather, Yahweh did not desire such offerings from *disqualified Israel*, who "eats and drinks unworthily" in Yahweh's presence. Indeed, says that ancient voice: "[Your offerings] have become a burden to me,/I am weary of bearing them" (1:14b). Offerings given by an unworthy people are an exhausting chore to Yahweh. Moreover, a prophetic psalm suggests that such offerings are in principle unwelcome to Yahweh:

> "I will not accept a bull from your house,
>   or goats from your folds.
> For every wild animal of the forest is mine,
>   the cattle on a thousand hills. . . .
> If I were hungry, I would not tell you,
>   for the world and all that is in it is mine."
>   (Psalm 50:9–10, 12–13)

Yahweh has no need of anything Israel can bring.

In our text, however, Yahweh rebukes Israel for not bringing offering and sacrifices. It is as though, in a situation of dispute with Babylonian gods, Yahweh wants and must have visible, dramatic, generous acknowledgments of allegiance from Israel. Paul Hanson observes:

> The meaning behind God's accusation that Israel has withheld offering is clearly this: Israel's niggardliness is a sign of the deadness of its heart in what should be the most precious of all relationships; Israel is incapable of extending even the simple gesture of gratitude symbolized by food (*Isaiah 40–66*, 77).

Whereas Yahweh had wearied of Israel's much worship in 1:14, here Yahweh is wearied with Israel's sin and iniquity. Yahweh has not made excessive liturgical demands on Israel, demands that make Israel "serve Yahweh" and "weary Yahweh." The field, however, is now reversed because of Israel's recalcitrance. Israel, who should have "served" Yahweh, now requires that Yahweh "serve" Israel: "But you have burdened me with your sins;/you have wearied me with your iniquities" (v. 24b). The literal rendering of the Hebrew in the first line is "You have caused me to serve."

Everything is distorted. The true relationship between Yahweh and Yahweh's people is perverted, and Yahweh will no longer tolerate the distortion.

43:25 **I, I am He**
>   **who blots out your transgressions for my own sake,** *(in. 4:5 Gosph.)*
>   **and I will not remember your sins.**

In the midst of this heavy-duty dispute, verse 25 provides a surprising and welcome pause. Yahweh now moves against Israel's self-destructive sin. Yahweh's self-announcement in the double first-person pronoun ("I, I"), reiterating the same rhetoric from verse 11, now promises forgiveness. As 40:1–2 announced forgiveness for the sins that caused exile, so here forgiveness is offered for sins committed in exile, for refusal to go public in liturgical ways for Yahweh in the face of the Babylonians. Yahweh is endlessly committed to this people and will yet again disrupt the serious indictment with an act of forgiving and forgetting.

43:26 **Accuse me, let us go to trial;**
>   **set forth your case, so that you may be proved right.**
> 27 **Your first ancestor sinned,**
>   **and your interpreters transgressed against me.**
> 28 **Therefore I profaned the princes of the sanctuary,**
>   **I delivered Jacob to utter destruction,**
>   **and Israel to reviling.**

It is, however, as though the generosity of verse 25 is only a passing thought. In verse 26, the harsh tone of verses 22–24 is resumed. The NRSV rendering of verse 26 misses the delicacy of the rhetoric. In verse 26, the first verb is "cause me to remember," that is, "remind me." The verb is the same Hebrew term that ends verse 25, that says, "Yahweh will not remember." Thus in verse 26, accused Israel is invited by Yahweh to make a case so that it may be vindicated. Yahweh is prepared both to forget and to remember as may benefit Israel.

But as Yahweh has not waited for the evidence to be presented on behalf of the Babylonian gods in 41:21–23, so here there is not much pause for evidence on behalf of Israel. Indeed, Yahweh as judge already knows and has already decided. Yahweh has long known about Abraham, "your first ancestor." Israel is marked by recalcitrance, disobedience, and unfaith from the outset. The second line of verse 27 and its reference to "interpreters" perhaps refers to Moses and Aaron. The whole history of Israel is enough to provoke Yahweh (on which see Psalm 106). For that reason, destruction has come.

The judicial sentence of verse 28 is exceedingly strong. The first verb suggests that Israel is so polluted as to make it unworthy for worship of Yahweh. The second verb (*ḥrm*) is the ancient term used for massive, total annihilation (see 34:2, 5). The verse anticipates harsh termination of Israel. The indictment of verse 27 uses the terms of sin and transgression already named and forgiven in verse 25. But obviously, in the flow of the poetry, the sins forgiven still linger with power in Israel. It is possible to take verse 25, which clearly disrupts the flow of the dispute, as an intrusion in the text. It is preferable, in my judgment, to respect the disjunction as a reflection of the convoluted relationship between Yahweh and Israel that is deeply marked both by savage hostility and by genuine affection. In verses 22–28, the tone of hostility is pervasive, interrupted only by verse 25. But of course these harsh verses do not stand alone. They occur in the midst of the profound affirmation of the salvation oracles before (43:1–7, 14–21) and after (44:1–8).

We may notice one other rhetorical feature that is particularly poignant. In 43:14, it is affirmed that Yahweh will act "for your sake." Yahweh will break Babylon for the sake of the well-being of Israel. In verse 25, however, forgiveness is "for my own sake," for the sake of Yahweh, that is, because it is in Yahweh's character and nature and passion to forgive Israel. Now it may be that *the external rescue of Babylon* (vv. 14–15) and the *intimate act of forgiveness* (v. 25) evoke different groundings and motivations. I prefer to think, however, that Yahweh's motivations are mixed and unclear, as they often are in relationships of deep love and intense pain. One is not sure, ever, that the generous act is done to enhance the other or to satisfy one's own propensity toward the other. Both characteristically operate; both operate for Yahweh. Perhaps in the end, in a relationship of deep care and passion as is the case of Yahweh and Israel, the two merge so that one does not know what is "for your sake" and what is "for my sake." Yahweh is not a principle or an automaton or a one-dimensional force. Yahweh, in the imagination of Israel, is a real live player, able to enact and to give voice to a mix of inclinations and emotions that are powerful and serious but not fully sorted out. Israel characteristically is on the receiving end of this God so peculiar, so inscrutable, so forthcoming, so elusive, so decisive, so irresistible. In the end, what is known in this transaction of forgiveness and harshness is that this is the God of "new things." Israel testifies to it, and the nations can see it happening.

GOD AGAINST THE GODS
44:1–23

This complicated passage uses the literary genres with which we are now familiar (salvation oracle and speech of disputation) and sounds the theological accents we have come to expect: Yahweh is attentive to Israel; Yahweh is stronger than the other gods. The text begins and ends with assurances to Israel: verses 1–5 are a salvation oracle with the crucial phrase "do not fear"; the concluding small units (vv. 21–22, 23) do not bear the marks of the salvation oracle, but in any case offer assurances to Israel. Between these framing assurances, the text is filled out with a speech of disputation (vv. 6–8) that is expanded and supplemented by a long negating section on idols (vv. 9–20). As we will see, this middle section of the unit breaks rhetorical convention in important ways but nonetheless stays focused upon Yahweh's incomparable power. The effect of the whole is to assure Israel that life in a world well governed by Yahweh is indeed a viable, reliable alternative to a Babylonian-construed reality.

I Belong to the Lord (44:1–5)

44:1 **But now hear, O Jacob my servant,**
  Israel whom I have chosen!
 ²**Thus says the LORD who made you,**
  who formed you in the womb and will help you:
 Do not fear, O Jacob my servant,
  Jeshurun whom I have chosen.
 ³**For I will pour water on the thirsty land,**
  and streams on the dry ground;
 I will pour my spirit upon your descendants,
  and my blessing on your offspring.
 ⁴**They shall spring up like a green tamarisk,**
  like willows by flowing streams.
 ⁵**This one will say, "I am the LORD's,"**
  another will be called by the name of Jacob,
 yet another will write on the hand, "The LORD's,"
  and adopt the name of Israel.

This salvation oracle, congruent with 41:8–13, 14–16, and 43:1–7, offers an intense assurance to Israel. It also serves with the disjunctive "but now" in verse 1 (as in 43:1) to contradict and override the heavy indictment of 42:22–28. This beginning point declares that abrasiveness is over and done with, so that Israel may now receive the newness of Yahweh's present tense. In the first verse, Israel is addressed and identified according to its traditional claim of chosenness. This identification is complemented in verse 2a by an identification of Yahweh with three strong verbs: Yahweh is the one who *made* and *formed*, and Yahweh is the one who will now *help*. Thus the two parties are the faithful *initiator* and the needful *receiver*. The interaction between the two is from Yahweh's side: "Do not fear." The phrase assures Yahweh's commitment to Israel and Israel's consequent well-being.

What follows is the ground for the banishment of Israelite fear, an exposition of Yahweh's verb "help." The *help* of Yahweh (see Psalms 121:1–2; 124:8; 146:5) consists of *water* in an arid environment and *spirit* on the next generation, so that there is flourishing in Israel (vv. 3–4). The imagery portrays dry, barren, hopeless Israel in the desert of Babylonian ideology, now richly transformed by the water of Yahweh, who has the power to enliven what is dead and to give futures to those who are hopeless. The language of verse 3 echoes the trusted promises of the ancestral narrative of Genesis. The promise, moreover, links water and spirit; that is, a concrete reference and an elusive assurance in faith, a combination that appears to refer back to the working of creation in which the "spirit" moves in the "waters" (Gen. 1:2). Christians, moreover, will be quick to connect the imagery to the inscrutable sacramental power of baptism, with its focus upon water and spirit.

The outcome of this transformative activity on the part of Yahweh is that Israel in exile will receive a clear, fresh identity as Yahweh's people. The naming (renaming) consists of four names for Israel. The second and fourth (Jacob, Israel) are conventional and allude to Genesis memory. It is, however, the first and third ("I am the Lord's, The Lord's") that are especially suggestive. Both of these terms have the Hebrew proposition "*le*," which here means "belonging to, linked decisively to Yahweh." The usage is commonly thought to be a stamp that is put upon a ceramic jar handle when tax is paid in kind. When the jar of grain is sent to the royal government, the jar bears the mark "belonging to the king," not unlike making a check out to "Internal Revenue Service."

In the imaginative world of exile, it is as though these displaced people had stamped on their hopeless bodies "belonging to the king of Babylon, belonging to the Babylonian gods." And now, a new name, a new identity, a new relationship is stamped on the life of Israel. Israel belongs, it is asserted, not to Babylon but to Yahweh, belongs both in terms of being safe and well-beloved (see 43:4) and in terms of obedience. Indeed, the whole story of Yahweh with Israel is to secure Israel as a special treasured possession of Yahweh: "For they are my servants, whom I brought out of the land of Egypt; they shall not be sold as slaves are sold" (Lev. 25:42; see Exod. 19:5). Even though by outward appearance Israel is still the property and possession of Babylon, it is not so! Therefore Israel need not fear or trust or serve Babylon. In the later development of Christian baptism, one can see the marks of the same disjunctive process, for it is "by water and spirit," claims the Christian sacrament, that a new identity is given to the baptized, free of old identities, old slaveries, old obediences, old fears, and old trusts. The "fear not" of Yahweh gives to Israel a new life, a new identity, a new way to be in the world.

Witnesses to the Redeemer (44:6–8)

44:6 Thus says the LORD, the King of Israel,
    and his Redeemer, the LORD of hosts:
  I am the first and I am the last;
    besides me there is no god.
  7 Who is like me? Let them proclaim it,
    let them declare and set it forth before me.
  Who has announced from of old the things to come?
    Let them tell us what is yet to be.
  8 Do not fear, or be afraid;
    have I not told you from of old and declared it?
  You are my witnesses!
  Is there any god besides me?
    There is no other rock; I know not one.

We are shifted abruptly back to a speech of disputation in which Yahweh abrasively invites challenge. As in 41:2–4, 42:23–24, the defiant speech of Yahweh is introduced by a double "who?" The stated answer is "no one." There are no gods comparable to Yahweh. Again and predictably, Yahweh dominates the court case. Beyond that, however, we may identify three features of this speech of disputation that are distinctive. First, Yahweh the creator, the first and the last, is peculiarly linked to Israel. That is, the peculiar claims of history move in on the large claims of creation. This is "King of Israel," "his Redeemer." The term "redeemer" here is especially telling, for it concerns the rescuing activity of this kinsman Yahweh, who has purchased a weaker relative from economic bondage. Thus the term belongs to the same circle of imagery as the "exchange" in 43:3–5. The *redeemed* belong to the one who *redeems* and to no other.

The second point, as in 43:9–10, is that Israel is *witness* for Yahweh in a trial situation. Israel tells the truth about Yahweh to the court, the truth that Yahweh is the first and the last, the truth that Yahweh is the only God. Israel's truth telling, moreover, is rooted in its own dealing with Yahweh. The truth is that Yahweh has redeemed Israel; that is, rescued Israel from the power of the fake gods, the rescue that demonstrates and establishes the large claims of incomparability for Yahweh. Third, this role of witness illumines why in a speech of disputation we have in verse 8 "do not fear." This phrase, as we have seen (41:10, 13, 14; 43:1; 44:2), belongs to the salvation oracle. But here it is at the center of a speech of disputation.

Thus the themes of "do not fear" and "witness" are juxtaposed. The interface of the two occurs because being witness to Yahweh in the hostile environment of Babylonian ideology is a scary thing. It is to place one's self in jeopardy, because the claim of Yahweh challenges the ideological, socioeconomic-political-military claims of Babylon. Truth telling for this witness is not a thin religious statement but a claim that touches the core pretensions of the great empire. Israel is summoned to dangerous work, with only the assurance that the redeemer who is the first and the last is a "rock" of reliability. Thus the poet has skillfully drawn from quite distinct literary genres to voice a quite new reality: The salvation oracle provides guarantees for the participants in the disputation of the trial.

The Nothingness of Idols and Their Witnesses (44:9–20)

44:9 **All who make idols are nothing, and the things they delight in do not profit; their witnesses neither see nor know. And so they will be put to shame.** [10] **Who would fashion a god or cast an image that can do no good?** [11] **Look, all its devotees shall be put to shame; the artisans too are merely human. Let them all assemble, let them stand up; they shall be terrified, they shall all be put to shame.**

[12] **The ironsmith fashions it and works it over the coals, shaping it with hammers, and forging it with his strong arm; he becomes hungry and his strength fails, he drinks no water and is faint.** [13] **The carpenter stretches a line, marks it out with a stylus, fashions it with planes, and marks it with a compass; he makes it in human form, with human beauty, to be set up in a shrine.** [14] **He cuts down cedars or chooses a holm tree or an oak and lets it grow strong among the trees of the forest. He plants a cedar and the rain nourishes it.** [15] **Then it can be used as fuel. Part of it he takes and warms himself; he kindles a fire and bakes bread. Then he makes a god and worships it, makes it a carved image and bows down before it.** [16] **Half of it he burns in**

the fire; over this half he roasts meat, eats it and is satisfied. He also warms himself and says, "Ah, I am warm, I can feel the fire!" [17] The rest of it he makes into a god, his idol, bows down to it and worships it; he prays to it and says, "Save me, for you are my god!"

[18] They do not know, nor do they comprehend; for their eyes are shut, so that they cannot see, and their minds as well, so that they cannot understand. [19] No one considers, nor is there knowledge or discernment to say, "Half of it I burned in the fire; I also baked bread on its coals, I roasted meat and have eaten. Now shall I make the rest of it an abomination? Shall I fall down before a block of wood?" [20] He feeds on ashes; a deluded mind has led him astray, and he cannot save himself or say, "Is not this thing in my right hand a fraud?"

This long presentation of idols is peculiar in exilic Isaiah and has few parallels in the Old Testament text (see Psalm 115:4–8 and Jer. 10:1–16). It is commonly recognized as a distinct unit that has been inserted into the midst of more familiar types of speech. Whereas the primary rhetorical agenda of Isaiah in exile is to persuade exiles of Yahweh's power and reliability, here the alternative strategy is undertaken to dismiss the claim and force of Babylonian gods. The primary verdict of the court is the succinct opening statement: "All who make idols are nothing. . . ." The makers of idols are *tôhû*, a Hebrew term meaning "chaos," that is, embodiments of disorder and practitioners of disorder. The strategy is to mock, belittle, and dismiss the other gods so that Yahweh is made conspicuous by contrast.

The general theme is that whereas Yahweh "makes" Israel (and the world) (v. 2), here Babylon "makes" its gods. These gods have no inherent power or force but are manufactured. As a consequence, they can have no more power or force than their "makers" can bestow upon them, which is nil. The direct contrast of Yahweh and these gods is evident in the verb "fashion" in verse 10, the same verb as "form" in verse 2, except that here the gods are object of the verb and not subject.

In order to stress the *production* of gods who are no center of power or authority, the text slowly, carefully, and in great detail traces the productive sequence for making a god. It takes many skilled craftspersons to "make a god." It requires an ironsmith who works so hard he becomes faint (v. 12). It requires a carpenter who not only hones the wood but must cut down the tree, who not only cuts down the tree but must plant it (vv. 13–14). It takes much foresight and a long time to make a god!

The poet clearly intends Israel to enjoy the scenario by making fun of these seductive alternatives in the life of Israel. The development of the text almost sounds as though the speaker plays to the audience. If the audience laughs (as it is supposed to), then there is evoked an even more ridiculous comment about these gods and their producers. The carpenter, the real maker of gods, is a foolish figure, almost clownish, enjoying the fire made by the wood (v. 16). But in the same breath, he speaks an imperative petition to it, "Save me" (v. 17). How could the carpenter be so obtuse that at the same time that he comments on the delightful warmth, he then expects rescue!

The Babylonian gods are overcome and defeated by ridicule. We may note here an ancient argument that has been replicated in the modern world by Ludwig Feuerbach, who argued in the nineteenth century that gods are simply "human projections." Feuerbach's argument, moreover, is taken up by Freud, who regarded religion as an "illusion," albeit one "necessary" to human community. We may notice two things about this ancient–modern assault on "the gods." First, it is important to recognize that Feuerbach's critique of religion is, in the end, almost unanswerable. Even Karl Barth, with his enormous theological courage and daring, could not finally answer Feuerbach but could only override the objection by firmer, more determined affirmation.

Second, in the ancient text and in contemporary faith still haunted by Feuerbach, Israel's (and the church's) claim about God is simply excluded in principle from the critique. The exception of Yahweh is not argued. Thus in our text, the poet asserts Yahweh and bids allegiance but cannot make a logical case. Everything depends, in the ancient text of Israel and in the contemporary faith of the church, upon the premise that "our God" is an exception to the rule that gods are "human projections." Thus the church, in its primal claim of faith, insists that its God is not like the other gods.

In order to appreciate this text as a resource for faith, it is necessary to contrast Yahweh to the would-be gods of our time and place. In the United States (it would be different elsewhere), the rival gods are likely the icons of free market capitalism that run from entertainment celebrities and sports heroes to the "bull market" to the generative power of television ads, all of which seek to seduce us into a cozy world of private safety and happiness. From the perspective of this text, these "idols" are fake precisely because they have no power to keep their promises. Thus such "adored" icons as Coke or Nike cannot in the end keep their promises, either to make us happy or to make us secure.

This twofold awareness that the *issue of "production" is not answerable* and that *Yahweh is excepted in principle from the critique* makes clear why the rhetoric of disputation is required. Truth is disputed, and Israel is an exposed, endangered witness. The faith of this community is always contested, and the community is always engaged in advocacy, seeking to show why its faith claims are valid when other faith claims are projections.

Although this long polemic is surely inserted in its context, we may ask why it is here in this place. The answer, I suggest, is that although the text concerns *rival gods*, the real emphasis is upon *rival witnesses*. Calvin comments:

> And in this passage there is a contrast between the testimony of the people of God and that of idolaters. The former will give an illustrious testimony of the glory of God from his works and promises and predictions; the latter will be constrained to be dumb, if they do not choose to bring forward contrivances which have no certainty whatever, and therefore are false and vain (*Isaiah* III, 369).

As Yahweh has a witness in Israel (v. 8), so the idols have witnesses (v. 9) who are also "devotees" (v. 11). But these witnesses are not here permitted to speak as they were invited to do in previous speeches of disputation. Here speaks someone (Yahweh?) from Israel in their behalf, to their great negation. They are intentionally reduced to silence, and derision is the only proper assessment that can be made. The final failure concerns not the gods but the Babylonian adherents who cling to their absurd loyalties. They are the foolish ones with whom Israel is to join issue. Thus again, although the argument is God versus gods, the case comes down to truth versus truth and witness versus witness, in a trial in which Babylon no longer enjoys the privilege of power.

The witnesses for the Babylonian gods are stupid, end in shame, and are terrified (vv. 9–11). The poetry invites Israel to reflect on what a sorry state these Babylonian witnesses are ultimately in, even if for an instant they seem to prevail. The assault on the Babylonian witnesses continues in verses 18–20. It is ironic that they are now in a position to be as obdurate and obtuse as Israel had been fated to be in 6:9–10; 42:18–19; 43:8. They do not understand and cannot figure it out. The climactic statement about these witnesses is "a deluded mind has led him astray" (v. 20). The Babylonian enterprise that has seemed so learned and stable and sophisticated is theologically misguided. There is no *saving* for the empire (vv. 17, 20).

The focus of our interpretation should be, I suggest, on the rhetorical effect of this polemic. The ostensible effect is to denude Babylonian confidence; the practical effect, more likely, is to embolden Israel by the systematic exposure of the adversary. In the end, the effect is to empower Israel to see and think and know and trust and act Yahwistically!

Israel Remembered and Forgiven
(44:21–22)

44:21 **Remember these things, O Jacob,**
    and Israel, for you are my servant;
  I formed you, you are my servant;
    O Israel, you will not be forgotten by me.
  [22] **I have swept away your transgressions like a cloud,**
    and your sins like mist;
  return to me, for I have redeemed you.

The jarring rhetorical demand of verses 6–20, in which Israel is pushed to dangerous, counterempire testimony, perhaps leaves Israel in a spent and anxious state. It is, on such a supposition, not surprising that the text now turns again to assurance. The mood of these verses is like a salvation oracle, though without the phrase "do not fear." The primal assurance in verse 21 is bracketed by "remember/forget." In 43:18–19, Israel is urged to "forget." Now, against that imperative, Israel is summoned to "remember" and is assured that Yahweh does not forget. It is a recurring sense of Israel in exile that Yahweh has forgotten Israel and Yahweh's own covenant obligations to Israel (see 49:14; Lam. 5:20). Here, against that propensity, Israel is assured that Yahweh persists in care and attentiveness for Israel. The inner two lines of the verse twice reiterate the term "my servant," together with the decisive verb "form" (see vv. 2, 21). Israel is a creature bound to Yahweh and the product of Yahweh's generative work, and is not abandoned. Even when Israel is fearful before the realities of Babylonian power, Yahweh's assurance trumps such intimidation.

Verse 22 cites the decisive action of Yahweh that demonstrates Yahweh's intense remembering of Israel. Yahweh has "swept away" Israel's sin and transgression. Already in 40:2, it is clear that exile results from sin; it is equally clear in the gospel announcement of 40:2 that punishment is fulfilled and now ended. Forgiveness is the primal message to Israel in exile. The verb here is the same as that used in 43:25 and in Israel's quintessential prayer for forgiveness (Psalm 51:1, 9). The affronts held against Israel have evaporated like clouds and mist, and are no more. The key evidence for Yahweh's governance is the reality of forgiveness. Yahweh has indeed acted like *redeemer* (see v. 6), the one who emancipates Israel and permits new life.

All that remains is that Israel "return." All that is necessary is that Israel should turn away from the world of Babylonian ideology and situate itself afresh in the world of Yahweh's assurances. Yahweh has completed the possibility. Israel now need only act on that possibility.

Once More Redeemer (44:23)

44:23 **Sing, O heavens, for the LORD has done it;**
shout, O depths of the earth;
break forth into singing, O mountains,
O forest, and every tree in it!
For the LORD has redeemed Jacob,
and will be glorified in Israel.

This final verse in this long sequence is a vigorous doxology to which all elements of creation are invited—heaven and earth, mountains and forest. The anticipated exuberance of all creation is not unlike Psalm 96:11–12, only there it is Yahweh's rule over all the earth that evokes praise (v. 10). Here the motivation for praise is the rescue of Israel. Yahweh is seen by all creation to be redeemer; thus the concluding line again sounds the reassuring title "Redeemer." It may well be that this verse forms a parallel to 41:1. In that verse a great summons is issued to the trial (to coastlands and peoples). Now in our verse, a different set of creatures is invited to celebrate the verdict that vindicates Yahweh. The rescue of Israel has cosmic significance, for it is the great example of Yahweh's sovereignty. Indeed, the last two lines juxtapose *the redemption of Israel* and *the glorification of Yahweh*. Israel is the test case for Yahweh; everybody can see in this rescue that Yahweh is more powerful than Babylonian gods, ostensibly the most powerful of all the gods. The boasts Yahweh has made in the speeches of disputation are all justified! Everybody knows: Israel is free!

THE GENTILE MESSIAH
44:24–45:13

This section of the text marks a major turn in the focus of the exilic poetry of Isaiah. Until now, the accent has been completely upon Yahweh and Yahweh's power, fidelity, and incomparability. The point of the poetry has been to permit the exiles to "see your god" (40:9), the God whom Babylonian ideology had eliminated as a serious factor in the life of the world. The intense concern for the reality, viability, and availability of Yahweh in these chapters has allowed for almost no attention to *human agency* in the rescue of Israel and the overthrow of Babylon. The work of rescue and overthrow has been directly and singularly the work of Yahweh. The only exceptions have been reference to "a victor from the east" (41:2) and "one from the north" (41:25), a human agent summoned and authorized by Yahweh but not yet named.

In the present unit of poetry, by contrast, the imagination of exilic Israel is led intentionally toward the prospect of human agency. The initial doxology (44:24–28) begins in large scope (v. 24) and moves to the concreteness of Cyrus (v. 28). Cyrus is directly addressed in a "royal oracle" (45:1–6) that culminates in a sweeping self-affirmation of Yahweh (v. 7). The whole of 44:24–45:7 is followed by a resounding doxology (v. 8) that is perhaps matched by the brief doxology of 44:23 (though I have placed that verse with the preceding poetic unit).

It is clear in 45:9–13 that the Yahwistic designation of Cyrus as Yahweh's agent evokes (unreported) resistance on the part of Israel, resistance that is answered by Yahweh in the chiding rebuke of verses 9–11. The unit ends with yet one more self-announcement of Yahweh, who reaffirms Cyrus as Yahweh's agent and chosen one in the turn of the world (vv. 12–13). Thus the sweeping, sovereign resolve of Yahweh is intimately and inalienably connected to the coming rule and ultimate domination of Cyrus and the Persians. This entire unit is of peculiar interest because it demonstrates the way in which biblical faith characteristically links *the rule of Yahweh* and *the concreteness of the historical.* That linkage is all the more compelling and problematic, because the historical side of the equation here is a non-Jew, an outsider to the faith horizon of the exilic community.

"The Lord Who . . ." (44:24–28)

44:24 Thus says the LORD, your Redeemer,
      who formed you in the womb:
  I am the LORD, who made all things,
      who alone stretched out the heavens,
      who by myself spread out the earth;
   25 who frustrates the omens of liars,
      and makes fools of diviners;
  who turns back the wise,
      and makes their knowledge foolish;
   26 who confirms the word of his servant,
      and fulfills the prediction of his messengers;
  who says of Jerusalem, "It shall be inhabited,"
      and of the cities of Judah, "They shall be rebuilt,
      and I will raise up their ruins";
   27 who says to the deep, "Be dry—
      I will dry up your rivers";

[28] who says of Cyrus, "He is my shepherd,
    and he shall carry out all my purpose";
and who says of Jerusalem, "It shall be rebuilt,"
    and of the temple, "Your foundation shall be laid."

These verses are a divine decree out of the mouth of Yahweh, the God who governs the council of the gods (6:1–8; 40:1–11), who rules over heaven and earth. The initial assertion "I am Yahweh" (v. 24) is followed and substantiated through a series of participial verbs that express Yahweh's most reliable and characteristic activity: "who formed, who made, who stretched, who spread, who frustrates, who makes, who turns back, who makes, who confirms, who fulfills, who says, who says, who says, who says." The flow of these participial affirmations is from the most general and comprehensive (all things, heavens, earth) to the most particular (Cyrus, Jerusalem). The connection of the general and the specific makes clear that all the power of the creator is now mobilized around the particularities of the rise of Cyrus and the rescue of Israel. The accent of the passage clearly falls on the four "who says" in verses 26–27. Yahweh addresses: (1) Jerusalem and its dependent cities; (2) the deep; (3) Cyrus; (4) Jerusalem and its temple. The purpose of the oracle is to focus the imagination of the exiles upon the restoration of the city (and the rehabilitation of Judaism) by the agency of Cyrus. The odd factor in this fourfold sequence is the address to "the deep," which may be a reference to the taming of chaotic waters or to the Exodus (Exod. 14:21). Either way, it is an allusion to Yahweh's demonstrated power to reorder the world in behalf of Israel. The address to Cyrus (v. 28) is most remarkable, for it is a direct linkage of Israel's God and a Gentile ruler, on the clear assumption that even Gentile rulers operate at the behest of Yahweh (see 10:5; Jer. 25:9; 27:6). This address to Cyrus points us to the next section of the text.

Cyrus Summoned (45:1–6)

45:1 Thus says the LORD to his anointed, to Cyrus,
        whose right hand I have grasped
    to subdue nations before him
        and strip kings of their robes,
    to open doors before him—
        and the gates shall not be closed:
[2] I will go before you
        and level the mountains,
    I will break in pieces the doors of bronze

and cut through the bars of iron,
  ³I will give you the treasures of darkness
      and riches hidden in secret places,
  so that you may know that it is I, the LORD,
      the God of Israel, who call you by your name.
  ⁴For the sake of my servant Jacob,
      and Israel my chosen,
  I call you by your name,
      I surname you, though you do not know me.
  ⁵I am the LORD, and there is no other;
      besides me there is no god.
  I arm you, though you do not know me,
  ⁶so that they may know, from the rising of the sun
      and from the west, that there is no one besides me;
  I am the LORD, and there is no other.

These verses exhibit Yahweh addressing Cyrus, summoning him to do the geopolitical work intended by Yahweh in behalf of Israel. Such a mode of address is a "royal decree" wherein God addresses a king in order to authorize, empower, legitimate, and instruct. Scholars suggest that the closest biblical parallel is Psalm 2, wherein Yahweh addresses David as king, a psalm incidentally used often in the New Testament for God's authorization of Jesus as "king" (Messiah) and "Son" (Matt. 3:17, 17:5; Mark 9:7; Luke 3:22, 9:25). The first words of verse 1 are among the most remarkable in the Bible, first because Cyrus, the coming leader of the coming superpower, is named by Yahweh, and second, because the name Cyrus is linked to the Jewish title "Messiah." The NRSV translation "anointed" is a rendering of the noun "anointed one," that is, "Messiah," which translated into Greek is "Christ." That is, in Old Testament parlance, this Gentile is "the Christ," the royal designee to enact the salvific intention of Yahweh. What a mouthful! Some scholars believe, moreover, that in this utterance Cyrus the Persian receives and takes over the claims of the Davidic dynasty, so that he is now the bearer of Davidic promises.

The breathtaking affirmation is that Israel will be saved by a non-Jew. Isaiah in exile thinks very large about God's future in the world and is not contained by Israel's conventional categories of faith and hope. Rescue by such an agent is scarcely acceptable in the community of exiles (see vv. 9–11). When this affirmation is pushed into the New Testament, moreover, the church is confronted by the same scandal when it is confessed that God's work is done by Jesus. On the one hand, Jesus is an uncredentialed nobody who comes from a no-place (Nazareth; see John 1:46). On the other hand, it is not only *Jesus of Nazareth* but it is *"him crucified,"* the staggering affirmation that God's power is enacted in Friday weakness. The early church (and the subsequent church) faced the same scandal as did the exiles, only more completely so in the claim that Jesus is "the Word enfleshed."

Beyond Cyrus and Jesus, moreover, we may observe that the same gospel reality continues to operate wherever God's purposes for the future are carried by "unacceptable" human agents: so Marx and Freud may be prophets in their time and place, and all sorts of conventionally unacceptable people—like minorities, women, the poor, homosexuals—may turn out to be bearers of God's possibilities in the world. In our text it is clear that God's future for Israel is not to be enacted in the way the Jews either expected or preferred.

The address to Cyrus is a powerful authorization (45:1) to enable Cyrus to have the authority and capacity (according to Yahwistic imagination) to storm the defenses and treasures of Babylon, which he did without firing a shot (vv. 2–3). Moreover, the oracle intends that Cyrus may "know" Yahweh (v. 3), even though "you do not know me" (v. 4). That is, those who enact Yahweh's purposes in the world ofttimes do not knowingly respond to Yahweh's initiative but may act for other reasons. The daring expectation of this poetry is that Cyrus may come to acknowledge that the move west by the Persian Empire is not just imperial policy but belongs to the larger purpose of the real Governor of international politics. Thus it is Yahweh who "names" Cyrus, who gives Cyrus identity and authority.

Beyond Cyrus, however, the rise of his realm from the east has two larger purposes. First, it is "for the sake of my servant Jacob" (v. 4). The entire international process is for the beloved, treasured people Israel. The "scandal of particularity" that Christians find in Jesus of Nazareth is already voiced here. Second, it is "that they may know"; that is, that all the world, beyond Persia and beyond Israel, may acknowledge Yahweh as the creator and only ruler of the world (v. 6). Thus the rescue of Israel characteristically has a larger purpose. Israel—and often the church—wants to contain and limit the purposes of God to its own life. Here it is clear that Yahweh always looks well beyond the beloved community. The rescue of Israel is in part instrumental, even as was the Exodus in part instrumental, for it was so that Yahweh should "get glory over Pharaoh" (Exod. 14:4, 17).

Lord of All These Things
(45:7)

45:7 **I form light and create darkness,**
   I make weal and create woe;
   I the LORD do all these things.

This verse as a climactic claim for Yahweh is among the most sweeping in the entire Bible (see Deut. 32:39; 1 Sam. 2:6; Job 5:18). The first word pair—light/darkness—alludes to the work of creation, for "darkness is as light to you" (Psalm 139:12). The second word pair—*shalom*/evil (translated here as "weal/woe")—refers back to historical relations of prosperity and suffering. In both phrases, the verbs include not only the conventional "make, form," but a double use of "create," the most exalted and majestic term the Old Testament has for Yahweh's generative capacity. It is likely that the two word pairs—light/darkness, *shalom*/evil—mean to be inclusive, that is, everything from A to Z in creation and in history. Yahweh is the one, the only one, who is responsible for what is, and that surely includes Cyrus, the fall of Babylon, and the emancipation of Israel.

Taken out of context, the claim of this verse is problematic, for it is affirmed that *Yahweh creates evil*, a statement sure to vex and puzzle. Taken in context, however, the doxological claim wants to eliminate all rival claims, either about the power of the Babylonian gods or the autonomy of Cyrus or the voice of Israel in its dissenting mistrust (as suggested in vv. 9–11). None of these count: Babylonian gods have no voice in the future of Babylon. Cyrus has no clout in the rise of his empire. Israel has no vote on its destiny. Everything is settled on Yahweh's terms, for Yahweh is without rival, adviser, competitor, or aide. What is now to happen through Cyrus is sure, because it is the resolve of Yahweh.

A Doxological Interlude (45:8)

45:8 **Shower, O heavens, from above,**
       and let the skies rain down righteousness;
    let the earth open, that salvation may spring up,
       and let it cause righteousness to sprout up also;
       I the LORD have created it.

This brief verse, a sweeping doxology for the creator, corresponds to the doxology of 44:23, but there is an important difference between the two verses. In 44:23, it is the redemption of Israel that is celebrated. Here it is the gift of creation that causes the earth to prosper. The horizon of Yahweh's sovereignty is pushed to its most comprehensive claim, a claim well beyond the future of Israel. The double use of "righteousness" makes clear that a theology of blessing is intimately linked to the creator's intent for a rightly ordered, life-sustaining creation. Israel's praise here pushes well beyond any conventional affirmation. The exuberance of Israel is to celebrate "all these things" (v. 7), that "what is" is the gift of Yahweh. The singing community is invited to praise, awe, amazement, and gratitude that are boundless, to note the limitless sovereignty and generosity of Yahweh.

Implied Questions, Explicit Answers (45:9–13)

45:9 **Woe to you who strive with your Maker,**
      earthen vessels with the potter!
  Does the clay say to the one who fashions it, "What are you making"?
  or "Your work has no handles"?
  ¹⁰**Woe to anyone who says to a father, "What are you begetting?"**
      or to a woman, "With what are you in labor?"
  ¹¹**Thus says the LORD,**
      the Holy One of Israel, and its Maker:
  Will you question me about my children,
      or command me concerning the work of my hands?
  ¹²**I made the earth,**
      and created humankind upon it;
  it was my hands that stretched out the heavens,
      and I commanded all their host.
  ¹³**I have roused Cyrus in righteousness,**
      and I will make all his paths straight;
  he shall build my city
      and set my exiles free,
  not for price or reward,
      says the LORD of hosts.

We are hardly prepared, after such comprehensive praise, for the abrupt reversal of tone in verse 9. The opening word "woe" voices a threat of judgment, sadness, and grief, as we have already seen in the tone of 5:8–23. The term and its mood are indeed a non sequitur after 44:24–45:8 and its exuberant affirmation. Thus we may suppose that something happened between verses 8 and 9 to evoke this rebuke from Yahweh. It makes most sense that Israel in exile responded negatively and resistantly to the Cyrus announcement of a non-Jewish messiah. Israel apparently has asserted that rescue should not come from a Gentile and wants to be saved in a clearly Jewish way. That is, recalcitrant Israel wants to be saved in its own way by its own kind and doubts the viability of the "Cyrus project." Israel, so we imagine, believes it has a right to doubt and question and refuse Yahweh's resolve for the future, because the resolve just announced is too shocking and unconventional and scandalous.

In response to such a supposed objection, verses 9–11 make good sense. It has just been affirmed that Yahweh acts decisively and alone and needs no help (v.7). Thus the assumed objection of Israel moves precisely against that claim, and Yahweh will have none of it! In order to demonstrate the absurdity and objectionable quality of Israel's resistance, the poetry employs two images. In verse 9, the relation of potter and pot is reviewed. The potter holds initiative, and the pot is the object acted upon. It cannot be otherwise. The clay has no voice in what happens in the work of the potter. This thought is expressed in the romantic, pietistic hymn *Have Thine Own Way, Lord:* "Thou art the potter, I am the clay." But Israel—the clay—has tried to question and correct the potter. The question of verse 9 requires a negative answer: *no*, the clay does not ask what is being made; *no*, the clay does not comment on the handles being formed.

In verse 10 an even more daring image is used. These lines imagine a father in the act of impregnating the mother, and then the mother in labor. *No*, the sperm does not question the father. *No*, the fetus does not interrogate the mother in labor. *No*, the creature does not question the creator. *No*, the exiles do not interrogate the Lord of history. *No*, Israel does not cross-examine Yahweh. *No, no, no!* Verse 7 had defined the proper relation between the two parties. Yahweh decides, decrees, intends, plans, and executes. Israel receives. Yahweh may indeed do what Yahweh's people do not want; Yahweh is not captive to the conventional expectations of Yahweh's people. The messiah can be a Gentile!

The divine response to the alleged objections of Israel comes in verses 11–13. The one who speaks is holy, the one who has formed Israel. That is, Israel has no standing ground outside Yahweh, but as Yahweh's creation Israel is contained completely within the rule of Yahweh. Thus the question of verse 11 is in fact a rebuke: *No*, you will not ask me! The role of creator and creature will not be confused or inverted. Israel is object, recipient, creature; that is all. Yahweh's plans are not decided in consultation with Israel, any more than they are decided in discussion with the gods (see 41:28).

The scolding rebuke of verse 11 is reinforced by the first-person assertion of verses 12–13: "I made, I created, my hands stretched out, I commanded, I aroused, I will make." Yahweh does all this. The purpose of the assertion is to silence Israel, to override the protests and questions that Israel has no right to voice.

Notice again that the sweeping claims of creation, as in 44:24–28, move by verse 13 to Cyrus. The verb "arouse" is the same verb we have found in 41:2, 25. The Hebrew does not here include the name "Cyrus" as it does in 44:28 and 45:1, contrary to the reading of the NRSV. But the antecedent is clear. The large purpose of the creator devolves upon Cyrus. Cyrus will free the exiles by an act of power, not an act of barter or ransom (see 43:3–4). Yahweh is not talked out of Cyrus as the way of the future, any more than Jesus is talked out of the cross as a way to the future (see Mark 8:31–34), any more than God is ever talked out of scandalous modes of activity. It is the business of the community of God's people—in the contemporary world as in the ancient world—to "take no offense at me" (Luke 7:23). Yahweh is not moved by such protests. Yahweh's purpose in history is to emancipate, even if in ways taken by the faithful to be objectionable. Such objections impinge upon "the Lord of hosts" not at all.

EITHER YAHWEH OR . . .
45:14–25

These verses constitute a series of brief poetic units only loosely connected to each other. The core theme of the several units is the sovereignty of Yahweh that speaks in favor of Israel and against the Babylonian idols and their makers. As we will see, the by now familiar theme of sovereignty evokes several images and phrases that are more broadly important for biblical faith.

Saved and Not Shamed (45:14–17)

45:14 **Thus says the LORD:**
> **The wealth of Egypt and the merchandise of Ethiopia,**
> > **and the Sabeans, tall of stature,**
> **shall come over to you and be yours,**
> > **they shall follow you;**
> > **they shall come over in chains and bow down to you.**
> **They will make supplication to you, saying,**
> > **"God is with you alone, and there is no other;**
> > **there is no god besides him."**
> 15 **Truly, you are a God who hides himself,**
> > **O God of Israel, the Savior.**
> 16 **All of them are put to shame and confounded,**
> > **the makers of idols go in confusion together.**
> 17 **But Israel is saved by the LORD**

with everlasting salvation;
you shall not be put to shame or confounded
to all eternity.

These verses move abruptly from one mode of address to another. Israel is addressed in verse 14 and again in verse 17. But in verse 15 God is addressed. Thus there is no smooth flow through the verses but only a series of brief, disconnected statements. In verse 14 Israel is addressed with a most uncommon assurance, namely, that the wealth of the most exotic states and cultures will come in submissiveness to Judah. The theme is perhaps an echo of 43:3–4, only now the promise is aggressively materialistic. The tone is almost imperialistic: Israel will receive and enjoy the material wealth of others, perhaps an affirmation to be understood as "the last becoming first." But the *material* concession of other people will be accompanied by a *theological* recognition as well. In the end, other peoples will come to acknowledge Yahweh. The last two lines of the verse make two very distinct theological affirmations. First, Yahweh is allied *only with Israel*; second, Yahweh is the *only God*. Although the two statements may turn out practically to be equivalents, the second line is a sweeping advance beyond the first. The several peoples learn belatedly what every people must learn. In the end, even ancient Pharaoh had to acknowledge Yahweh as the God with whom he must deal: "Let us flee from the Israelites, for the LORD is fighting for them against Egypt" (Exod. 14:25; see Exod. 10:16). Before Pharaoh, Laban had confessed similar awareness: "If you will allow me to say so, I have learned by divination that the LORD has blessed me because of you" (Gen. 30:27). After Pharaoh, the Gibeonites knew and confessed the same truth about Yahweh:

> "Because it was told to your servants for a certainty that the LORD your God had commanded his servant Moses to give you all the land, and to destroy all the inhabitants of the land before you; so we were in great fear for our lives because of you, and did this thing. And now we are in your hand: do as it seems good and right in your sight to do to us" (Josh. 9:24–25).

Soon or late, Yahweh is confessed because the evident role of Yahweh in the life of the world cannot be denied.

The address of verse 15 shifts to Yahweh. Now a remarkable confession about Yahweh is made, apparently by Israel: "You are a God who hides himself." This theme is an exceedingly important theological motif, even if its intent here is not self-evident. It is clear that Yahweh's hiddenness is intrinsic to Yahweh's character and is not simply a response to human sin.

Hiddenness belongs to Yahweh's unfettered freedom and refusal to be contained or even known by conventional categories. In that ancient world, Yahweh is hidden in the coming of Cyrus, a way of Yahweh's coming not at all evident in the world. Luther, moreover, had understood that hiddenness not only characterizes God's freedom from control and domestication, but that God's *power* is hidden in the *weakness and vulnerability of the cross*. God works and impinges on the world in ways not discernable except to the faithful. With the rise of Enlightenment modes of rational, autonomous discernment, moreover, Blaise Pascal is moved to put God beyond all such decipherment: "A religion which does not affirm that God is hidden is not true" (so rendered by Samuel Terrien in *The Elusive Presence*, xxv).

It is not self-evident that verse 16 is linked to verse 15, because it seems to be a general polemic against idols and their makers. If, however, we see here an intentional contrast between *hidden God* and *idol*, then it is clear that an idol is an available, visible, palpable object completely exhaustible upon contact. Such gods are truly "pornographic" because they leave nothing to the imagination and have no density of power or will in reserve. (That is already quite clear in 44:9–20.) By contrast, Yahweh is hidden, not completely visible or available, not exhaustible on contact, but always with more power and more fidelity, more elusiveness and more incomparability in reserve, living well beyond the sight and decoding and discernment of human eyes or human reason. Thus the contrast of *Yahweh hidden* (v. 15) and the confused *idol-makers* (v. 16) nicely results in the double use of "save" in verse 17. It is God hidden—beyond domestication—who has the power to emancipate Israel and to make all things new.

The Creator beyond Chaos (45:18–19)

45:18 **For thus says the LORD,**
    who created the heavens (he is God!),
    who formed the earth and made it
      (he established it;
    he did not create it a chaos,
      he formed it to be inhabited!):
    I am the LORD, and there is no other.
    [19] **I did not speak in secret,**
      in a land of darkness;
    I did not say to the offspring of Jacob,
      "Seek me in chaos."
    I the LORD speak the truth,
      I declare what is right.

Although the tone and tenor of these verses is clear enough, the point being made by the poetry is not clear. The positive affirmation concerning Yahweh is dominated by powerful verbs "created, formed." Indeed, the positive affirmation about Yahweh occurs at the beginning (v. 18a), in the middle (the end of v. 18), and at the end (v. 19). Sandwiched in between, in verses 18b–19a, are three negative statements (*not* create, *not* speak, *not* say) that are linked to the double use of "chaos" (*tôhû*). Thus the contrast is total, a contrast between creator God and chaos that echoes the contrast between hidden God and idols in verses 15–16.

The creator God intends a fruitful, life-giving, inhabited earth. It is not clear what chaos (*tôhû*) refers to in this context, and perhaps it is not meant to be clear. On first reading, the contrast between creator and chaos alludes to something like the creation liturgy of Genesis 1:2 (perhaps dated at the same time as Isaiah in exile), wherein chaos is treated as precreation material and as the anticreation force of nothingness. We do not, however, expect Isaiah in exile to reiterate such a large or generic theme. Thus we may suggest that here chaos more particularly refers to the *death-dealing context* of Babylonian exile; or to the confused *idol-makers* who are the rulers of the empire, who are termed *tôhû* in 44:9; or to the *idols* themselves who are purveyors of deathly disorder (see 41:19). Or perhaps the term refers to all of these. Yahweh is in sharp contrast to all of them. Consequently, those who subscribe to Yahweh's rule may expect a different life in a different world. Although we do not know the precise intent of "chaos" in this usage, we can be very clear about Yahweh, who is offered as an alternative who makes an ordered, viable, fruitful life possible.

"No Other God" (45:20–21)

45:20 **Assemble yourselves and come together,**
  draw near, you survivors of the nations!
 They have no knowledge—
  those who carry about their wooden idols,
 and keep on praying to a god
  that cannot save.
 [21] **Declare and present your case;**
  let them take counsel together!
 Who told this long ago?
  Who declared it of old?
 Was it not I, the LORD?
  There is no other god besides me,

> a righteous God and a Savior;
> there is no one besides me.

These verses are a brief speech of disputation in which the poet once more imagines a trial between Yahweh and the other gods (see 41:1–7, 21–29). Again there is a summons to assembly, and again there is an invitation to testify, and again there is the defiant question "Who?" By now we are not surprised that the answer to "Who?" is: "Was it not I, the Lord?" (v. 21). The peculiar, singular claim of Yahweh culminates again in the appellation "Savior," thus echoing verse 17.

We are now able to identify the radical either/or in this peculiar section of brief poetic units: either hidden God or shamed idols (vv. 14–17); either created habitation or chaos (vv. 18–19); either saving God or wooden idols who cannot save (vv. 20–21). The radical either/or is characteristically addressed to Jewish exiles who are required to decide their faith and consequently their destiny. But here, in verse 20, the address is to "you survivors of the nations," suggesting that the either/or is addressed beyond Israel to what is left of Babylon, given the expected onslaught of Cyrus. Even Babylon is invited to choose its future, and it may choose Yahweh. Even Babylon may choose the *hidden God* (v. 15), *created habitation* (v. 18), and *saving God* (v. 21). What is offered to exilic Jews is offered to the Gentile world as well!

The Ultimate Turn (45:22–23)

45:22 **Turn to me and be saved,**
        all the ends of the earth!
    For I am God, and there is no other.
   23 **By myself I have sworn,**
        from my mouth has gone forth in righteousness
        a word that shall not return:
    "To me every knee shall bow,
        every tongue shall swear."

On the basis of this threefold "either/or," a massive imperative summons is now issued. The summons is to *turn* and face a different way. The consequence of such turning is *being saved*, but the being saved is dependent upon turning. Without turning, there is no saving, and one is fated to idols and their consequent hopeless chaos. Most remarkably, this mighty summons is issued to "all the ends of the earth!" All peoples are invited to the rule of Yahweh as an alternative to the coming destruction.

The final quotation from the divine decree in verse 23 is the pivot point of the entire either/or in this extended collection of brief units. On the basis of the new summons of verse 22, it is now all "either" with no "or." That is, this decree entertains no alternative possibility. The anticipation of total deference to Yahweh is perhaps a *command*, telling the summoned nations what must now happen. Or perhaps it is a *promise*, anticipating what must inevitably happen because the nations will come to see that any alternative choice is a bad choice. The rhetoric of the summons that moves between promise and command is not unlike the first commandment, "You shall have no other gods before me" (Exod. 20:3). Although this assertion is conventionally taken as commandment, H. Graf Reventlow has nicely shown that it is not a command, but simply a promise for the commands that follow (*Gebot und Predigt*). The initial assertion of the Decalogue anticipates and insists upon a world from which all other gods are banished, and, consequently, there are no possible inclinations toward any other god. All will bow down "to me." All such possibilities toward other gods are eliminated by the dominant, compelling reality of Yahweh.

The promise/command verdict of verse 23 is taken up in the New Testament in two quite different contexts. In the more familiar use of Philippians 2:11, the formula of our text is given a christological nuance: The One obediently crucified is subsequently fully honored by God. In Romans 14:11, the lyrical quality of Philippians 2 is crowded by the severity of judgment. It is affirmed that all finally must submit to God and be held accountable for right or wrong conduct. Thus the either/or of our poetry serves the early church both to express the singular, unrivaled, uncompromised rule of Christ and to press the church community to a mode of conduct congruent with God's uncompromising rule. The statement in Philippians is a *promise;* in Romans it has the texture of *command.*

Only Yahweh (45:24–25)

45:24 **Only in the LORD, it shall be said of me,**
　　are righteousness and strength;
　all who were incensed against him
　　shall come to him and be ashamed.
　25 **In the LORD all the offspring of Israel**
　　shall triumph and glory.

These verses are a reprise over themes now familiar. In Yahweh, surely in Yahweh, only in Yahweh, are the sources for an alternative life:

"righteousness, strength, triumph (righteousness), and glory (praise)." The rule of Yahweh assures everything that is needed for a buoyant, joyous, exuberant, celebrated life. The negative alternative for those who reject is shame (see v. 16).

The final line of our unit contains a surprise. It has appeared from verses 20 and 22 that the offered either/or of Yahweh is available to all peoples. In the end, however, the promise is peculiarly to "all the offspring of Israel," a phrasing from Genesis that pertains only to this particular community. In the acknowledgment of Yahweh as *only God* comes the affirmation of Israel as Yahweh's *only people.* This phrasing seems to revert to the self-aggrandizing tone of verse 14.

There can be no doubt that exilic Isaiah is singularly focused on the future well-being of Israel. Of course, since Genesis 12:3 the well-being of Israel had at its center the additional affirmation "in you all the families of the earth shall be blessed." That counterpoint that reaches beyond Israel seems to be reiterated in these verses. The poet knows that the horizon of creation extends to all creatures. That further reach, however, is not consistently maintained in this exilic rhetoric. It is as though the poet suggests the larger horizon and then pulls back to more conventional ground. We might wish it were otherwise.

However, we who live in the church know that constant intentionality is required in order to keep focused on "the others." When that intentionality relaxes, as it often does, the easier cadences of Israel sound again. Both elements are here, assurances both to Israel and to "the others." Both Israel and the Gentiles face a decision. Although the prospects for the internal community of Israel are most readily available and most fully appreciated, there is evidence here of a passion in the gospel rule of Yahweh that extends far beyond the bounds of Israel. But it requires endless attentiveness. Otherwise the either/or is kept closer to home, against the larger sweep of the vision of this poetry.

THE POWERFUL, ACTIVE,
DECISIVE "I" OF YAHWEH
46:1–13

It is likely that chapters 46 and 47 are to be seen together. Chapter 46 dismisses (by name) the key gods of Babylon, and chapter 47 dismisses the political power of Babylon. As Karl Marx has understood, the "criticism of politics" begins in a "criticism of theology." The judgment against Babylonian politics is rooted in a dismissal of Babylonian theology, for the purpose and function of the gods is to guarantee and authorize political rule.

In chapter 46, we are again given a reflection upon the decisive contrast between Yahweh and the other gods who are Yahweh's competitors and rivals. Yahweh is an active subject and agent, whereas the gods of Babylon are passive, immobile, mute objects. The intent of the chapter is to empower and persuade exilic Israel to switch its allegiance and trust from failed imperial gods to the God of Israel by whom an alternative future in the world is offered.

46:1 **Bel bows down, Nebo stoops,**
> **their idols are on beasts and cattle;**
> **these things you carry are loaded**
> **as burdens on weary animals.**
> 2 **They stoop, they bow down together;**
> **they cannot save the burden,**
> **but themselves go into captivity.**

This chapter begins with an explicit reference to the Babylonian gods, who are identified by name, who give credence to Babylonian power. It is likely that the ridicule of these gods, ridicule as a means of delegitimation, pictures the gods in a solemn religious procession, being carried on the backs of animals—"beasts and cattle." That is, they are like religious "floats" in a parade. An alternative reading is that they are being carried out of town in a panic after an imagined defeat. The intended mockery is that each time the carrying animal takes a step forward, the god (statue, image) mounted on the back of the animal tilts, thus giving the impression of tottering instability. The dismissive poet crudely reduces the "god" to the image, something the Babylonian believers themselves would never do.

But the dismissive mockery not only wants to make the gods appear ridiculous. The more serious theological claim is that they cannot "rescue" the burden. They cannot protect or make safe the very bulk of their material form, that is, their own images. Indeed, these gods shall themselves be carried away into exile, presumably humiliated by the coming Persians with their more powerful theological claim (from Yahweh). Though these verses are not a speech of disputation, the dismissive charge of impotence functions like a legal verdict that seeks to discredit the gods completely.

46:3 **Listen to me, O house of Jacob,**
> **all the remnant of the house of Israel,**
> **who have been borne by me from your birth,**

> carried from the womb;
> ⁴ even to your old age I am he,
>   even when you turn gray I will carry you.
> I have made, and I will bear;
>   I will carry and will save.

The initial two verses, however, are only a foil for the positive affirmation of Yahweh in verses 3–4. Now Israel is summoned to *listen*. The address is to the "remnant" of Israel, that is, the exiles who have survived the great devastation wrought by Yahweh through Babylon. It is this smaller community of Jews that is always on the horizon of the book of Isaiah. But the exiles are not a thinly rooted, one-generation community. They are summoned to recall the entire history of Yahweh with Israel: From birth (and even prenatal care) to old age, Yahweh has been attentive to and protective of Israel. The imagery here is intensely personal, but it surely refers to the life of the community by appealing to the sorts of images of intimacy given in Hosea 11:1–3; Ezekiel 16; 20; 23. Indeed, "from the womb" suggests a maternal metaphor. With reference to Psalm 22:10, John Calvin concludes:

> I do not object to extending the words so far as to mean, that they were brought, as it were, out of the bowels of God into a new life and the hope of an eternal inheritance. . . . If it be objected, that God is everywhere called "a Father" . . . I reply that no figure of speech can describe God's extraordinary affection towards us. . . . God who has manifested himself to be both their Father and their Mother, will always assist them.

Israel's entire existence has been nurtured and made possible by Yahweh, the endlessly reliable guardian and advocate of Israel.

After the retrospective of verses 3–4a, the remainder of verse 4 makes a particularly strong promise with four first-person verbs. The verbs contrast sharply with those of verses 1–2 wherein Bel and Nebo need to be *carried* and have been *made* and will not *save*; Yahweh will perform all of those verbs. These verbs belong characteristically, singularly, and reliably to the way in which Yahweh attends to Israel. The verbs, moreover, are reinforced by the intensive first-person pronoun used four times. In conventional verbal form, the pronoun is only a suffix to the verb. Here it is an independent element used for emphasis. The accent is "I—not Bel," "I—not Nebo," "I—not Babylonian gods," "I—not any other!" Yahweh is the key and sole actor in Israel's life, upon whom Israel may count for its future.

46:5 **To whom will you liken me and make me equal,**
     and compare me, as though we were alike?
      ⁶ **Those who lavish gold from the purse,**
     and weigh out silver in the scales—
   they hire a goldsmith, who makes it into a god;
     then they fall down and worship!
      ⁷ **They lift it to their shoulders, they carry it,**
     they set it in its place, and it stands there;
     it cannot move from its place.
   If one cries out to it, it does not answer
     or save anyone from trouble.

Now the poetry returns to the negative critique of the idols as in verses 1–2. The opening line of verse 5 echoes the formula of incomparability we have seen in 40:18. The question is not unlike the "who" questions of the speeches of disputation in 41:2–4, 26. But the particular point here does not concern the incomparable Yahweh. Rather, the poetry moves immediately and at some length to mock the gods of Babylon, echoing the parody of 44:9–20 concerning the manufacture of gods who are pitiful and impotent. Thus the goldsmith (see 41:7), like the ironsmith and carpenter of 44:12–13, does his best work. As with the work of the carpenter in 44:15–17, the "produced" god is worshiped—of course to no effect. The "produced" god is an object with no inherent power, so that it must be lifted and carried and set where it is to remain, quite in contrast to the God of 46:4, who lifts and carries and saves. The point of course is the powerlessness of the Babylonian gods who cannot save Babylon, let alone do anything for Israel. These gods have no available evidence, support, or testimony, no record or memory of efficaciousness. According to the poet, they are sadly contrasted with Yahweh who has a long "track record"—from birth to old age—of caring concern and efficacious power.

46:8 **Remember this and consider,**
     recall it to mind, you transgressors,
    ⁹ **remember the former things of old;**
   for I am God, and there is no other;
     I am God, and there is no one like me,
  ¹⁰ **declaring the end from the beginning**
     and from ancient times things not yet done,
   saying, "My purpose shall stand,
     and I will fulfill my intention,"
  ¹¹ **calling a bird of prey from the east,**
     the man for my purpose from a far country.

> I have spoken, and I will bring it to pass;
>   I have planned, and I will do it.
>
> ¹² Listen to me, you stubborn of heart,
>   you who are far from deliverance:
> ¹³ I bring near my deliverance, it is not far off,
>   and my salvation will not tarry;
> I will put salvation in Zion,
>   for Israel my glory.

As verses 3–4 affirm Yahweh following the dismissive verdict of verses 1–2, so in these verses the dismissive verdict of verses 5–7 is answered by an affirmation of Yahweh in two parts. In verses 8–11, Israel is summoned to remember. Two things about this opening imperative of verses 8–9a are noteworthy. First, the summons to "remember former things" sharply contrasts with the imperative of 43:18. Now Israel is not to forget for the sake of newness as in 43:18, but is to recall the entire history of care—from birth to old age—in order to have data about Yahweh's reliability. Yahweh's availability to Israel in the present depends upon the living tradition of attentiveness. Second, Israel is addressed as "you transgressors" (see 42:24–25; 43:22–28). The transgression is not specified. It may be a general indictment, or it may refer more particularly to Israel's propensity in exile to be responsive to Babylonian seductions. The point worth noting is that Yahweh is now completely committed to the well-being of Israel in exile—"the survivors"—transgression or no (as in 43:25).

The self-assertion of Yahweh in verses 9b–11 is enormously rich and freighted. Verse 9b is an assertion of Yahweh's sole claim to be God. The line echoes the by-now familiar formula of incomparability, but perhaps also refers "in former time" to the decree of Sinai in the first commandment (Exod. 20:1). In any case, this sole God has a *plan and purpose* that is rooted in antiquity but is about to be enacted in the present. The "plan" apparently does not refer to a specific course of action but rather to an enduring resolve for the well-being of Israel, the intention Yahweh has had for Israel "from your birth" (v. 3). That purpose, in the stringent circumstance of exile, now calls for an extreme measure. Indeed! The extreme measure in order to achieve an extreme end is "a bird of prey from the east," yet another reference to Cyrus the Persian. Cyrus will now enact in this concrete moment, as Yahweh's Gentile messiah (45:1), the long-term intention of Yahweh for Israel's well-being.

The depth of resolve on the part of Yahweh—not unlike 14:14, 27 (also concerning a superpower)—is expressed again in four strong first-person verbs. Unlike verse 4, however, these verbs have only the suffix pronoun and not the more emphatic independent pronoun. Nonetheless, the fourfold assertion is closely paralleled to verse 4 and reiterates the same claim that Yahweh is a resolved agent and decisive actor who is now to work a newness for the sake of Israel.

The conclusion of the chapter in verses 12–13 reiterates the cadences of verses 8–11. Again there is an initial summons, "Listen," as in verse 3. The address to the stubborn from whom righteousness is remote is clearly parallel to the address of verse 8. And the core promise of verse 13 is an echo of the resolve of verses 4 and 11, again dominated by first-person verbs. Israel is far from "righteousness" (v. 12). But Yahweh's saving righteousness is not remote but near to Israel. Indeed, the saving righteousness of Yahweh is about to happen, presumably through Cyrus, "the bird of prey." The double use of "salvation" is a promise and assurance that Israel's life—so long skewed by Babylon—is about to be made whole. The promise is to *Zion*, now about to be resettled in Jerusalem. Thus the final verse sounds the ultimate aim of this portion of Isaiah, the reconstitution of Judaism among the "survivors" of exile.

The deep contrast between "no-gods" (vv. 1–2, 5–7) and "true God" (vv. 3–4, 8–13) is complete. The difference is power and resolve to effect a difference in the life of Israel. It is remarkable to notice that Yahweh's passionate and powerful assurance to Israel in exile takes into full account the inadequacy and failure of Israel. But Yahweh's resolve is not thereby diminished. It is for this inadequate, failed people that this active, resolved, passionate God will now make a difference. The difference is rooted in Yahweh's readiness to move past transgression in fidelity, thus relying on the assertion of forgiveness with which Isaiah in exile has begun (40:1–2; see 43:25).

As elsewhere, the contrast is a rhetorical one. The speech does not make an argument as much as it offers a persuasive appeal. The listening community of exiles in that ancient time must still decide whether to risk its future on the utterance of this God. And subsequent generations of this listening community (such as we), still caught in the like seductions of imperial gods and systems of power, must always again decide whether this rhetoric is a basis for a risky alternative commitment. The poetry, with its vigorous affirmation and its relentless debunking, makes the choice seem more clear than it ever is in practice. The either/or is a summons to a "new regime," which Jesus later terms "the kingdom of God" (Mark 1:15).

"YOU SAY . . . BUT EVIL
SHALL COME"
47:1–15

When *the Babylonian gods* are exposed and delegitimated in 46:1–2, 5–7, it follows readily and inevitably that *Babylonian political power* will promptly be ridiculed and dismissed in chapter 47; the sole purpose of *the gods* is to lend ideological support and legitimacy to *human power*. When the gods go, imperial power is seen to be feeble, illusionary, and without credibility. The purpose of the present chapter is to enact, before the ears of listening Israel in exile, the dismissal and defeat of the empire. To be sure, the dismissal is only poetry, and the defeat is likely lyrical; but then, empires survive and prosper only because of their seeming formidableness lent to them by poetry, liturgy, and other forms of propaganda. And when the legitimacy fails, raw power cannot persist. The chapter is an address to Babylon intended for the hearing of the exiles. The speaker is not identified but is unmistakably known by what is said: It is the Holy One of Israel who speaks.

The chapter concerns the demise of Babylon that will lead to the liberation of Israel. This is the only chapter in Isaiah of the exile that is directly against the empire, though much else is against Babylon by implication. This text is to be seen in connection with Isaiah 13—14 in the structure of the book. Both chapters assert the rule of Yahweh that is deeply inimical to the rule of Babylon.

47:1 **Come down and sit in the dust,**
      virgin daughter Babylon!
  Sit on the ground without a throne,
      daughter Chaldea!
  For you shall no more be called
      tender and delicate.
  ² Take the millstones and grind meal,
      remove your veil,
  strip off your robe, uncover your legs,
      pass through the rivers.
  ³ Your nakedness shall be uncovered,
      and your shame shall be seen.
  I will take vengeance,
      and I will spare no one.
  ⁴ Our Redeemer—the LORD of hosts is his name—
      is the Holy One of Israel.

The initial three verses of the poem are a song of grief over a city that has been devastated. The mourners gather around to describe the situation of ruin and to express their sadness. The genre of this grief is well known in the ancient world. In the Old Testament, the poetry of the book of Lamentations is of the same genre, whereby Israel grieves destroyed Jerusalem (see, e.g., Lam. 1:1–2). Here the grief is over destroyed Babylon. In a series of parallel statements, the poetry characterizes and contrasts *the good past* that is gone and the *present misery* that is overwhelming:

> virgin daughter . . . sit in the dust,
> tender and delicate . . . sit on the ground,
>   grind meal,
>   remove your veil,
>   strip off your robe,
>   uncover your legs.

Babylon used to be an elegant, extravagant, impressive, attractive city, described in the rhetoric of femininity. But such past affirmation is only a foil for the present, wherein this erstwhile beauty will now become an exposed, vulnerable, exploited slave, with none of the protections of social decor, now completely at risk and humiliated. The radical reversal characterized (anticipated) is not unlike the radical reversal of Jerusalem that the Isaiah tradition has already portrayed, there also in terms of feminine comfort, elegance, privilege, and beauty:

> Instead of perfume there will be a stench;
>   and instead of a sash, a rope;
> and instead of well-set hair, baldness;
>   and instead of a rich robe, a binding of sackcloth;
>   instead of beauty, shame. (3:24)

The time is at hand when former wonder will yield to terrible degradation. It is enough to make one weep "for the glory that was Greece and the grandeur that was Rome." The poetry invites a moving embrace of pathos and loss for what was and is no more.

However, the poetry is a setup, ostensibly addressed to ruined Babylon, in fact addressed to watchful Israel in exile. The expressed grief is a pseudo-grief that is in fact dismissive mockery. Israel sheds no tears for Babylon, too long cruel. The artistic offer of tears is in fact an invitation to joy. The exiles can only celebrate the demise of hated, resented, feared

Babylon. That great city had been too long established, seemingly safe and guaranteed forever.

The reason we know that the song of grief, which uses familiar genres of lament as parody, is a ploy is the vigor of verses 3b–4. The agent of demolition is none other than Yahweh, the one who had refused any longer to protect Jerusalem in its recalcitrance. The God who could relinquish beloved Jerusalem to suffering is the one who will undo Babylon; Yahweh will do so soon. Yahweh will retaliate without compromise or compassion: "For the LORD has a day of vengeance, / a year of vindication by Zion's cause" (34:8). The one who is about to act is the one already known in the poetry of Isaiah as the redeemer of Israel, the Lord of hosts, the Holy One of Israel (v. 4). The poetry stacks up the most awesome, formidable titles for Yahweh so that there will be no mistake. The *redeemer* will act for the sake of Israel. The *avenger* will reassert sovereign rule that Babylon has usurped. The *redeemer-avenger* will make a wholesale correction in geopolitics that had, in the guise of Nebuchadrezzar, been massively distorted. The deep loss that is coming is the ground of deep joy for Israel. Who would have thought such a turn possible in imperial history! Only those who speak the name of the Holy One. Israel's poetry is saturated with hope and expectation over the ruin of the oppressor (e.g., Jer. 50:2; Ezek. 33:21).

The fall of Babylon is a datable moment in the rise and fall of great powers who characteristically and bafflingly act to their own destruction. The fall of Babylon in the imagination of Israel, however, is not simply another passing event in imperial history. It is rather the foundational event whereby the rule of Yahweh is restored and Israel's future is again made possible. The event evokes the lyrical power and passionate resolve that in Christian parlance is reserved for the Easter defeat of death. Thus the mocking lament here is like feeling sad over the demise of death. It is not a real sadness. It is instead a pretended sadness that issues in release and dancing and joy and finally homecoming. The joyous future of the exiles turns on the deep and unqualified readiness of Yahweh to invert history, whereby oppression is turned to emancipation and sorrow to joy (see John 15:20–22).

47:5 **Sit in silence, and go into darkness,**
> **daughter Chaldea!**
For you shall no more be called
> **the mistress of kingdoms.**
>> [6]**I was angry with my people,**
>> **I profaned my heritage;**

I gave them into your hand,
  you showed them no mercy;
on the aged you made your yoke
  exceedingly heavy.
⁷You said, "I shall be mistress forever,"
  so that you did not lay these things to heart
  or remember their end.

The grief continues—pretended grief. The great city Babylon had been opulent and affluent, indulgent, arrogant, surely the preeminent city of its world. The language of "mistress" concerns the elegance of the grande dame, the loveliness of a stunning debutante—but now *silence and darkness*, the end of endless frivolity and confident self-assertion, a power failure, the great lights dimmed, sports events canceled, the theaters dark and failed.

And why? Verse 6 offers, in succinct form, a complete prophetic philosophy of history in three parts. Given the cruciality of Yahweh, the destiny of Babylon is clear:

1. Yahweh was angry with Judah ("my people") and Jerusalem ("my heritage"). Of course! That is what the entire early recognition of the prophets was all about. Israel refused torah, rejected widows and orphans, disregarded Yahweh—and Yahweh could bear it no longer.

2. Yahweh in rage gave beloved Judah and Jerusalem into the power of Babylon. That is why Jerusalem is leveled in 587 B.C.E. That is why Jews were deported—not because Babylon was aggressive and autonomous, and not because Yahweh loved Nebuchadrezzar, but because Babylon was a useful, ready-at-hand instrument for the rage of Yahweh.

3. The fourth line of the verse is stunning: "You showed them no mercy!" Babylon is reprimanded by Yahweh for not showing mercy to Israel. This is an astonishing rebuke that provides the basis for the denunciation of Babylon that follows. Babylon is now to be destroyed precisely for a lack of mercy to Israel. There are at least two great oddities about this conclusion. First, Yahweh did not show mercy to Israel, and so expects Babylon to do for Israel what Yahweh does not do (see Jer. 42:11–12). Indeed, Babylon must have gotten a different implicit message from Yahweh by Yahweh's own action toward Israel. Second, there is no hint here or elsewhere that Babylon had been urged by Yahweh to show mercy. Indeed, the very opposite would have seemed to be Yahweh's intent.

But, implies the poet, Babylon should have known. Everybody—Jew and non-Jew—should have known that Yahweh is a God of mercy and intends mercy, everywhere and always, but especially toward Israel. One may conclude that such an expectation of Babylon is completely unfair, and therefore such a judgment against Babylon is gratuitous. But so prophetic faith works. The empire is now to be dismantled for not knowing what everyone should have known. The superpower should have known that the reality of Yahweh curbs the brutalizing propensity of even the superpowers.

The final verse of this subunit of poetry is derivative from the preceding argument (v. 7). The prophets often delight to place in the mouth of an opponent what they "say" by their actions and policies. Thus Babylon's way in the world "said . . . " Babylon's life is one of self-indulgent autonomy, imagining that the empire would remain on top of the heap forever. Babylon could recognize no restraints, no limits, no obligations, no qualms, imagining itself completely unfettered and following its own self-indulgent desire. And the self-indulgent desire of an empire is characteristically economic greed that is imposed on occupied territories by taxation and aggressive military adventurism. Babylon imagined its world without the counterreality of Yahweh. It is no wonder, says the poet of Yahweh, that now comes the end in silence and darkness. It could not be otherwise, because in the end, no power is so great or so free or so guaranteed as to conduct itself without reference to Yahweh, especially Yahweh's determined commitment to mercy.

47:8 **Now therefore hear this, you lover of pleasures,**
    who sit securely,
  who say in your heart,
    "I am, and there is no one besides me;
  I shall not sit as a widow
    or know the loss of children"—
  [9]**both these things shall come upon you**
    in a moment, in one day:
  the loss of children and widowhood
    shall come upon you in full measure,
  in spite of your many sorceries
    and the great power of your enchantments.

These verses continue the accents we have already heard and are organized around the predictable elements of a speech of judgment. Babylon is summoned to hear and is addressed in an *indictment* (v. 8). Babylon is self-indulgent and self-preoccupied, thinking that it has enough wealth and wisdom and arms to satisfy itself. Again, the poet imagines the utterance of the superpower: There is no one else, no one to whom to give account, that is, no Yahweh. The boastful self-announcement of Babylon echoes and parallels the self-announcements of Yahweh. As Yahweh has claimed, "There is no one besides me" (43:11; 45:5, 6, 21; 46:5, 9), now the empire makes the same claim, a claim deeply scandalous from a Yahwistic perspective. This boastful imperial power, moreover, imagines itself to be immune to the dangerous vagaries of history. Its self-congratulation projects its prosperity and security to be assured to perpetuity, so that no grief or loss or vulnerability can come here.

The *sentence* sure to follow such self-deceiving autonomy is massive (v. 9). All at once, the two most elemental threats will penetrate this facade of well-being. The great city, as in verses 1–2, is imagined as a refined, elegant woman. Such a woman, in that ancient patriarchal world, is guaranteed by her husband and celebrated in her children. And now—abruptly—much to her surprise, she will lose her guaranteeing husband and her pride of children. The loss that cuts to the heart of well-being, moreover, matches the claim of arrogance in verse 8, so that the punishment corresponds precisely to the pride. The very signs and sources of well-being are assaulted and jeopardized. The loss that is not even on the horizon of the empire is assured by Yahweh. The imagined safety of the empire is quickly penetrated and undone. Nobody is immune to Yahweh! Yahweh must be reckoned with. If Yahweh is not acknowledged, then Yahweh comes as the Great Devastator. Nothing will stop the loss, not Babylonian religion, not Babylonian technology, not Babylonian learning. The ideological claims and theological resources of the empire are completely ineffective. They will not be able to stop the loss any more than the ancient Egyptian "magicians" could foil Yahweh (Exod. 8:18; see Isa. 19:11–15). The self-deceived empire is shown to be completely impotent and helpless in the face of Yahweh. There is only one source of power and well-being, and Babylon long ago rejected that. Now comes the sure consequence of such a foolish way in the world.

47:10 **You felt secure in your wickedness;**
  you said, "No one sees me."
 Your wisdom and your knowledge
  led you astray,
 and you said in your heart,
  "I am, and there is no one besides me."
 [11]**But evil shall come upon you,**
  which you cannot charm away;

> disaster shall fall upon you,
>   which you will not be able to ward off;
> and ruin shall come on you suddenly,
>   of which you know nothing.

These verses reiterate themes already offered in this chapter and are ordered as a speech of judgment. The indictment of verse 10 concerns the illusion of well-being that imagines that power can cover over wickedness. The self-deception of the mighty, prosperous empire is to imagine autonomy without accountability to anyone for anything. The two quotations of verse 10 are not utterances of oral statement but utterances made through policy and practice. The double assumption that "no one sees" and "there is no one besides me" authorizes and permits a shameless, exploitative, self-aggrandizing policy. The assumption of course is false; One does see, and there is One besides Babylon, and it is Yahweh. The empire, the exiles are assured, does not live in a Yahweh-less world, even though the second claim of the empire rivals Yahweh, who also declares "there is no one besides me."

The sentence of verse 11 is introduced with a powerful adversative preposition that contradicts the assumption of verse 10. "Evil" will come, the very "evil" in which Babylon sits secure. The evil consequence of evil policy and evil practice cannot be avoided. The evil will be "disaster and ruin" that are not even on the horizon of the empire, about which all the learning of Babylon produces no clue, because it is all learning without reference to Yahweh. In context, the "disaster and ruin" apparently refer to the coming of Cyrus. But the rhetoric intends to communicate an awesome threat that resists naming it as a historical event.

The ultimate (unnamed) threat that is to come from Yahweh is that Babylonian religion and learning are no resources for resistance to the threat of Yahweh. As in verse 9, so here "sorceries and charms," the protective practices of Babylonian religion, are no resources because Yahweh will indeed overrule and override all such stratagems. The rhetoric imagines a secure, massive reversal of the empire, a reversal before which the empire is reduced to helplessness. The rhetoric mediates Babylon's impotence and therefore the fate of the great empire not to be saved by its several technologies.

47:12 **Stand fast in your enchantments**
>   **and your many sorceries,**
>   **with which you have labored from your youth;**
>   **perhaps you may be able to succeed,**

perhaps you may inspire terror.
¹³ You are wearied with your many consultations;
    let those who study the heavens
stand up and save you,
    those who gaze at the stars,
and at each new moon predict
    what shall befall you.

¹⁴ See, they are like stubble,
    the fire consumes them;
they cannot deliver themselves
    from the power of the flame.
No coal for warming oneself is this,
    no fire to sit before!
¹⁵ Such to you are those with whom you have labored,
    who have trafficked with you from your youth;
they all wander about in their own paths;
    there is no one to save you.

The overcoming of imperial learning and technology echoes a like judgment against Egypt in 19:11–15. In our verses, the poet mockingly invites Babylon to rely on its conventional practices of control and protection. We know that astral religion and astronomy were well advanced in ancient Babylon. Indeed, such study was a formidable industry in the empire, belatedly reflected in the "wise ones" who follow the star (Matt. 2:1–12). In Matthew's legend, the coming of the Magi signifies the submission of Babylonian learning, the quintessential learning of the Gentile world, to the rule of Yahweh. Here that same submission is anticipated, forcibly and not willingly as in the Matthew narrative. The mocking tone of the poetry is unmistakable in the double "perhaps" of verse 12. "Perhaps" the ways of the empire will work, but we know better! "Perhaps" it will be formidable, but we doubt it!

The transition to the threat of verses 14–15, introduced by "See," is abrupt. The "fire next time," the burning of what is precious and treasured in the empire, is bracketed in these verses by a double negative. The learned "cannot deliver themselves" (even as the gods in 46:2 "cannot save"); there is "no one to save." The situation of the empire is hopeless. There is no agent able to rescue because of the overriding negative resolve of Yahweh, who cannot be resisted or averted.

The poetry imagines a conflagration of the empire. This is no cozy fire, no comfortable fireplace, no nice warming (v. 14; see 44:15–16). This a fire from which to flee, for Yahweh's resolve is sure and beyond recall. The future of the empire is determined and beyond challenge.

This chapter offers a mighty contrast of the present of a well-situated empire and the coming future that is at the behest of Yahweh. The empire, contrary to appearance, is helpless and resourceless. As the gods are no source of hope in chapter 46, so here the political apparatus is impotent. The exiles must not look upon the pretentious appearance of the empire. Everything needs to be reassessed in the presence of "the Holy One of Israel," before whom the empire has no chance. The text ostensibly is addressed to the empire, but it is in reality intended for the exiles. Conversely, in our listening we are tempted to hear as exiles and to be reassured; it is possible, however, that our own proper hearing is from the angle of the empire. We also have much learning and great power. The fire cannot be averted, and much religion cannot cover (not then, not now) for policies of unrestrained autonomy, greed, and exploitation.

"FOR MY OWN SAKE"
48:1–22

This chapter continues the themes now familiar to us: (a) the exaltation of Yahweh, (b) the dismissal of Babylon, and (c) the emancipation of Israel. The themes are presented in a peculiar way here, however, because the poetry is an odd and sustained juxtaposition of *affirmation* and *rebuke*. Although it is suggested that the poetry was initially affirmative and only subsequently edited toward rebuke, it may be more interesting and compelling to suggest that this theological tension that concerns the behavior and destiny of Israel is rooted in the tension deep within the character of Yahweh, who is both wondrously caring and demandingly sovereign.

James Muilenburg has observed how the verb "hear" recurs in this poem, both as an invitation to hear (obey) and as a rebuke for refusing to hear (*Isaiah 40–66*, 553). (In addition, the term šāma' is used in ways not evident in English, for the terms "made known" [v. 3], "announced" [v. 5], and "proclaim" [v. 20] are in Hebrew "cause to hear.") Israel is a community whose future depends upon *listening to the promises* of Yahweh and *heeding the commands* of Yahweh. The hearing is urgent for the future well-being of Israel, for hearing means to cede life over to the good rule of Yahweh and to leave off other loyalties.

Former and New Things, to the Glory of Yahweh (48:1–13)

This section of poetry has an introductory summons to hear (vv. 1–2), a concluding summons to hear (vv. 12–13), and three intermediate units concerning "former things" (vv. 3–5), "new things" (vv. 6–8), and an affirmation of Yahweh's self-regard (vv. 9–11).

48:1 **Hear this, O house of Jacob,**
    who are called by the name of Israel,
    and who came forth from the loins of Judah;
  who swear by the name of the LORD,
    and invoke the God of Israel,
    but not in truth or right.
  ² **For they call themselves after the holy city,**
    and lean on the God of Israel;
    the LORD of hosts is his name.

Israel is summoned to hear, that is, to listen, obey, and trust. Except for one phrase, these verses are a remarkable affirmation of Israel, linking Israel intimately and peculiarly to Yahweh, and drawing upon the rich imagery from Israel's memory of life with Yahweh. This rhetoric portrays Israel as an object of Yahweh's special attention and concern.

The odd phrase that jeopardizes everything is at the end of verse 1. It asserts that all of these connections between Yahweh and Israel are not done in good faith, so that the positive review is subverted. John Calvin suggests, in a way that clearly overrides legitimate Jewish faith claims, that this negation (and the ones to follow) is a rejection of the Jews. Claus Westermann prefers to say that the negatives are late additions (*Isaiah 40–66*, 197). James Muilenburg simply concludes that "the contradictions are more apparent than real" (*Isaiah 40–66*, 553). There is no clear way to resolve this question, except to notice that the affirmations are at least placed in question by the negatives. The relationship to Yahweh may be definitive, but it is neither easy nor settled. Paul Hanson nicely states the point:

> [In Isaiah 48] the prophet addresses a human condition that is filled with ambiguity. Even the promises of God at a time of renewed hope retain a bittersweet quality given the inconsistency of human commitment. The ebb and flow of this chapter skillfully reflect the prophet's realistic awareness of the convolution of the human response to divine initiative. Any attempt to sort out pure promise from pure judgment tears apart a skillfully balanced message (*Isaiah 40–66*, 123).

The only modification to the words of Hanson suggested here is that the text is not addressed to "a human condition" but specifically to an Israelite community at the brink of emancipation.

48:3 **The former things I declared long ago,**
  they went out from my mouth and I made them known;
  then suddenly I did them and they came to pass.
 ⁴**Because I know that you are obstinate,**
  and your neck is an iron sinew
  and your forehead brass,
 ⁵**I declared them to you from long ago,**
  before they came to pass I announced them to you,
 so that you would not say, "My idol did them,
  my carved image and my cast image commanded them."

The reference to "former things" recalls the interpretive troubles and possibilities already noticed in 43:16–21. Whereas in many places the "former things" appear to be past saving deeds by Yahweh (such as the Exodus), here we seem on better ground to accept "former things" as punishments, reflected in the first part of the book of Isaiah. This interpretation would take the negativity of verse 4 seriously. Attention to verse 5, on the other hand, would seem to require a positive deed by Yahweh, for which Israel is tempted to thank its idols. Again we can only notice interpretive options, noting that the text is ambiguous and admits of no clear, single sense.

48:6 **You have heard; now see all this;**
  and will you not declare it?
 From this time forward I make you hear new things,
  hidden things that you have not known.
 ⁷**They are created now, not long ago;**
  before today you have never heard of them,
  so that you could not say, "I already knew them."
 ⁸**You have never heard, you have never known,**
  from of old your ear has not been opened.
 For I knew that you would deal very treacherously,
  and that from birth you were called a rebel.

Whatever the "former things" of verses 3–5 may be, there can be little doubt that "new things" here refer to acts of rescue and deliverance now to be performed for the sake of the listening, contemporary community late in the book of Isaiah. The acts are not specified, but they surely refer to deliverance from Babylon to be accomplished by the majestic, irresistible power of Yahweh. It is curious that these lines repeatedly assert that these new actions are not previously known by Israel: "not known," "never heard," "never known." These actions and awareness of them have been deliberately withheld from Israel. Perhaps Israel has not known them because they are to be such stupendous acts that there are not preexisting categories or precedents by which they may be anticipated. We might suppose they have been withheld from Israel because in their timeliness any earlier clue would have been premature and misleading.

It is also likely, however, that these new deeds have been withheld because Israel would "deal very treacherously." It is as though Israel is not to be trusted with good news—even about "new things"— because Israel might be exploitative of Yahweh's rescues, might take advantage of them, might be tempted to self-sufficiency and self-congratulation. Yahweh apparently has withheld the wonder of rescue from Babylon until the last moment, so that the miracle would not be distorted or used against its true purpose. It is remarkable that not only are "former things" troubled by Israel's "iron sinew" (v. 4), but even the "new things" are readily and quickly perverted into something not intended by Yahweh.

48:9 **For my name's sake I defer my anger,**
    for the sake of my praise I restrain it for you,
    so that I may not cut you off.
10 **See, I have refined you, but not like silver;**
    I have tested you in the furnace of adversity.
11 **For my own sake, for my own sake, I do it,**
    for why should my name be profaned?
    My glory I will not give to another.

Yahweh's anger toward Israel is considerable. It is enough that Yahweh might be warranted in "cutting off" Israel, that is, eliminating Israel as a visible community. Thus far in the poem the negatives are weighty (vv. 1b, 4, 8). All of this resistance to Yahweh on the part of Israel is cause of profound anger on Yahweh's part and ground for extermination. The present verses of necessity must provide ground for Yahweh's goodness toward Israel other than Israel's merit or even Yahweh's love for Israel. That ground, in an assertion that parallels Ezekiel 36:22–32, is found in Yahweh's self-regard. The emancipation soon to be enacted for Israel is: "for my name's sake . . . for the sake of my praise . . . for my own sake, . . . for my own sake . . . for my name . . . my glory." There is a strand of Old Testament faith that asserts that Yahweh has not given Yahweh's full self over to the care of Israel in love. Yahweh retains a sense of Yahweh's own self and is determined to maintain the dignity, majesty, effectiveness, and honor of Yahweh's own reputation. Yahweh wants and will have glory, exaltation, and honor in the eyes of the nations. There is much more to Yahweh, asserts the poet, than *self-giving* love. There is also *self-regarding* majesty.

The problem for Yahweh is that Yahweh has been for so long committed to Israel and for so long perceived by the nations as the God of Israel that Yahweh's glory in the eyes of the nations can be sustained and enhanced only by the rescue of Israel. Thus Israel will be rescued, not out of love but out of self-regard, for Yahweh jealously and attentively cares about an honorable reputation. This concern is evident in the peculiar text of Numbers 14:13–19. It is, however, given its fullest articulation in Ezekiel, a prophet who does not speak of God's love for Israel, but characteristically only of Yahweh's holy self-regard: "It is not for your sake, O house of Israel, that I am about to act, but for the sake of my holy name, which you have profaned among the nations to which you came" (Ezek. 36:22). The linkage between Yahweh's reputation and Israel's well-being is vigorously affirmed by the prophet: "Now I will restore the fortunes of Jacob, and have mercy on the whole house of Israel; and I will be jealous for my holy name. . . . Then *they shall know that I am the LORD* their God because I *sent them into exile* among the nations, and then *gathered them* into their own land. I will leave none of them behind" (Ezek. 39:25, 28).

Our passage asserts the same. Israel is an instant in Yahweh's self-enhancement, with good, albeit derivative, results for Israel.

48:12 **Listen to me, O Jacob,**
  and Israel, whom I called:
 I am He; I am the first,
  and I am the last.
 [13] **My hand laid the foundation of the earth,**
  and my right hand spread out the heavens;
 when I summon them,
  they stand at attention.

This conclusion returns to the summons of verse 1. Israel is to pay attention and heed Yahweh's resolve. What Israel is to hear is *the glory of Yahweh* articulated, in the mouth of Yahweh, as doxology. The doxology links (a) the choice of Israel, (b) the first-and-last quality of Yahweh, who overrides all the transactions of worldly powers such as Babylon, and (c) the work of Yahweh as creator. Thus the resolve of Yahweh is an occurrence on the scale of creation power. The detail of verse 13 is suggestive: The earth and the heavens are like cadets among Yahweh's troops. When Yahweh musters them, they stand sharply at attention, ready to obey. The God who summons the extremities of creation is the God who will save Israel. And the reason is the same—not love of the world or love of Israel but yearning for glory and enhancement. The ground of Israel's hope is here removed from Israel. The rescue of Israel from the empire is not really about Israel, but Israel receives good gifts as a by-product of Yahweh's self-regard (as in Exod. 14:4, 17).

Wistfulness and Assurance (48:14–22)

The second half of this long poem reiterates familiar themes. It begins with an assertion that Cyrus will crush Babylon, a theme prominent in chapters 44—45 (vv. 14–16). It expresses Yahweh's wistfulness over Israel, who has not listened, thus echoing the negativities of verses 1–9 (vv. 17–19). And finally it invites Israel's departure from Babylonian exile (vv. 20–22).

> 48:14 **Assemble, all of you, and hear!**
> **Who among them has declared these things?**
> **The LORD loves him;**
> **he shall perform his purpose on Babylon,**
> **and his arm shall be against the Chaldeans.**
> 15 **I, even I, have spoken and called him,**
> **I have brought him, and he will prosper in his way.**
> 16 **Draw near to me, hear this!**
> **From the beginning I have not spoken in secret,**
> **from the time it came to be I have been there.**
> **And now the Lord GOD has sent me and his spirit.**

The text begins with a summons to assembly. Apparently the summons is addressed to Israel, though it is not impossible that the addressee is the nations or even the other gods (see 41:1). In any case, the rhetoric is again a disputation, asking if Yahweh or some other nominee is the true God. As in the previous disputations, Yahweh of course prevails and is established by the rhetoric as the true God.

The question of verse 14b is answered in verses 14c–15, so that from the answer we can determine the point of the question. *It is Yahweh* who has declared, summoned, initiated. The subject though unnamed, it seems clear, is Cyrus. Who has dispatched Cyrus the Persian? The answer is: "I, even I, have spoken and called him, I have brought him" (v. 15). Cyrus is offered as evidence that Yahweh is the true God. Yahweh, moreover, has been quite public and open about geopolitical intentions. The exiles are

here led to identify, trust, and heed the true Dispatcher of imperial
history.

48:17 **Thus says the** LORD,
      your Redeemer, the Holy One of Israel:
   I am the LORD **your God,**
      who teaches you for your own good,
      who leads you in the way you should go.
  ¹⁸ **O that you had paid attention to my commandments!**
      Then your prosperity would have been like a river,
      and your success like the waves of the sea;
 ¹⁹ **your offspring would have been like the sand,**
      and your descendants like its grains;
   their name would never be cut off
      or destroyed from before me.

The God who voiced the sweeping claim in verses 14–16 now speaks in a
different tone. The one who speaks is Israel's redeemer. The remainder of
verse 17 further identifies Yahweh in relation to Israel. The formulation is
not unlike the familiar words of Exodus 20:2: "I am the LORD your God,
who brought you out of the land of Egypt." The reference in verse 17 is
not to the Exodus, but it uses two freighted verbs—"who teaches, who
leads"—that probably refer respectively to the commands of Mount Sinai
and to the protective leadership of Yahweh amid the risks of the wilderness sojourn. As is characteristic, Yahweh is here identified with narratives
about past saving miracles that constitute "former things."

In verse 17, Yahweh is fully identified with a gracious past. Given that
affirmative memory, we are scarcely prepared for the tone of verse 18, for
we might expect continuing affirmation. Instead, the verse turns negative,
as in the earlier verses: "O that you had" is a wistful negative that means
"You did not!" You did not "pay attention" to the commandments. The
God who teaches has not been heeded!

The tone of verse 18a is clearly paralleled in the negations of three
"prophetic psalms":

> "*Hear*, O my people, and I will speak,
>   O Israel, I will testify against you. . . .
> You give your mouth free rein for evil,
>   and your tongue frames deceit.
> You sit and speak against your kin;
>   you slander your own mother's child." (Psalm 50:7, 19–20)

> "*Hear*, O my people, while I admonish you;
>   O Israel, if you would but *listen* to me! . . .
> But my people did not *listen* to my voice;
>   Israel would not submit to me. . . .
> O that my people would *listen* to me,
>   that Israel would walk in my ways!" (Psalm 81:8, 11, 13)

> O that today you would *listen* to his voice! (Psalm 95:7b)

These psalms, and our oracle with them, recall the resistance and recalcitrance of Israel. The remainder of verses 18–19 state the rich promises of Yahweh, but they are all in the subjunctive. That is, they are all "contrary to fact." This is what could have happened, but it will not.

It could have been that:

- Israel could have prosperity like a river—but it will not;
- Israel could have success like the waves of the sea—but it will not;
- Israel could have offspring like the sand of the sea—but it will not;
- Israel could have descendants as numerous as grains of sand—but it will not;
- Israel could have an enduring name—but it will not.

This harsh verdict is rooted in the old theology of *šāmaʿ*. No listening—no future!

48:20 **Go out from Babylon, flee from Chaldea,**
    declare this with a shout of joy, proclaim it,
  send it forth to the end of the earth;
    say, "The LORD has redeemed his servant Jacob!"
²¹ **They did not thirst when he led them through the deserts;**
  he made water flow for them from the rock;
  he split open the rock and the water gushed out.

Then comes a pause between verse 19 and verse 20. It is a pause for a changed tone—a pause for reconsideration on the part of Yahweh. And then abruptly, inexplicably, there is a positive imperative: *Go out!* The verb is an Exodus verb. The departure from Babylon now to happen is likened to the Exodus from Egypt. Israel has a gospel to announce. It is to be announced far and wide, vigorously, with exuberance. The message, the decisive message, the only message that counts is "Yahweh has redeemed Israel!" The theme reiterates Yahweh's titles from verse 17. That is who Yahweh is; consequently, that is who Israel is—Yahweh's redeemed and emancipated!

The Exodus theme is extended in verse 21. Now the old Exodus memory is reiterated without any interpretive connection to present events. *This* event is *that* event (see Josh. 4:23–24). The journey of the wilderness sojourn is from Egypt/from Babylon. Verse 21 looks back to the wonder of Exodus 17:1–6, concretely Yahweh's miracle, a sign of Yahweh's sustaining, life-giving promise to Israel as Israel departs the food-chain and water supply of the empire. As Israel remembers the gushing waters of the rock, so the exiles are now assured of gushing, life-giving waters on the way (see 41:18).

Verses 17–21 are saturated with memory and allusion. The verbs "teach" and "lead" (v. 17) look back to Moses' leadership, anticipating the negative on the commandments in verse 18 and the miracle of verse 21. The reference to sand and grain (v. 19) recalls the promise to the Genesis ancestors (Gen. 22:17; 32:12), and the gushing of verse 21 recalls wilderness wonders. The unit invites exilic Israel to resituate its life in the old narrative of the Torah, now replicated and reiterated in the sixth century.

The affirmation of verses 20–21 is a vast non sequitur after the negative "contrary to fact" of verses 18–19. We are not told how this leap to the positive is accomplished or how Yahweh manages to make such an affirmation to such an unresponsive people. Nonetheless, Israel's life with Yahweh is characteristically given in such non sequiturs, which in Christian confession swirl around the supreme non sequitur of Easter.

Perhaps our best clue for making the leap from the negation of verses 18–19 to the affirmation of verses 20–21 is in the assertion of verses 9–11 that I take to be the pivotal point of the entire chapter. The ground of affirmation for the exiles is not found in Yahweh's love for Israel. It is found, rather, in Yahweh's self-regard. The new Exodus and new wilderness sustenance out of Babylon here are not for the sake of Israel. They are for the sake of Yahweh's reputation and honor. Israel is a fortunate by-product of Yahweh's honor. Yahweh's self-regard produces miracles for Israel, because Israel is Yahweh's best visible credential in the eyes of the nations.

48:22 "There is no peace," says the LORD, "for the wicked."

The poet (or editor) cannot quit without one more negative, thus reminding us yet again of the ambiguity of Israel's life with Yahweh. This lean verse is perhaps a freestanding cliché, as in 57:21. It does not in any case refer to the common problem of restless workaholism. In context, "the wicked" refers to those who are alienated from the promises of Yahweh, who refuse the commands of Yahweh, who doubt the gushing waters of

Yahweh, who refuse to situate their life in this construal of reality. In a word, the wicked are those who will not depart Babylon for the risk of life with Yahweh.

"Peace like a river" is given to the attentive. There is no such peace for "the wicked." Rather, they are assigned to the endless chaos, anxiety, and insecurity of life in the empire by the norms of the empire. Yahweh is the only real source of "peace," and that peace requires a venturesome departure. For those who trust the empire more than they trust Yahweh, the future is sure to be taxing, unsettled, and endlessly demanding.

Israel faces a terrible choice in exile, not unlike the choice given the disciples of Jesus who are always between "two masters" (Matt. 6:24–33). Only one master banishes anxiety. It is no wonder our text exudes ambiguity and ambivalence. The rhetoric of contradiction that pervades this chapter reflects the choice Israel must now make. The text requires an intentional redeciding among exiles, without which the future is endlessly restless and unresolved.

A SERVANT AS LIGHT AND AS COVENANT
49:1–12

These verses constitute an enormous problem in Isaiah studies because they celebrate "the servant of the Lord," whose identity is unfathomable. It is characteristic that Jewish interpretation identifies the servant as the community of Israel. More classical Christian interpretation (as in John Calvin) has found here anticipatory allusion to Jesus, whereas standard historical criticism has sought to identify a nameable, known historical character (see Christopher North, *The Suffering Servant in Deutero-Isaiah*). The question of identity is at the present time an enigma beyond resolution. Several things can be noted, however:

1. It is possible to understand how this poetry suggested Jesus to the early church, without in any way making the claim that such an anticipation was intended by the poet or the canonizers of the book.

2. The identification of a historical person in the Old Testament has been a futile enterprise, because there is no consensus among scholars and because each such proposed candidate only accommodates the poetry in incidental details and never in comprehensive ways.

3. The most likely interpretation is to regard the servant as Israel, as is the case elsewhere in exilic Isaiah. There is, however, a major obstacle to

such a sense, because in verses 5–6 the servant has a ministry to Israel, so that it could not be Israel as servant to Israel.

4. It is likely that David J. A. Clines, in *I, He, We, and They*, has offered the best counsel—to wit, that we give up the quest for identity of the historical servant and pay attention only to the imagery and force of the poetry as such; that is, to move from historical to literary-rhetorical considerations. From such a perspective, it is enough to see that Yahweh has designated some human agent to be about the work of healing and emancipation in the world with particular reference to Israel. Such an approach permits us to attend to the text and to forgo questions of historical identity that in any case did not seem to interest the poet.

In this unit of poetry, the servant speaks (vv. 1–4), first addressing the coastlands and peoples (vv. 1–2), quoting what Yahweh has said to the servant (v. 3), and reiterating a response of futility coupled with trust and affirmation (v. 4). Then Yahweh speaks (vv. 5–12). These verses seem to be a series of brief utterances addressed to the servant that are marked in verses 5–8 by a series of rhetorical indicators. Although the poetry appears to be a series of distinct speeches, together they amount to a forceful commissioning whereby Yahweh has authorized human, emancipatory agency in the historical process.

49:1 **Listen to me, O coastlands,**
      pay attention, you peoples from far away!
  The LORD called me before I was born,
      while I was in my mother's womb he named me.
  ²**He made my mouth like a sharp sword,**
      in the shadow of his hand he hid me;
  he made me a polished arrow,
      in his quiver he hid me away.

The servant speaks to announce his mandate from Yahweh. The address to "coastlands and peoples" is ambiguous. (See the same word pair in 41:1.) It may be that this is a global invitation to all peoples. Conversely, it may be that it is an address to Jews who have been scattered in the diaspora in the wake of the destruction of Jerusalem. In either case, the servant is to be recognized in a very large vista, with a sweeping mandate and a large ambition. The servant announces that he was selected by Yahweh even before birth (see Jer. 1:5), has been equipped by Yahweh to be an effective instrument (weapon) for Yahweh, and has been safely hidden by Yahweh. These phrases assert that the servant is indeed to be reckoned with, assured beyond his own resources for the purposes and resolves of Yahweh.

49:3 **And he said to me, "You are my servant,**
      Israel, in whom I will be glorified."
   [4] **But I said, "I have labored in vain,**
      I have spent my strength for nothing and vanity;
   yet surely my cause is with the LORD,
      and my reward with my God."

The servant announces in a quotation from Yahweh, moreover, that he has been claimed and commissioned by Yahweh, so that through the work of the servant, Yahweh will be honored (v. 3). Thus the self-assertion of the servant (vv. 1–2) and the quotation from Yahweh (v. 3) assure that the servant is referred beyond self and is to be regarded as a force in the world by and for Yahweh. The servant is Yahweh's device for Yahweh's purposes.

At the outset, the servant expresses discouragement, defeat, and exhaustion, acknowledging that enactment of the mission has been a failure and concluding that the mission is futile (v. 4a). The first lines of verse 4 use a series of three terms—"vain, nothing, vanity"—a powerful triad of negations. Remarkably, the second half of the verse reverses field, introduced by a powerful adverb "yet surely." Nonetheless, the servant is confident that "my cause" and "my reward" are with God, and this linkage to Yahweh counters the futility and discouragement of the first lines. The concluding line suggests that the servant is still resolved and prepared to do the work assigned by Yahweh, discouragement notwithstanding.

49:5 **And now the LORD says,**
      who formed me in the womb to be his servant,
   to bring Jacob back to him,
      and that Israel might be gathered to him,
   for I am honored in the sight of the LORD,
      and my God has become my strength—
   [6] **he says,**
   "It is too light a thing that you should be my servant
      to raise up the tribes of Jacob
      and to restore the survivors of Israel;
   I will give you as a light to the nations,
      that my salvation may reach to the end of the earth."

Yahweh has been quoted in verse 3, but now speaks directly for the first time. Verse 5 is not yet the substance of address but is only an appositive further identifying Yahweh who speaks. Yahweh is the one who found the servant, thus reiterating verse 1. And now we learn, for the first time, the work of the servant. It is to *return and gather* Israel, that is, to end exile and bring Israel home (v. 6). The homecoming had long been announced in chapters 40—48 and is to be made possible by the triumph of Cyrus. But it is the servant who will effect the wonder of gathering. That has been Yahweh's mandate to the servant, even prior to birth.

But now, in verse 6, in one of the oddest verses in exilic Isaiah, it is as though Yahweh has second thoughts contradicting verse 5. The servant is to restore the remnant of Israel, but that is too "light," too trivial. The servant is now assigned a greater task. The servant is now dispatched to "the nations," "the end of the earth." It is possible that these phrases continue to refer to scattered Jews; it is also possible, however, that in this remarkable phrasing Israel's exilic horizon is pushed beyond the needful Jewish community to a concern for Gentiles. One way or the other—to Jews or also to Gentiles—the servant is to be "light" and "salvation" (victory). We may take the two terms as rough synonyms, both of them referring to the full offer of well-being as intended by the creator. "Light" is the antithesis of darkness, disorder, and chaos; and "salvation" is the counter to oppression, exploitation, and despair. The mandate intends that the servant will effect a complete reversal of fortunes according to the full resolve for life and well-being by the creator. At the least, it is a reversal for the Jews; at its largest potential, this is a vision for a renewed world for all peoples.

49:7 **Thus says the LORD,**
       the Redeemer of Israel and his Holy One,
    to one deeply despised, abhorred by the nations,
       the slave of rulers,
    "Kings shall see and stand up,
       princes, and they shall prostrate themselves,
    because of the LORD, who is faithful,
       the Holy One of Israel, who has chosen you."

This verse seems to be a reprise, one more time affirming and celebrating the servant. The verse is bracketed in the first and last lines by the identification of the God of Israel, who has designated and empowered the servant. This is indeed a Yahwistic enterprise. Because of the solidarity and resolve of Yahweh, the servant will succeed even when appearing to be defeated. It may be that the image of one "despised and abhorred" anticipates chapter 53; but such an appearance notwithstanding, eventually the powerful of the earth (the Babylonians?) will stand up in respect and will bow down in deference. It is no wonder the Christians find here cadences of the affirmation of Jesus, the one who is "humbled and exalted" (Phil. 2:5–11). The imagery here is bold and radically new in Israel. We do not know why the poet presents the servant in this way. This presentation in any case serves as a harbinger of the riddle of strength and weakness that characterizes the life enacted by Jesus. Everything for the servant, who has no self-possessed resources, depends on Yahweh. But Yahweh is faithful. As a consequence, this servant, who holds little promise of effectiveness, will not fail. The mission is as sure as is Yahweh's own fidelity—utterly sure! The transformative intention of the servant is reliable and is as good as done.

49:8 **Thus says the LORD:**
> **In a time of favor I have answered you,**
>> **on a day of salvation I have helped you;**
> **I have kept you and given you**
>> **as a covenant to the people,**
> **to establish the land,**
>> **to apportion the desolate heritages;**
> ⁹**saying to the prisoners, "Come out,"**
>> **to those who are in darkness, "Show yourselves."**
> **They shall feed along the ways,**
>> **on all the bare heights shall be their pasture;**
> ¹⁰ **they shall not hunger or thirst,**
>> **neither scorching wind nor sun shall strike them down,**
> **for he who has pity on them will lead them,**
>> **and by springs of water will guide them.**
> ¹¹ **And I will turn all my mountains into a road,**
>> **and my highways shall be raised up.**
> ¹² **Lo, these shall come from far away,**
>> **and lo, these from the north and from the west,**
>> **and these from the land of Syene.**

Yahweh speaks again to the servant, assuring the servant of support and solidarity. The accent, however, is not upon support but upon the assignment of the servant. The servant is to be "a covenant," as in 42:6. The sense of the phrase is not clear, but it apparently means a powerful agent and partner in the practice of loyal solidarity that makes a new future possible. The servant as "covenant" is empowered to speak two imperative verbs: to the prisoners, the servant is to command "come out." To those in darkness, the servant is to command "appear" (v. 9a). If we take prison and darkness as images of exile and the despair resultant from exile, then the verbs mean to counter the despair of exile by summoning, authorizing, and empowering the exiles to assert themselves, to claim their Yahweh-given freedom. The verb "come out" is an exodus verb, asking the Babylonian exiles to leave the thralldom of Babylon as their ancestors left the certitudes of Egypt (see 52:11). We may imagine that over time a sense of distinctiveness had eroded in Israel and with it a loss of purpose, hope, and possibility. The work of the servant is to enliven the exilic community with new intentionality and courage that will eventuate in homecoming, a life outside the contours of the empire.

Then follows a lovely, idyllic scenario of the emancipated, now with courage to go, on their way home. We have already seen the image of "highway," that is, an especially prepared route of passage that is safe, speedy, and well protected (v. 11; see 35:8; 40:3). However, here the imagery is of a flock of sheep on its way under the caring supervision of a shepherd. En route home "the flock" will find adequate protection. It will be safe from all dangers of weather and environment, not at risk because of wind or sun or shortage of water or food.

The flock will be safe and well cared for because the shepherd (here not named but alluded to) will have "pity" upon them, will care for them, guide them, and provide adequate water. This language echoes the assurance of 40:11 and of course calls to mind Psalm 23. Indeed, that familiar psalm may best be understood as a meditation upon the protection of the "good shepherd" for all those who "like sheep have gone astray" (Isa. 53:6). The imagery, moreover, anticipates the parable of Jesus concerning the shepherd who seeks the lost (Luke 15:3–7) and the Johannine reflection upon the shepherd who gives his life for the sake of the sheep's abundance (John 10:10). Indeed, we may be able to see that the shepherd metaphor, when used of Jesus, suggests that Jesus is still at work in the ending of the "scattering" that has been the long-suffering circumstance of displaced Jews. The work of the servant as shepherd is the *gathering of the scattered* (see v. 5; Jer. 31:10). The scattered are in many places. They shall now come home from everywhere they have been scattered, from all directions (v. 12). The imagery anticipates the gospel announcement of the great global ingathering and homecoming soon to be enacted: "Then people will come from east and west, from north and south, and will eat in the kingdom of God" (Luke 13:29). The rhetoric concerns a complete reversal of fortunes for the scattered now to be gathered. It is to be accomplished by the work of the servant in the service of "The Good Shepherd." The servant figures crucially in the vision of newness here uttered over the exiles.

THE JOY OF HOMECOMING
49:13–26

This section of the chapter is a series of brief utterances with a variety of literary forms and modes of speech. All through the variation, however, there is a constancy of theme: Yahweh's fidelity will cause an end to exile and will enable Israel to return joyously to Jerusalem.

49:13 Sing for joy, O heavens, and exult, O earth;
      break forth, O mountains, into singing!
  For the LORD has comforted his people,
      and will have compassion on his suffering ones.

    14 But Zion said, "The LORD has forsaken me,
      my Lord has forgotten me."
    15 Can a woman forget her nursing child,
      or show no compassion for the child of her womb?
    Even these may forget,
      yet I will not forget you.
    16 See, I have inscribed you on the palms of my hands;
      your walls are continually before me.
    17 Your builders outdo your destroyers,
      and those who laid you waste go away from you.
    18 Lift up your eyes all around and see;
      they all gather, they come to you.
    As I live, says the LORD,
      you shall put all of them on like an ornament,
      and like a bride you shall bind them on.

This text consists in a hymnic affirmation (v. 13), an expression of doubt on Zion's part (v. 14), and an affirmative response by Yahweh that seeks to override the doubt of Zion (vv. 15–18). The *hymnic affirmation* is in the characteristic pattern of a hymn: a *summons* (lines 1 and 2) and *reason* (lines 3 and 4). The summons is that the whole cosmos might sing in praise of Yahweh. The reason is that Yahweh has "comforted" and had "compassion" on Israel. The cosmos is to celebrate the comforting of Israel! The first verb, "comfort," echoes the initial announcement of forgiveness in 40:1. The second verb, "have compassion" (as in v. 10), reflects the attentive concern of a mother for a child.

The affirmation, however, evokes *the doubt of Jerusalem* (v. 14). The lament on the lips of Israel likely reflects the stylized, liturgical utterance of Israel in exile, as in Lamentations 5:20. With good reason, Israel in its present circumstance of exile might have doubted the comfort and compassion of Yahweh. The two verbs, "forget, forsake," signifying total abandonment, seek to nullify the assurance of comfort and compassion. The complaint of Israel in exile seeks to nullify the hymn, thus reflecting despondency in exile. The hymnic utterance of verse 13 anticipates a good future, but complaining Israel in verse 14 is still caught in present-tense circumstances in which Yahweh is no visible player.

The *affirmative response* Yahweh makes to the doubt of Israel, however, reiterates the accosting verbs of verse 14, "forget, forsake," and then vetoes them. It is completely improbable that a nursing mother would forget her child, improbable but not impossible. For Yahweh, however, such forgetting and forsaking is not even a possibility, for Yahweh's commitment and compassion are stronger and more intense than that of any nursing mother. Yahweh will not forget Israel, not abandon Zion. Even in the depth of exile, Yahweh has not forgotten and has not abandoned, contrary to what the circumstance may suggest. And the reason for such intense remembering is that Israel's name is engraved on the palm of Yahweh's hand; that is, cut like a carving on stone or like a tattoo, in order to assure the attentiveness of Yahweh. The image here is complementary to that of 44:5. In that verse, Israel has "The Lord's" written on its hand to indicate a relation to Yahweh. Now Yahweh has written "Israel" on Yahweh's hand in order to affirm the relationship. Yahweh is inextricably for Israel as a mother is inextricably for a suckling child, only more so.

From this intimate, maternal imagery, the assurance of verses 16b–18 becomes more public and anticipates reclamation of a restored Jerusalem. The dominant verbs are "build" and "gather," referring in turn to the reclamation of the physical city and to the rehabilitation of its inhabitants. It is rooted in nothing less than the enduring resolve of Yahweh that Jerusalem will be rebuilt and reinhabited. It is no wonder that the heavens and the mountains will sing (v. 13). The cause for cosmic rejoicing is the revival of Jerusalem that now becomes a dominant theme for the tradition of Isaiah. The renewal of the city is an event of cosmic interest, importance, and urgency.

49:19 **Surely your waste and your desolate places**
   and your devastated land—
 surely now you will be too crowded for your inhabitants,
   and those who swallowed you up will be far away.
 20 **The children born in the time of your bereavement**
   will yet say in your hearing:
 "The place is too crowded for me;

> make room for me to settle."
> ²¹ Then you will say in your heart,
>   "Who has borne me these?
> I was bereaved and barren,
>   exiled and put away—
>   so who has reared these?
> I was left all alone—
>   where then have these come from?"

The ultimate image of judgment and ruin is that the city should be uninhabited, so that it becomes either a place for thorns and briers or a place of wild, unclean animals. It is the language of desolation that characterizes Jerusalem while the exiles are absent. Now, in an abrupt rhetorical reversal, the city will be repeopled with the exiles from Babylon. It will be "too crowded" (v. 19) with people, that is, cramped, full to overflowing. Indeed, children born in exile, the time of grief and desolation, will sense the overcrowding and will say "too crowded" (v. 20).

These verses play upon the contrast of barrenness and birth. Barrenness bespeaks failure, judgment, and exile. Birth in such fecundity alludes to the elemental creation promise "be fruitful" and the ancestral promise that the heirs of Israel will be as numerous as the stars of the heavens and the sand of the sea (see 48:19). That is, the power of Yahweh's blessing is fully generative of new life. But exile had seemed a termination of such blessings, as though the promises of Yahweh had been defeated.

Now, says the poet, Israel will be dazzled by its multiplication. It will be bewildered and will not understand how barrenness has turned to generativity. The forsaken has become the blessed precisely because Yahweh has comforted and had compassion, because Yahweh has not—ever—forgotten or forsaken.

49:22 Thus says the Lord GOD:
>   I will soon lift up my hand to the nations,
>   and raise my signal to the peoples;
>   and they shall bring your sons in their bosom,
>   and your daughters shall be carried on their shoulders.
> ²³ Kings shall be your foster fathers,
>   and their queens your nursing mothers.
>   With their faces to the ground they shall bow down to you,
>   and lick the dust of your feet.
>   Then you will know that I am the LORD;

> those who wait for me shall
>   not be put to shame.
>
> ²⁴ Can the prey be taken from the mighty,
>   or the captives of a tyrant be rescued?
> ²⁵ But thus says the LORD:
>   Even the captives of the mighty shall be taken,
>   and the prey of the tyrant be rescued;
>   for I will contend with those who contend with you,
>   and I will save your children.
> ²⁶ I will make your oppressors eat their own flesh,
>   and they shall be drunk with their own blood as with wine.
> Then all flesh shall know
>   that I am the LORD your Savior,
>   and your Redeemer, the Mighty One of Jacob.

The imagery changes slightly. Now the image is not of newborn children. Rather, the subject is the already birthed children of Israel who have been carried away into exile by many nations. There they have become war booty, cheap labor, abused slaves. It has seemed that any future was lost as Jews had disappeared into the woodwork of the larger imperial economy.

But now, Yahweh will give a signal. Yahweh will motion to the nations. It is as though all powers in the earth keep their eye on Yahweh. They are watching their leader. Their leader, Yahweh, need only beckon, and immediately, without hesitation, the kings and queens of the earth, in full obedience to Yahweh, not only release Jews kept too long in bondage. They also carry them and attend to them and in submissive deference gladly bring the Jews back to Jerusalem. The poetry imagines a great flood of foreigners readily returning Jews home. There are here echoes of 43:4–6, wherein Yahweh bargained and made trades for the release of the exiles. But here there are no bargains or trades, simply a modest gesture. The nations know and respond. They know Yahweh is the commander, and they know Jews are treasured by Yahweh and belong in Jerusalem. The great homecoming to the heretofore emptied city is supreme evidence of Yahweh's full sovereignty. Everybody can see it—Jews and Gentiles.

Whereas verses 22–23 seem to suggest that the nations yield their Jewish captives willingly, verses 24–25 suggest that the nations are resistant and reluctant. The loss of such captive Jews entails both an economic loss and a loss of face. The poet wonders for us, "Do you think they can be rescued?" The imagery of verse 24 suggests the attempt to rescue a lamb from the mouth of a ferocious lion (see 1 Sam. 17:34–36). It is as though Babylon is a ravenous lion, and the lamb Israel would seem to be lost. The first line of verse 24 states the metaphor, and the second line interprets for the intention of the poem.

The unlikely rescue of the lamb from lion will be done. Yahweh will do it. Yahweh will decisively intervene and contest in behalf of Israel. Yahweh will effect a complete reversal, permitting Jews to come home and creating a situation of desperate impossibility for the captive nations (Babylon?), who will be so crazed and so needy and so desperate as to devour each other in insane, self-destructive war. The great reversal is testimony to Yahweh. The concluding assertion of verse 26 echoes verse 23, except that in verse 23 it is "you" who shall know; in verse 26 it is "all flesh," all the heavens and mountains summoned in verse 13, all the watching nations, all who wonder at Yahweh's governance (see 40:5). All shall know, understand, and accept this rule for the world.

In verses 1–2, it is the servant who will effect the emancipation and homecoming of Israel. But in verses 13–18, the servant is no longer mentioned. Now it is directly and only Yahweh. It is Yahweh who will have compassion and who will gather. It is Yahweh who will effect the radical reversal. Everyone now knows: Israel is free and Yahweh has done it. The nations end up completely devastated, for they have resisted Yahweh and refused Yahweh's intention. None can withstand Yahweh, the sure source of Israel's future.

YAHWEH'S POWER AND RELIABILITY
50:1–11

This chapter contains three brief rhetorical units that do not seem to be related to each other in any evident way. Verses 1–3 constitute a speech of disputation on the part of Yahweh against Israel, of the sort we have found in 42:18–25 and 43:22–28. In verses 4–9 the servant reappears, apparently the figure to whom reference is made in 42:1–9 and 49:1–12. Finally, verses 10–11 are something of a fragment that invites trust (v. 10) but harshly condemns the disobedient.

50:1 **Thus says the LORD:**
    Where is your mother's bill of divorce
      with which I put her away?
    Or which of my creditors is it to whom I have sold you?
    No, because of your sins you were sold,

> and for your transgressions your mother was put away.
> ² Why was no one there when I came?
>   Why did no one answer when I called?
> Is my hand shortened, that it cannot redeem?
>   Or have I no power to deliver?
> By my rebuke I dry up the sea,
>   I make the rivers a desert;
> their fish stink for lack of water,
>   and die of thirst.
> ³ I clothe the heavens with blackness,
>   and make sackcloth their covering.

This oracle in the mouth of Yahweh is a disputatious challenge to Israel. It is more characteristic in exilic Isaiah that Yahweh should dispute with rival gods. There is evidence, however, that a quarrelsome debate continued in the Exile concerning the cause of the Exile. Some wondered, was exile just punishment given Israel by Yahweh? Or was it a result of Yahweh's inattentiveness or impatience? That is, is Yahweh *at fault* for the Exile? This oracle is Yahweh's self-defense, an assertion that Yahweh is not at fault; it is Israel's own transgression that caused exile. Thus the verses participate in the ongoing issue of theodicy that so occupied Israel in the Exile.

The oracle begins with two rhetorical questions that in turn ask: (a) Did Yahweh arbitrarily divorce wife-Israel as it was a husband's right to do in that patriarchal society (see Deut. 24:1–4)? (b) Did Yahweh arbitrarily sell Israel for profit as a bond-servant? The required answer to both questions is "no," Yahweh did not arbitrarily divorce nor did Yahweh sell Israel out. Yahweh is not the cause of exile. The cause of divorce is Israel's fickleness, not the arbitrariness of Yahweh; the cause of being sold into exile is Israel's forfeiture of claim, not the avarice of Yahweh. The next line takes up the same charges in reverse order and places responsibility upon Israel: (a) Israel is sold because of sin; (b) Israel is divorced for cause.

With that argument made, verse 2 moves on to invite a counterargument in the imagined court case. But as with the gods who are mute (41:28), so Israel is silent. There is "no one," "no one." It can only be implied that Israel has no case to make in its own defense. That is, Yahweh's initial argument carries the day without challenge.

In verse 2b, Yahweh returns to self-defense and self-justification with a double rhetorical question concerning Yahweh's unrivaled power. Some in exile must have charged that Yahweh lacked power to prevent exile. The rhetorical questions again require a negative response: "No, my hand is not shortened!" The image refers to the characteristic way in which Yahweh's hand is "outstretched" in power to do a transformative deed (Deut. 26:8, and negatively in Jer. 21:5). No, Yahweh does not lack power! The questions are in fact directly answered in verses 2c–3 with a series of three powerful, decisive verbs: "I dry up," "I make," "I clothe," and again, "I make." Yahweh's power is exhibited in the massiveness of creation, whereby Yahweh can invert waters to dryness and can cause darkness and devastation. There need be no doubt of Yahweh's capacity to govern. The Exile, it is clear, is not a consequence of Yahweh's neglect or default. It is rather a justly deserved punishment over which Yahweh has intentionally presided.

50:4 **The Lord GOD has given me**
     the tongue of a teacher,
 that I may know how to sustain
     the weary with a word.
 Morning by morning he wakens—
     wakens my ear
     to listen as those who are taught.
 [5] **The Lord GOD has opened my ear,**
     and I was not rebellious,
 I did not turn backward.
 [6] **I gave my back to those who struck me,**
     and my cheeks to those who pulled out the beard;
 I did not hide my face
     from insult and spitting.

 [7] **The Lord GOD helps me;**
     therefore I have not been disgraced;
 therefore I have set my face like flint,
     and I know that I shall not be put to shame;
 [8]   **he who vindicates me is near.**
 Who will contend with me?
     Let us stand up together.
 Who are my adversaries?
     Let them confront me.
 [9] **It is the Lord GOD who helps me;**
     who will declare me guilty?
 All of them will wear out like a garment;
     the moth will eat them up.

It is not clear that these verses have any connection to the foregoing. It is as though these verses provide a reflective interlude concerning the urgent, contested vocation of the servant of Yahweh, who is to bring Israel home from exile. The most prominent rhetorical feature of this unit is the fourfold reiteration of the title "Lord God" (vv. 4, 5, 7, 9), each time with an active, decisive verb of which Yahweh is the subject and the servant is the recipient: "The Lord God has given me . . . ; the Lord God has opened . . . ; The Lord God helps . . . ; The Lord God helps. . . . " The speaking servant pushes the focus of his vocation away from himself to Yahweh. The work is the work of Yahweh. It is only as an obedient, trustworthy respondent that the servant acts:

The Lord God has given a tongue (v. 4a). That is, the servant is credible and persuasive in utterance, and knows how to give support and sustenance to the weary. The "weary" are those who are exhausted by the demands and anxieties of Babylonian requirements. Presumably, the sustaining word of the servant is a word about Yahweh, an insistence that the truth of Yahweh contradicts and denies the power and erodes the authority of Babylon. Thus the sustaining word to the weary is not just any pastoral word; it is a word energizing the exiles to their own distinctive identity in a context where that identity is at risk.

The Lord God has given an ear (vv. 4b–5). The servant has learned how to listen and how to be instructed, how to be attentive to Yahweh's address and how to accept the fresh identity and vocation that comes from such obedient listening. The teacher of the exiles is taught and is fully prepared to run the risks of obedience to the peculiar and uncompromising mandates of Yahweh. As a result, the servant is steadfast and unflinching in obedience, even in the face of abusive opposition. It is possible that the abuse comes from Babylonian authorities who seek to intimidate and silence such subversive teaching. It seems more likely to me that the abuse comes from other members of the exilic community who have worked out a sustainable compromise between Yahweh and the empire, who do not want to have the compromise exposed or questioned, and who do not want to be pressed to decide for Yahweh and for the disruptive venture of homecoming in a distinctive identity. The vocation of the servant is singularly and leanly Yahwistic, and so is at odds with more accommodating ways of faith.

The Lord God helps me (vv. 7–9). The servant is exposed to challenge and dispute, and may face formal accusation as a troublemaker or perhaps only the endlessly hostile distraction of resisters. But the servant will not give in. Yahweh is indeed a "helper" (Psalm 121:2). Being helped, the servant is utterly resolved and will not be dissuaded. The servant is fully confident of Yahweh as a sufficient support to do what Yahweh has mandated.

The poetry conjures a judicial context. There are adversaries who would condemn, but Yahweh is the one who will vindicate (or acquit). The terms *vindicate* and *declare guilty* (or condemn) are a deliberate word pair stating the alternative available outcomes of a judicial procedure. The speaker is completely confident that Yahweh presides over the court and will acquit, and therefore the opponents have no power to indict, condemn, or punish.

The judicial word pair is taken up by Paul to make the same point in a very different context: "Who will bring any charge against God's elect? It is God who *justifies*. Who is to *condemn?* It is Christ Jesus, who died, yes, who was raised, who is at the right hand of God, who indeed *intercedes* for us" (Rom. 8:33–34). In his christological formulation, Paul is so sure of vindication (justification) that every attempt to condemn (in his case by the power of sin, law, and death) is futile, for the power of negation cannot withstand the affirmation of the gospel given in the court over which God presides. The futility of accusation and attack is abundantly clear. The servant will "wear out" (v. 9) his opponents. They will fail in their effort to negate the servant and his vocation. They will last no longer than a garment exposed to moths. That is, it is not possible for the opponents of the servant to resist the vocation of homecoming. The summons to distinctiveness cannot be resisted.

Here speaks a voice of complete certitude, grounded in nothing other than the utter reliability of Yahweh. But that utter reliability is enough. Consequently, the servant will not desist even in the face of great adversity. Therefore the mission will not fail. The power of Yahweh has been reasserted in verses 1–3. Here that power, enacted through the servant, is to do good for Israel, even if some in Israel resist.

50:10 **Who among you fears the LORD**
     and obeys the voice of his servant,
  who walks in darkness
     and has no light,
  yet trusts in the name of the LORD
     and relies upon his God?
      11But all of you are kindlers of fire,
     lighters of firebrands.
  Walk in the flame of your fire,
     and among the brands that you have kindled!
  This is what you shall have from my hand:
     you shall lie down in torment.

These two verses seem to be a curious, disconnected fragment. It is possible, however, that the two parts of this brief section, positive and negative, draw together the earlier elements of the chapter. Verse 10 offers a positive portrayal of what a serious worshiper of Yahweh may do. The verse is dominated by positive verbs: "fear, obey (listen), walk, trust, rely upon." Such an adherent to Yahweh, however, would do so in spite of any circumstance of darkness (= exile?). Not only is such faith (trust) linked to Yahweh, but it is intimately connected to "his servant." That is, the concrete form of trust in Yahweh is to follow the teaching and mandate of the servant. If the mission of the servant is the emancipation of Israel from exile, then obedience to Yahweh consists in accepting the emancipation and departing from Babylonian definitions of reality. The positive verse, however, is governed by the interrogative "Who among you . . . ?" which implies a negative response: None of you *fear, trust, or rely upon.* Such faith is possible, but it is not evident in the community of exiles, who do not trust Yahweh enough to risk the summons and leadership of the servant.

The negative implication of the interrogative of verse 10 is made explicit in verse 11. In this condemnation, the poetry does not seem to discriminate concerning part of the community that is unresponsive. The negative is wholesale and pertains to the entire community that is hesitant and reluctant about the offer of homecoming by way of distinctive identity. The precise intention of the verse concerning fire, flames, and firebrands is by no means clear. Claus Westermann inclines to take the imagery of fire as an allusion to destruction: They are to perish "by their own weapons, those they used against the righteous." Calvin, by contrast, appeals to the phrase "flame of your fire" and understands the verse to comment on an effort at autonomy that contrasts the light of the human community with Yahweh's own light of rescue and salvation. In such a contrast, the human light will surely fail, and the community shall "miserably perish." The reference to fire is difficult, but Calvin's reading seems to me to have great merit. The theme of "darkness" may suggest a connection back to Isaiah 9:2, wherein darkness refers to something like Assyrian oppression. Here, in a later context, the "darkness" may be the Babylonian exile. Israel is not able on its own strength (by its own light) to deal with the problem of exile but must finally trust in Yahweh—which here it refuses to do. Israel could have trusted in Yahweh (v. 10); refusing that, Israel here is destined to a sorry end (v. 11).

The chapter is not a unity in any obvious way. We may suggest, however, that the positive of verse 10 reflects the affirmation of verses 4–9, whereas the negative of verse 11 echoes the theme of transgression from verses 1–3. If we see the chapter in terms of these motifs, it is evident that Israel has an urgent choice of life or death, blessing or curse (see Deut. 30:15–20). The servant of verses 4–9, at great cost, teaches the way of life.

Israel, however, rejects that way, abuses the servant, chooses death, and ends with "fire." This is the same unresponsive Israel of 49:14, who is preoccupied with its evident abandonment by Yahweh but is unaware of the compassion of Yahweh that overrides the abandonment. The consequence for such resistance is "torment," a term suggestive of extreme punishment, a horror nearly unutterable.

"LISTEN, LISTEN, LISTEN"
51:1–8

Three times in this unit of poetry, Israel is called to "listen" (vv. 1, 4, and 7). Yahweh has a crucial dramatic announcement to make that turns out to be life-or-death for Israel. Each of the three sections that comprise this unit begins with a series of *summoning imperatives* and moves to a statement of *reasons for listening*, each time expressing an assurance of Yahweh's saving initiative (vv. 1–3, 4–6, 7–8).

51:1 **Listen to me, you that pursue righteousness,**
      you that seek the LORD.
   Look to the rock from which you were hewn,
      and to the quarry from which you were dug.
   ² **Look to Abraham your father**
      and to Sarah who bore you;
   for he was but one when I called him,
      but I blessed him and made him many.
   ³ **For the LORD will comfort Zion;**
      he will comfort all her waste places,
   and will make her wilderness like Eden,
      her desert like the garden of the LORD;
   joy and gladness will be found in her,
      thanksgiving and the voice of song.

This summons to Israel is addressed to "the pursuers of righteousness" and "the seekers of Yahweh," that is, the ones deeply serious about faith. They are addressed by three imperatives. The first imperative, "listen," (*šāmaʿ*) is a broad call to attention echoing the decisive *šāmaʿ* of Deuteronomy 6:4. The two imperatives that follow, "look . . . look," invite Israel to recall the Abraham-Sarah narratives of the book of Genesis, for Abraham and Sarah are the true ancestors of the community of exiles. The single crucial point made here about the ancestors is that Abraham was one but

Yahweh made him many. This is a fair summary of the entire Abraham narrative that is endlessly preoccupied with the promise of a son and an heir. The gift of a son, Isaac, to Abraham, when he was "as good as dead" (Hebrews 11:12), permitted the family of Israel to prosper according to Yahweh's life-giving promise. The exiles are to recall the ancestors in order to ponder the memory that Yahweh gives miraculous blessing to this people in the most unlikely circumstance. In verses 1–2, it is to be inferred that what Yahweh did of old to that hopeless people Yahweh will do again in this present needy generation of exiles. The same people may now anticipate the same miracle from the same God.

The initial "for" (= because) of verse 3 turns the summons to reason: "listen, look, look" *because* Yahweh will "comfort" Jerusalem. The verb is the characteristic verb of 40:1. To comfort is to make new life possible, even as Yahweh "comforted" Abraham and Sarah long ago. That is, Yahweh is about to act decisively in the restoration and rehabilitation of Jerusalem. The earlier Isaiah tradition, accenting judgment and anticipating exile, had imagined the reduction of Jerusalem to waste places, wilderness, and desert.

Now there is to be a mighty inversion. Those places, bereft of life resources, are now to be "comforted" and blessed like the very Garden of Eden; they are to exude the wondrous power for life. The news to exiles is that the force of "new creation" will be enacted in that wounded, beloved city. No wonder the restored city will be a place of unending doxology—joy, gladness, thanks, song—a doxology commensurate with the marvelous gift of new life! The utterance in imperative and assurance defies present exilic circumstance and looks to renewal assured by Yahweh, who is now again the dominant force in Israel's life.

51:4 **Listen to me, my people,**
    and give heed to me, my nation;
  for a teaching will go out from me,
    and my justice for a light to the peoples.
 [5]**I will bring near my deliverance swiftly,**
    my salvation has gone out
    and my arms will rule the peoples;
  the coastlands wait for me,
    and for my arm they hope.
 [6]**Lift up your eyes to the heavens,**
    and look at the earth beneath;
  for the heavens will vanish like smoke,
    the earth will wear out like a garment,

**and those who live on it will die like gnats;
but my salvation will be forever,
and my deliverance will never be ended.**

With important rhetorical variation, these verses echo verses 1–3, both in terms of structure and substance. Here there are two imperatives to listen, addressed to "my people, my nation" (v. 4a). The *address* is not as precise or as intense as that of verse 1, but we may assume this address also assumed an Israel fully prepared to be faithful to Yahweh.

The *reason* for listening is here more complex (vv. 4b–6). In verse 4b, the reason is "my torah, my teaching," "a light to the peoples." The phrasing is closely parallel to 42:4, 6 and 49:6, and apparently asserts Yahweh's good governance, which is sharply contrasted with the exploitative governance of Babylon. As in those texts, here the rhetoric of "light to the peoples" may indeed suggest international governance or, alternatively, a governance of rescue for all Jews from among the nations. Either way, it is a promise of new governance to which Israel is to pay close attention.

The imagery of verse 5 much more directly bespeaks Yahweh's transformative governance—in the phrasing of "my deliverance," "my salvation," and "my arms" (= power)—for which there is great expectation. The language suggests that the world of the exiles is alive with great hope of newness, a newness not to be disappointed.

The dramatic claims of verses 4b–5 are reinforced in the sweeping imagery of verse 6. The "salvation" and "deliverance" of Yahweh (v. 6), in the same phrases as those used in verse 5, are contrasted with the condition of "heavens and earth." The poetry in verse 6 employs three quite concrete images: "the heavens . . . like smoke; the earth . . . like a garment; and those who live on it [the earth] . . . like gnats." All will vanish while Yahweh's new governance persists. The point is not the termination of the earth but the assertion that as permanent as heaven and earth manifestly are, Yahweh's new governance is more durable and more reliable. The rhetoric is not unlike that of Jeremiah 31:35–36, which also asserts the staying power of Yahweh's intention (see Mark 13:31). The most trustworthy, most reliable, most durable reality is Yahweh's coming good governance that will be for all foreseeable, all thinkable, all imaginable time to come.

51:7 **Listen to me, you who know righteousness,
you people who have my teaching in your hearts;
do not fear the reproach of others,**

    and do not be dismayed when they revile you.
    ⁸For the moth will eat them up like a garment,
      and the worm will eat them like wool;
   but my deliverance will be forever,
    and my salvation to all generations.

In yet a third utterance, the same affirmations with the same pattern of speech are reiterated. Here there are, as in verse 1, three imperatives addressed to those intending righteousness in response to Yahweh's purposes. The second and third imperatives are of special interest. Given in the negative, they are in fact salvation oracles with the characteristic phrasing we have already seen in 41:8–13, 14: "do not fear; . . . do not be afraid." This utterance on the lips of Yahweh is a response to a complaint of Israel in need. In exilic Isaiah, the complaint characteristically concerns the condition of exile, so that the salvation oracle is to be understood on the lips of Yahweh as a sovereign, exile-ending assurance. Although the "reasons" of verses 3, 4b–7 do not have the tag phrase "fear not" of the salvation oracle, they nonetheless function in the same way in order to offer a deep Yahwistic assurance to Israel in desperate need.

The double assurance of verse 7b is a sharp contrast to the double negative concerning those who "revile and reproach." The reference is not clear; it may be to the Babylonians who mock Israel's peculiar identity, or it is possible that the reproach and revilement reflect internal disputes in the community of Jewish exiles between those who accommodate to Babylonian insistences and those who resist any accommodation on the grounds of faith. It is most likely that this assurance is for the zealous in the community of exiles "who have my teaching in their hearts."

Verse 8 offers a sharp contrast not unlike that of verse 6. Positively, the word pair "deliverance, salvation" is a reiteration yet a third time after verses 5 and 6. Negatively, verse 8 uses two metaphors that are parallel to the metaphors of verse 6. The revilers and reproachers will be eaten away like a garment and like wool. The agents here, moth and worm, go along with garments worn out and dead gnats in verse 6. Again Yahweh's promise is durable; the only available alternative is transitory and unreliable.

These three brief summons function like salvation oracles. The addressee, Israel, is summoned to courageous counteridentity that is rooted in Yahweh's own promise. The imperatives in verses 1–2a, 4a, and 7 put a decision to the exiles. Israel must choose its true identity by heeding and trusting in Yahweh's promises that intend to override present circumstance so filled with despair.

"I AM HE . . . YOU ARE MY PEOPLE"
51:9–16

This extended passage is arranged in two parts. In verses 9–11, an urgent appeal is made to Yahweh, that Yahweh should act promptly. In verses 12–16, Yahweh speaks in the first person to offer assurance. It is most likely that the unit is arranged in dialogue fashion as *appeal* and *response*.

51:9 **Awake, awake, put on strength,**
   O arm of the LORD!
 Awake, as in days of old,
   the generations of long ago!
 Was it not you who cut Rahab in pieces,
   who pierced the dragon?
 ¹⁰ **Was it not you who dried up the sea,**
   the waters of the great deep;
 who made the depths of the sea a way
   for the redeemed to cross over?
 ¹¹ **So the ransomed of the LORD shall return,**
   and come to Zion with singing;
 everlasting joy shall be upon their heads;
   they shall obtain joy and gladness,
   and sorrow and sighing shall flee away.

As Israel has been addressed by imperatives in verses 1–2a, 4a, and 7, so here Yahweh is addressed with four imperatives that suggest boldness on Israel's part and a sense of deep urgency: "awake, awake, put on strength, awake." The appeal is that Yahweh's strength should be mobilized; the inference is that Yahweh has been asleep and neglectful. This likely suggests the daring thought that it is Yahweh's negligence that has permitted suffering at the hands of Babylon. Conversely, if mighty, faithful Yahweh can be aroused and motivated, the trouble from vexatious Babylon will be nullified, for no such power can withstand Yahweh's engaged governance.

The appeal to Yahweh in verse 9a is reinforced by a double question in verses 9b–10. "Was it not you?" The required answer: "Yes, *it was you* who acted powerfully in ancient times." Thus the question functions as a doxological affirmation celebrating Yahweh's past treasured actions of saving power. Two intimately related but distinct cases are cited. First, *it was you* who defeated and displaced the powers of chaos in order to make an ordered life in creation possible. The language appeals to a primitive tradition of Yahweh's combat with chaos that opposes Yahweh's plan for the "goodness" of creation. This language dominates verse 9b and probably continues in verse 10b. The imagery of verse 10a, however, is turned in verse 10b to refer to the Exodus, for here Yahweh controls the chaotic waters in order to permit safe passage for "the redeemed," that is, those rescued from Egypt. *It was you* who made the Exodus possible. The appeal is to both *creation* and *exodus*, but in Israel's doxological rhetoric the two memories are intimately linked as evidences of Yahweh's generous sovereignty. These remembered rescues (creation and exodus) are cited as precedents for what Yahweh has done when aroused, precedents that are now, it is hoped, to be replicated in the present tense.

In verse 11, the imperative and the appeal to the past are turned to the present circumstance of the exiles. It is assumed that Yahweh is now alert and mobilized. The confident expectation is that the "ransomed" will come joyously singing from Babylonian exile, so that the new event of rescue (from Babylon) is intimately paralleled to the old event of rescue (from Egypt). It is curious that what sounds like an urgent appeal in verse 9 has by verse 11 become an exuberant doxology, in certainty that Yahweh will be aroused and will act.

Verses 9–11 are not consistently a complaint. They are, nevertheless, answered directly by Yahweh in verses 12–16, as though these verses sound a characteristic response to a characteristic complaint.

51:12a I, I am he who comforts you;

This single line is the thesis of the response that follows. Now speaks Yahweh in the first person, with a double pronoun, "I, I." The "I, I" of Yahweh is the subject of the crucial verb comfort (see 40:1; 51:3). Yahweh intervenes decisively for the sake of Israel's well-being.

51:12b why then are you afraid of a mere mortal who must die,
a human being who fades like grass?
13 You have forgotten the LORD, your Maker,
who stretched out the heavens
and laid the foundations of the earth.
You fear continually all day long
because of the fury of the oppressor,
who is bent on destruction.

The assurance of verse 12a is followed by a rebuke to Israel. Israel has not fully trusted. Rather than trust, Israel in exile has been afraid. Israel has feared a mere mortal, one who fades like grass (see 40:6–8). The "mere mortal" is not named; presumably reference is to Nebuchadrezzar or one of his successors who is an ever-present, ever-intimidating, ever-visible threat. The reason Israel fears such a one is that Israel has forgotten the decisive difference Yahweh makes. The implication is that adherence to Yahweh will veto any trouble from Babylon. The reason is that Yahweh, according to Israel's doxology, is creator not only of Israel but of earth and heaven. Yahweh has all power, contrasted with this "mere mortal" who has no real power, has created nothing, and therefore need not be feared or obeyed. Israel, in its deep, weak-willed forgetfulness, however, is mesmerized by "the oppressor," endlessly aware of the danger of the oppressor, and therefore prone to obey that one instead of Yahweh, its proper object of trust and obedience.

51:13c   **But where is the fury of the oppressor?**
    ¹⁴ **The oppressed shall speedily be released;**
        they shall not die and go down to the Pit,
        nor shall they lack bread.

But, asks the poet in playful indignation: Where is the oppressor? The oppressor Babylon, when viewed on the horizon of Yahweh's intention, is nowhere and constitutes no threat. Indeed, Yahweh will promptly emancipate the oppressed so that they do not suffer, starve, or die. The power of the oppressor is as good as broken, so that Israel is in truth responding in fear to a phantom that has no real substance.

It is not easy to enter into this imagery when we are a people who resonate with no such notion of oppressor. The pertinence of the text will be accessible to us in such a circumstance only if we transpose the notion of oppressor into brutalizing, intimidating ideologies that hold us in thrall when in fact they have no real authority or creditability. In our contemporary world, we may readily identify two such ideologies that in twinlike fashion seem so formidable as to pressure and persuade us out of the gospel: namely, market ideology of autonomy and state ideology of conformity. The true power of Babylon to the exiles was not military or even economic but political and ideological. The gospel is an invitation to see clearly that views of reality apart from the holy power of Yahweh have no substance and warrant neither fear nor adherence.

51:15 **For I am the LORD your God,**
        who stirs up the sea so that its waves roar—

> the LORD of hosts is his name.
> ¹⁶ I have put my words in your mouth,
>   and hidden you in the shadow of my hand,
> stretching out the heavens
>   and laying the foundations of the earth,
>   and saying to Zion, "You are my people."

This concluding doxology looks back to verse 13 and exults in Yahweh's unrivaled power, and to verses 9b–10 concerning Yahweh's management of the chaotic waters. The one who can do that is all powerful—the Lord of hosts! As in 40:10–11, the assertion of Yahweh's power (v. 15) is followed in verse 16 by an assertion of Yahweh's attentive fidelity toward Israel (see also Deut. 1:30–31). The verse has Yahweh recognize the fragility of Israel, who must be held gently and is acknowledged as Yahweh's treasured people; in the midst of that, however, verse 16 has at its center yet one more doxology to the creator.

Our unit began with an appeal to Yahweh not yet awakened (v. 9). Now Yahweh is aroused, ready to act in power and fidelity. Israel's needful condition is about to be transformed. Israel need not fear; it belongs to Yahweh and is safe and cared for, redeemed, ransomed, released, hidden, held. No cause any more for fear!

"DRINK NO MORE"
51:17–23

The assurance of rescue stated in verses 12–16 here continues.

> 51:17a **Rouse yourself, rouse yourself!**
>   **Stand up, O Jerusalem,**

The imperatives addressed to Yahweh in verse 9 are now addressed in turn to Jerusalem. The same Hebrew term is rendered "awake" in verse 9 and "rouse" in verse 17. Jerusalem is summoned to be alert, for something is about to happen that will matter enormously to Zion. The imperative has a stronger force than those of verses 1–2a, 4a, and 7, but the content is the same.

> 51:17b **you who have drunk at the hand of the LORD**
>   **the cup of his wrath,**
>   **who have drunk to the dregs**

> the bowl of staggering.
> [18] There is no one to guide her
>> among all the children she has borne;
> there is no one to take her by the hand
>> among all the children she has brought up.
> [19] These two things have befallen you
>> —who will grieve with you?—
> devastation and destruction, famine and sword—
>> who will comfort you?
> [20] Your children have fainted,
>> they lie at the head of every street
>> like an antelope in a net;
> they are full of the wrath of the LORD,
>> the rebuke of your God.
>
> [21] Therefore hear this, you who are wounded,
>> who are drunk, but not with wine:

Verses 17b–21 and 22–23 are arranged as *before and after*, as *trouble and rescue*. Verses 17b–21 characterize the miserable condition of Israel in exile. In substance, this is a *complaint* describing the situation of exile; however, it is spoken to Israel and not by Israel. Its purpose is to be a foil for the good news to come in verses 22–23.

The specific characterization of Jerusalem in misery is rich in imagery:

1. Jerusalem has been made to drink "the cup" of Yahweh's wrath, a bitter drink that Israel must finish to the bottom of the cup (v. 17b). The imagery parallels that of Jeremiah 25:15–29, only there the cup is for the nations to drink. Here the bitter cup of harsh destiny is for Zion, who thus becomes drunk, staggering, out of control, out of balance.

2. The imagery changes abruptly in verse 18, in order to characterize a situation in which the city is left without any leaders, thus is in a state of anarchy. The imagery recalls 3:1–8 that long ago anticipated a complete lack of adequate leadership, perhaps a comment on the inadequacy and failure of the last kings in Judah or a comment on the termination of the dynasty.

3. Two facets of military invasion and occupation are described in a double word pair: "devastation and destruction," "famine and sword" (v. 19). It could be that these result from a lack of leadership just mentioned. Or it may more broadly refer to massive military invasion that could not have been resisted by any kind of leadership in the city. Either way, the most pathos-filled aspect of the poetry is the double rhetorical question:

"Who will grieve? . . . Who will comfort?" The second phrase is the common theme of exilic Isaiah since 40:1. However, here the required answer
is "no one"—none to grieve, none to comfort (see Lam. 1:2, 9, 17, 21).

4. Verse 20a returns to the imagery of verse 18. The cumulative effect
of this rich imagery is a deep sense of hopelessness, voiced finally in the
climactic statement of verse 20b concerning Yahweh's *wrath and rebuke*. It
is worth noting that this "wrath" is the same Hebrew word as "fury" in
verse 13, where it refers to the "fury of the oppressor." Devastated Jerusalem has nothing to fear from *that* wrath. It is only *Yahweh's* wrath that
matters, and it is total and inescapable. Verse 21 is something of a reprise,
referring to the judgment theme of verse 17b.

51:22 **Thus says your Sovereign, the LORD,**
            your God who pleads the cause of his people:
        See, I have taken from your hand the cup of staggering;
        you shall drink no more
            from the bowl of my wrath.
    [23] **And I will put it into the hand of your tormentors,**
            who have said to you,
        "Bow down, that we may walk on you";
        and you have made your back like the ground
            and like the street for them to walk on.

Now speaks the Lord Yahweh! The title is majestic. It is as though finally,
in response to the misery just reported, Yahweh is evoked to utter a decree
that will reverse the misery of Zion. Though none of the formal marks of
the genre are present, these verses function like *a salvation oracle* in divine
response to the implied complaint of verse 17b–21. Thus God now goes
to court in behalf of helpless, vulnerable Israel, taking the side of Israel in
the great cosmic contest for world justice.

The Sovereign announces two decisive actions. First, Yahweh has
removed "the cup of staggering" from Zion. Jerusalem's imbibing of
Yahweh's anger is spent. There is punishment, but it is now fully accomplished, a conclusion already indicated in 40:2. Second, Yahweh the Sovereign reassigns the cup of wrath, now putting it into the hand of Babylon
and forcing the mighty empire to drink. Thus the cup is transferred, and
the image of the cup is redeployed as good news for Judah. It was, during
exile, assigned to Israel; now, as exile ends, it is put to the lips of Israel's
tormentors. And the oppressor will have no more choice in the matter of
bitter drink than did Judah before it.

It is clear in this rhetoric that Yahweh is much more intensely angry with "your tormentors" than ever Yahweh was with Israel. The reason for Yahweh's fury, moreover, is that Babylon has been endlessly abusive to Israel. It is Babylon who has diminished and humiliated Israel and made it an international doormat to walk on. Babylon commanded Israel to bow down and Israel has complied, to become "like the ground and like the street." Perhaps Israel had no choice in the matter and could not have resisted. Perhaps Israel was overly impressed with Babylon and excessively intimidated. Either way, Israel is a victim who colluded with Babylon in its own subjugation.

Now, in this utterance of divine decree, all of that is changed. The mighty are brought low (see 2:11–17), and the humiliated one is to be exalted, lifted up in honor for all the nations to see. No wonder Jerusalem is to "rouse yourself" (v. 17). It is time to arise (an Easter verb) from suffering, misery, and humiliation. In an instant, Yahweh has, according to this poet, abruptly transformed the geopolitical situation of Israel. There is a rising and a falling; Yahweh causes both. Israel, as a consequence, may rejoice.

This entire long chapter is a series of assurances that what has been will no longer be. The *God of fury* becomes the *God of comfort, deliverance, and salvation.* (See the same change of Yahweh in Deuteronomy 4:24, 31 from a *"jealous God"* to *"a merciful God,"* a like change also wrought in exile.) The poet vetoes exilic circumstance. Israel is called to listen, to awaken, to look, to notice, and to accept the newness of Yahweh.

"AWAKE . . . DEPART"
52:1–12

Israel is now authorized to depart Babylon and return home to Jerusalem. The permit to go, evoking joyous expectation, is grounded in Yahweh's celebrated defeat of the powers of Babylon. This textual unit consists of four distinct elements, each of which voices exuberant expectation.

52:1 Awake, awake,
       put on your strength, O Zion!
    Put on your beautiful garments,
       O Jerusalem, the holy city;
    for the uncircumcised and the unclean
       shall enter you no more.
  2 Shake yourself from the dust, rise up,
       O captive Jerusalem;
    loose the bonds from your neck,
       O captive daughter Zion!

Israel in exile is addressed in a series of imperatives that urge preparation for departure for the empire. The initial double imperative, "awake, awake," reiterates in the same Hebrew word the imperative addressed to Israel in 51:17 and to Yahweh in 51:9. The inference is that exilic Israel had become dulled, inattentive, hopeless, and grief-stricken in exile. These verses consist of seven imperatives ("awake, awake, put on, put on, shake, rise up, loose"), all of which urge Israel to reject exilic status and attitude with all of its grief and despair, and so to be ready for departure in joy and vitality. The imagery is varied. The double command to "put on" suggests dressing in the rich apparel of success and joy, ready for participation in a great festal celebration, for the return home is envisioned as a hugely exuberant festal procession. The first two imperatives of verse 2, "shake yourself, rise up," portray a subject sunk in humiliation and abjection, perhaps so deep as to reach to the depth of death. Moreover, the final imperative, "loose," means to shake off the status of slave that Babylon had imposed. The imperatives are a summons to new energy grounded in new, God-given possibility.

The addressee is four times named, the names arranged in reverse order: "Zion/Jerusalem" (v. 1); "Jerusalem/Zion" (v. 2). Only one motivation is offered to support the seven imperatives. At the end of verse 2, the reason for legitimate expectation is that the uncircumcised and unclean are no longer present to jeopardize the community that is now completely purified. These particular concerns for purity likely reflect the postexilic preoccupation of Judaism with ritual cleanness and purity that qualifies the community as a proper place for Yahweh's presence (see 1:25; 4:3–4). This community, now purified and purged, is sharply contrasted with "the unclean people" from the prophetic vision of Isaiah 6:5. The Exile has been a process of smelting away the "dross and alloy" of the old community that had prevented the covenant people from being fully in communion with Yahweh.

52:3 **For thus says the Lord: You were sold for nothing, and you shall be redeemed without money. 4 For thus says the Lord God: Long ago, my people went down into Egypt to reside there as aliens; the Assyrian, too, has oppressed them without cause. 5 Now therefore what am I doing here, says the Lord, seeing that my people are taken away without cause? Their rulers howl, says the Lord, and continually, all day long, my name is despised. 6 Therefore my people shall know my name; therefore in that day they shall know that it is I who speak; here am I.**

These verses appeal especially to exodus imagery. Ancient Israel was "sold for nothing" into Egyptian bondage (v. 3). The phrasing is echoed in verse 5, "taken away without cause." These verses review the entire history of Israel that is one long history of oppression; they mention in turn Egypt and Assyria and imply Babylon as well. No explication is offered for this series of bondages, but the reality itself is not denied. Yahweh is here not implicated in these deathly realities, for Yahweh received no gain from the transactions, nor is any hint of punishment for Israel voiced. Rather, the oppression is cited as a foil for the happy announcement that follows.

The degradation of oppression under a series of superpowers is intensified with the imagery "their rulers howl." We may take that as a practice of gloating, arrogant mocking over defeated Israel that not only humiliates Israel but also scandalizes the name of Yahweh. Both Israel and Yahweh are savaged by the ways in which these empires have treated Israel.

The present oracle, however, does not dwell on the humiliation that is well known and beyond denial. It is, rather, to assert the radical reversal now to be enacted by Yahweh. Three statements voice the coming reversal:

1. Israel will be redeemed without money (v. 3). Yahweh will not bargain or purchase, but will commit an act of power that requires no consent by the oppressor state. This freedom to act unilaterally is congruent with the previous statement about redemption "without money." Yahweh received nothing in giving Israel over to the oppressors and so owes nothing in taking Israel back as Yahweh's own people.

2. Yahweh is acting here, now (v. 5). The deliverance is intensely present tense, "at hand" (see Mark 1:15). Although Egypt and Assyria are mentioned, it is clear in context that the declaration concerns Babylon. Babylon has no rightful claim on this people because there had been no exchange of money. Yahweh is perfectly entitled to take Israel back and now reclaim what is rightly Yahweh's own.

3. The name of Yahweh, which has been despised (v. 5), will now be known (= acknowledged as powerful) (v. 6). Yahweh, who has been invisible and inactive, now appears decisively on Israel's horizon. Yahweh is the initiator of newness, wrought simply by Yahweh's self-announcement "Here am I." The self-assertion of Yahweh is fully congruent with the initial gospel pronouncement of 40:9: "Here is your God!" Yahweh is back in play! And when that happens, Israel is free for homecoming, and Babylon can do nothing to prevent the departure home. The oracle anticipates an abrupt act of power that completely reverses the circumstance of Israel. Whereas verses 1–2 summon Israel by imperative, here the verbs are

all indicative, pointing to Yahweh's singular resolve and impending action.

52:7 **How beautiful upon the mountains**
    are the feet of the messenger who announces peace,
  who brings good news,
    who announces salvation,
    who says to Zion, "Your God reigns."
 8**Listen! Your sentinels lift up their voices,**
    together they sing for joy;
  for in plain sight they see
    the return of the LORD to Zion.
 9**Break forth together into singing,**
    you ruins of Jerusalem;
  for the LORD has comforted his people,
    he has redeemed Jerusalem.
10 **The LORD has bared his holy arm**
    before the eyes of all the nations;
  and all the ends of the earth shall see
    the salvation of our God.

These verses offer a scenario of Yahweh's triumph in which there are four dramatic roles:

1. The "*messenger*" is the one who runs with exuberance all the way from Babylon to Jerusalem in order to carry "the good news" that Yahweh has decisively defeated the powers of Babylon. This verse is a pivotal one for theological exposition, for it is the second use of the term "gospel" (after 40:9) and carries the "evangelical" news that Yahweh has won a victory and is therefore the ruling sovereign who has just come to decisive power. The phrase "Your God reigns" is probably taken over from older psalmic liturgies (as in Psalm 96:10) and provides the theme for the gospel of the New Testament: "The kingdom of God has come near" (Mark 1:15). The feet of the runner are said to be "beautiful" (welcome) because the runner runs lightly and exuberantly with the good news; one can tell at a distance by the way the messenger runs that the news for Israel is good. The "gospel" is the turn of world history; Yahweh has, in combat with the powers of death and negation, established a new governance.

2. The scenario includes the notion that *sentinels* are on the walls of ruined Jerusalem, partly to protect but primarily to await messengers from afar. They are at their observation posts, eagerly watching to see if any messengers come from the north to report the outcome of the deci-

sive conflict between Yahweh and Babylon. The sentinels watch intensely. Then they start shouting the news to the waiting inhabitants of ruined Jerusalem. The sentries are beside themselves with joy. They have seen the messenger at a distance. They know the news is good. They shout to the waiting populace, "Yahweh has won; we are free; exile is over!" The sentinels, however, see more than the messenger of verse 7. They also see Yahweh coming in majestic, regal procession, returning in power to Jerusalem. The imagery echoes 40:5, wherein Yahweh comes in splendor (glory) while all of creation watches in celebrative awe. In this regal procession, the power of life reenters Jerusalem from whence it had been absent. Jerusalem is again made the new center of Yahweh-governed reality.

3. The *ruins of Jerusalem* hear the report of the sentinels who relay the news of the messenger (v. 9a). The "ruins of Jerusalem" may be understood as the defeated, dependent people of the city who had given up all expectation of well-being. Or the phrasing may refer to the actual stones and ruined walls and buildings left since 587 in scattered disarray like a typical war-torn city. The very stones of the city cry out in joy for the restoration that is assured by the coming of Yahweh.

4. The imperative addressed to the "ruins of Jerusalem" in verse 9a is supported by the explanatory assertion of verses 9b–10. The reason the city rejoices, the reason the sentinel celebrates, and the reason the messenger runs eagerly are because of Yahweh. It is *Yahweh*, the fourth character in the drama, who matters decisively. Yahweh has *comforted*, by acting in transformative solidarity as Yahweh characteristically does in this poetry (40:1; 51:12). Yahweh has *redeemed* Israel from the bondage of Babylon as Yahweh did earlier from the bondage of Egypt and of Assyria (see v. 3). Yahweh *has bared* his holy arm like a warrior rolling up his sleeve so that all nations can see the powerful military muscle that assures Israel and intimidates the nations (see 40:10). Yahweh has come with unrivaled power to act decisively to reverse the circumstance of Israel. Everybody sees! Everybody notices! Everyone recognizes that Yahweh has now weighed in in behalf of Israel. This is the same Yahweh who seemed neglectful or perhaps impotent. Now everybody knows, and Jerusalem exults!

52:11 **Depart, depart, go out from there!**
   Touch no unclean thing;
      go out from the midst of it, purify yourselves,
      you who carry the vessels of the LORD.
   ¹² **For you shall not go out in haste,**

and you shall not go in flight;
for the LORD will go before you,
and the God of Israel will be your rear guard.

The double imperative "depart, depart" matches the double imperative of verse 1. The term "go out," the third imperative, is an Exodus term, thus alluding to the parallel already voiced in verses 3–6. In all, the verse opens with six imperatives ("depart, depart, go out, touch, go out, purify"). Four of these echo the Exodus and allude to an actual geographical movement. The other two imperatives ("touch, purify") look back to the term "unclean" in verse 1 and refer to Israel as a holy, now-purified people. In this rhetoric, the return home is understood as a liturgical processional wherein Israel enters into the holy place where dwells again the presence of Yahweh. Because the return is liturgical and will come to the presence of God, Israel must take care to stay pure. The final verb seems to allude especially to the priests who perhaps lead the procession and who carry in liturgical style the very temple accoutrements that were seized and confiscated by Babylon (see 2 Kings 25:13–17). The return envisioned here is not military and political, but it is liturgical. Israel will be a religious community whose life is properly focused on right worship.

The motivation for these imperatives is given in verse 12. This bold, joyous, highly visible theological procession will be unlike the Exodus. The "flight from Egypt" was undertaken "in haste," at great risk, barely escaping (see Exod. 12:11). Here there is no such risk or anxiety. There is no cause for alarm, hurry, or panic. And the reason is that Yahweh's victory here is more complete. Now Israel is well protected and utterly safe. Yahweh is before Israel as a guard and behind Israel as a protective escort. Israel is utterly safe (see Psalm 91:11–14).

In a rich variety of ways, this chapter invites Israel to a Yahweh-assured emancipation, no longer determined by Babylon. Our own appropriation of this text depends upon identifying the ideological grip over our lives wherein we are less than free and less than our true selves. The gospel message is precisely an invitation and authorization to be freed from all such distorting, coercive pressures: to be freely and completely Yahweh's own people, freed to live a life of unfettered worship, assured not only of safety from threat but assured of Yahweh's own person, who is the true joy of life. The departure from ideological alternatives is here offered. The community of faith is twice summoned to "awaken" (v. 1), twice authorized to "depart" (v. 11).

"MY SERVANT . . .
WHO PROSPERS AND BEARS"
52:13–53:12

We have already seen "the servant" mentioned in 42:1–9; 49:1–7; and 50:4–9. These three poetic units, together with our present text, have been regarded by many interpreters as a distinctive group of texts, commonly referred to as "the Servant Songs." There is, however, great interpretive uncertainty on two counts. First, it is disputed whether this was in fact a distinctive body of texts or whether these poems need simply to be taken in their present literary context. Second, the poems are concerned with a particular figure (historical or metaphorical?), but the identity of that figure is completely enigmatic. (See my comments in relation to 49:1–7.) It is one of the great oddities of Old Testament studies that the very text that is taken to be *abundantly rich and theologically suggestive* is at the same time undeniably *inaccessible and without clear meaning*. David J. A. Clines comments on the difficulty:

> What if the force of the poem . . . is in its very unforthcomingness, its refusal to be precise and to give *information*, its stubborn concealment of the kind of data that critical scholarship yearns to get its hands on as the building-blocks for the construction of its hypotheses? (*I, He, We, and They*, 25)

It is fair to say that although interpretation is completely bewildered by the specificity of the text that we simply do not understand, at the same time the broad thematic outlines of the text are enormously suggestive and continue to be generative of interpretation. Part of the problem is that the imagery is elusive. But the greater problem is that the Hebrew words are unusual and the text is seemingly disordered, so that every translation is to some extent speculative. My comments that follow are a statement of a rough interpretive consensus and are especially informed by the suggestive work of Claus Westermann.

52:13 **See, my servant shall prosper;**
he shall be exalted and lifted up,
and shall be very high.

Because the servant is one who serves only Yahweh, we take the verse as an utterance of Yahweh, who speaks of "my servant." This thematic verse voices the ultimate resolve of Yahweh that the servant (whoever that may be) will succeed in every way, will be honored and exalted. This motif at

the beginning of the poem is matched by a concluding affirmative assertion about the exaltation of the servant (53:10–12). These affirmations
form the final conclusion and assert the destiny of the servant. It is unmistakably clear, however, that such anticipated well-being is only at the end.
Before that glorious culmination, the remainder of the poem details the
life of the servant, a life of suffering and humiliation.

52:14 **Just as there were many who were astonished at him**
         —so marred was his appearance, beyond human semblance,
         and his form beyond that of mortals—
 [15] **so he shall startle many nations;**
         kings shall shut their mouths because of him;
      for that which had not been told them they shall see,
      and that which they had not heard they shall contemplate.

The double theme of *humiliation and exaltation* that constitutes the plot
line of the poem is well exhibited in these two verses. Verse 14 portrays the
servant as a marked, distorted figure. The assumption is that this was a
physical distortion. The servant is not one of the "beautiful people." He is
rather the kind of disfigured person toward whom one can hardly bear to
look and yet is one who is so mesmerizing that one will hardly look away.
The servant is distinguished by being exceptionally unattractive, and so no
doubt avoided and excluded, a genuine outcast.

This sorry portrayal, however, is abruptly countered in verse 15 by the
assertion that nations and kings—in keeping with the large geopolitical
horizon of the Isaiah tradition—are awed by the servant and assume a respectful silence before one who is so compelling in majesty and dignity. Indeed, the exalted appearance of the servant in this verse is something
utterly new, unexpected, and inexplicable.

We may suggest that the decisive theme of this entire poem is epito-
mized by the odd relation between the *marred* figure of verse 14 and the
awesome figure of verse 15. We do not know how to move from *marred* to
awesome, except by the powerful resolve of Yahweh, who transposes this
figure with an inexplicable firmness. Thus the theme is not simply humiliation and exaltation, but rather that it is the humiliated one who *becomes* the
exalted one by the intention of Yahweh. It is the will of Yahweh, moreover,
nothing else, that transforms and transposes. The remainder of the poem
explicates this theme. Before looking at the detail, however, we may consider the *Tremendum*—the massive, inscrutable coming of God's holiness
that defies explanation or resistance—that will propel the poem. The won-

der here announced is this transposition. We may suggest three paths of interpretation that are not mutually exclusive.

First, there is no doubt that the poem is to be understood in the context of the Isaiah tradition. Insofar as the servant is *Israel*—a common assumption of Jewish interpretation—we see that the theme of humiliation and exaltation serves the Isaiah rendering of Israel, for Israel in this literature is exactly the *humiliated (exiled) people* who by the powerful intervention of Yahweh is about to become *the exalted (restored) people of Zion*. Thus the drama is the drama of Israel and more specifically of Jerusalem, the characteristic subject of this poetry.

Second, although it is clear that this poetry does not in any first instance have Jesus on its horizon, it is equally clear that the church, from the outset, has found this poetry a poignant and generative way to consider Jesus, wherein *humiliation equals crucifixion* and *exaltation equals resurrection and ascension*. In the *Evangelical Catechism* on which I was nurtured, the most extended presentation (#72) offered the theme:

> *Question:* In which passage of Holy Scripture do we find the humiliation and the exaltation of Christ briefly described?
> *Answer:* We find the humiliation and the exaltation of Christ briefly described in the passage Philippians 2:5–11 which is as follows: " . . . he *humbled* himself and became obedient to the point of death. . . . Therefore God also highly *exalted* him."

The story of Jesus, summarized in this lyrical passage, is an account of how the humiliated Jesus, in the Easter miracle, is exalted "to the right hand of God." The church is not able to say how this "Saturday miracle" works, any more than we know how to move from 52:14 to 52:15, any more than the Isaiah tradition knew how to get from "former things" of punishment to "latter things" of deliverance. All that can be said in any of these cases is that a deep reversal of fortunes—in the life of Israel, in the life of Jesus— is evoked by the radical, powerful, inscrutable resolve of God to do something new.

Third, the Jewish conviction of Israel going from exilic humiliation to restored exaltation and the Christian confession of Jesus humiliated in crucifixion and exalted in Easter have for a long time been in deep tension, especially from the side of Christian triumphalism and, in response, from a Jewish fear of Christian usurpation of Jewish claims. My own judgment is that it is more important to recognize the commonality and parallel structure of Jewish claims and Christian claims at the core of faith than it is to dispute about which presentation of the claim is primary. The truth is that in understanding *the servant as Israel*—or as an unnamed one at work in ancient Israel—or derivatively using the servant imagery to understand *Jesus as servant* points to the definitional mark of both faiths, a claim both faiths have in common in their common trust in a common God to do something new. That claim is that both Jews and Christians have seen in their own history, in quite particular ways, the capacity and willingness of this God to *do something new through suffering.* This claim, verified for Jews in the restoration of Zion and for Christians in the life of Jesus, is a deeply inscrutable claim that speaks powerfully against common worldly insistences that *suffering is a dead end with no future* and *that there is no newness,* only endless derivations. Newness through suffering is the gospel that attests to *the power of God* at work *through human weakness* to bring to fruition God's intention for the world. This powerful dialectic, which propels the poem, is exhibited in the twofold "so" in verses 14–15, introducing in turn *the marred* quality and then *the awesome* quality of the subject.

53:1 Who has believed what we have heard?
   And to whom has the arm of the LORD been revealed?

This verse is not more than a rhetorical marker that stands between the theme announcement of verses 14–15 and the exposition of verses 2–12. The twofold question of "who" nicely links the themes of *belief and revelation.* The first clause of the verse recognizes that the poem *proclaims,* causes to hear, and expects a response of belief (= faith; *'amen,* incidentally the same term as in 7:9). The proclamation of humiliation-become-exaltation is an invitation to trust. The second clause goes to the substance of the proclamation, namely, to exhibit Yahweh's arm (= power). The theme of humiliation-become-exaltation is a disclosure of Yahweh's power; it is Yahweh's power that makes this newness effective. The disclosure invites faith, faith that moves beyond the categories acceptable to the world-without-faith. The questions are not answered. We may accept that the only "believers" on the horizon are the "us" of the following verses, the ones who can attest to what they have seen and know from their own experience. The proclamation is too much to believe, and no other can be expected to trust in such a strangeness. Thus the passage witnesses not only to the power of Yahweh and the destiny of the servant but also to the faith of the witnessing community that accepts this inexplicable transformation as the truth of their life.

53:2 **For he grew up before him like a young plant,**
   and like a root out of dry ground;
 he had no form or majesty that we should look at him,
   nothing in his appearance that we should desire him.
 [3] **He was despised and rejected by others;**
   a man of suffering and acquainted with infirmity;
 and as one from whom others hide their faces
   he was despised, and we held him of no account.

Westermann observes that the course of the poem offers a life story of the servant from birth ("grow up"; v. 2) to death ("buried"; v. 9). The beginning point is birth and growth. It was, however, not an auspicious beginning. Indeed, the servant began in something like humiliation—out of dry ground, no form, no majesty, nothing to notice or admire or value. These sentences interpret 52:14. He was a rejected person, not valued, perhaps ostracized, perhaps disabled, of whom nothing was expected. This is not, and never was, one of the great ones of the earth. This is one of the little ones, surely of no consequence.

53:4 **Surely he has borne our infirmities**
   and carried our diseases;
 yet we accounted him stricken,
   struck down by God, and afflicted.
 [5] **But he was wounded for our transgressions,**
   crushed for our iniquities;
 upon him was the punishment that made us whole,
   and by his bruises we are healed.
 [6] **All we like sheep have gone astray;**
   we have all turned to our own way,
 and the LORD has laid on him the iniquity of us all.

The grammatical particle opening verse 4 is an adversative of surprise, something like "Nevertheless." It was this one, this little one of no account, who now becomes the subject of active verbs. This nobody from whom nothing is expected is about to do something decisive. The second half of verse 4 picks up the theme of verses 2–3: "We did not expect anything."

In spite of such a dismissive prognosis over this "nobody," miracles happened. This very one—this marred, dismissed nobody—took on himself disabilities and diseases, hurts caused by sin, punishments. By taking all this on, this servant was wounded, crushed, and bruised—and "we" were healed! The poetry cannot be reduced to a rational formula. It must remain poetry that glides over rational reservation. We are not told how hurt and guilt can be reassigned and redeployed from one to another. We are not told how the suffering of one makes healing possible for another. But it is so here; "we" have thus been healed and made whole. We are here in this pastorally delicate transaction that is at the core of salvific faith, a mystery with which Christian faith has endlessly struggled through competing theories of atonement. This poet offers no such theory. Instead, the poem offers a confession, an admission, a dazzlement, and an acknowledgment. It is this deeply Jewish affirmation that has been transposed for us into the mystery of new life in Christ.

The wonder of the healing is linked in verse 6 to a confession of sin. "We" have all been wayward, all recalcitrant, like mindless, unresponsive sheep who graze off the path without heeding the summoning voice of the shepherd; in such autonomy we wander off into jeopardy and risk. The servant has been made to answer for such waywardness.

This poem, in addition to its stunning affirmation of the work of the servant, is dominated by first-person pronouns: "we, our, our, us, we, we, we, our, us." This is no cold, detached, reasonable statement. It is, rather, the voice of those who have been healed and are as bewildered as they are grateful. The "we" who speaks here is whoever voices the poem in bewilderment and gratitude. Critically, we imagine the voice to be that of exilic Jews who are dazzled by the turn of their life; derivatively, of course, it has become, in Christian parlance, all those who have relied on Jesus. But to ask this question from the outside is to miss the intimate, confessional tone of the pronouns. The lines of the poem are permitted on the lips of whoever it is who benefits from this indescribable transformation, this gospel calculus that denies the world that wants to assign and pigeonhole and locate when it turns out that the flow of healing works by suffering embraced. The "we" who speaks here knows that much, precisely because life has been transformed. It is known here that one life can be vulnerable enough to permit restoration of another. Indeed, the servant is not only effective one-on-one, one life in the place of another, but effects the new beginning for the entire community.

53:7 **He was oppressed, and he was afflicted,**
        yet he did not open his mouth;
    like a lamb that is led to the slaughter,
        and like a sheep that before its shearers is silent,
        so he did not open his mouth.

⁸**By a perversion of justice he was taken away.**
   Who could have imagined his future?
For he was cut off from the land of the living,
   stricken for the transgression of my people.
⁹**They made his grave with the wicked**
   and his tomb with the rich,
although he had done no violence,
   and there was no deceit in his mouth.

But "we" are not yet finished with our dazzlement. The life of the servant and the death of the servant are spectacular betrayals of genuine justice. Israel is never far away from legal language; we have seen much of it in exilic Isaiah. The servant was oppressed, afflicted, and done in by a "perversion of justice." He was not guilty; he should have received no punishment. He is the righteous sufferer of whom the Psalter endlessly sings. As a consequence, he is "cut off" (excommunicated), the ultimate humiliation. No, penultimate! The ultimate humiliation is that he is buried among the wicked, that is, outside the cared-for space where the righteous dead are kept and cherished. He is utterly rejected, treated to the end as utterly guilty, treated in death even as he had been in life. He is buried among "the rich." Among the pious who voice this poem, "the rich" are the hustlers who have exploited and taken advantage; that is, the wicked. He is grouped with the despised ones whom the world thinks have succeeded.

Congruent with his status as a nobody, even in court where he is wrongly accused, wrongly sentenced, and wrongly executed, he issues no protests, makes no defense, "never said a mumbling word" (v. 7). He had ample ground for a shrill litigious tone. But no, he is like a docile, timid sheep held by the shearers. He is silent and submissive, receiving what is dealt out. "We," in verse 6, are like sheep gone astray; the servant, unlike "us," is like a lamb led to slaughter, vulnerable, innocent, accepting—murdered. This silent, vulnerable sheep absorbs the deathly blows of hostility and—in derivative Christian cadence—is the lamb that was slain, "the Lamb of God who takes away the sin of the world!" (John 1:29). This is a life given for the life of others—no satisfaction of anger, no victory over the power of death, but only a gentle surrogate in punishment. It is as though the vicious cycles must be broken. But they cannot be broken by force, by power, by assertion, for such vigorous assertion only escalates and evokes more from the other side. The servant, this nobody with no resources, breaks the cycles of death and hurt precisely by a life of vulnerability, goes into the violence, and ends its tyranny.

53:10 Yet it was the will of the LORD to crush him with pain.
    When you make his life an offering for sin,
        he shall see his offspring, and shall prolong his days;
    through him the will of the LORD shall prosper.
 11   Out of his anguish he shall see light;
    he shall find satisfaction through his knowledge.
        The righteous one, my servant, shall make many righteous,
        and he shall bear their iniquities.
 12 Therefore I will allot him a portion with the great,
    and he shall divide the spoil with the strong;
    because he poured out himself to death,
        and was numbered with the transgressors;
    yet he bore the sin of many,
        and made intercession for the transgressors.

By verse 9, we have come to an ending of this savaged life. It is the end of a life; it is the end of a poetic scenario. It is the end of suffering and therefore of punishment—except, it is not yet an end. The poem is astonishingly continued by the phrase "Yet Yahweh" (v. 10). It is Yahweh who insists that the poem continue. It was the good pleasure of Yahweh to use up this servant in this way. It was part of Yahweh's large intention to deploy such an effective sufferer. Though the process was one of ultimate sacrifice, one can here glimpse a future for the servant, his days, and his offspring. The verb "Yahweh willed" is reiterated. Yahweh wills the servant to prosper; the verb, a different Hebrew verb, is a mate and parallel to "prosper" in 52:13. Yahweh intends the servant who *gave all* now to *receive all.* There will be light and satisfaction. In verse 11 the pronouns change, and now Yahweh again speaks as in 52:13 of "my servant." The servant is, in the end but only at the end, not abandoned.

In verses 11b–12, the words are on the lips of Yahweh. The entire transaction of the poem is here summarized. The servant "makes righteous"; that is, qualifies the others to receive the benefits due to a responsible torah-keeper, so that those who should be harshly judged are declared to be innocent. That is indeed humiliating work—to extend self in the service and interest of unwarranted vindication for the undeserving.

Finally comes the exaltation (v. 12): "Therefore . . . " as a consequence! The humiliation is the ground of God's exaltation. The one who was in the company of transgressors, who appeared as one of them, who prayed for them, who cast his lot as their advocate, who stood deeply in solidarity now receives the "therefore" of Yahweh. Yahweh will give to the servant a "portion" with the great and with the strong. The little, weak one will figure on the same footing with the great and the strong. The language is elusive. Some find here resurrection from the dead. The text, however, is not that explicit. Exaltation is enough, in whatever form it arrives.

Interpretation may legitimately cease in awe, refusing to decode the imagery, because we are very close here to what seems to be quintessential holy ground. Neither Christian nor Jew knows how to decode this poetry. There is here the extraordinary movement of God from guilt to healing, but the move is made through human agency, as surely it must be. Jews and Christians have always shared that conviction, even if they come to very different articulations and embodiments.

This poem is not tightly connected either to its Isaiah context or to its exilic context. In 54:1 the poet returns to the rhetoric of promise. But this poem, in its odd utterance, places wound in, with, and under newness. This is a wounded healer, wounded in a risk that gives wholeness; perhaps it is in chapters 54 and 55 that the newness here permitted is given its rich lyrical climactic statement.

This commentator is a Christian, and so the reading is probably more Christian than I know or intend. I am not in any case inclined to resist such a posture nor to restrain that reading, except to notice two caveats. First, the linkage to Jesus often made in interpretation of this text is not intrinsic to the poem itself. It is made among those who read through the humiliation and exaltation of Jesus who, we say, enacts what is here imagined. Second, authentic Christian reading is not, in my judgment, monopolistic. As this poem propels and feeds our Christian reading of our life through faith, so we may allow it to do the same feeding of other lives in faith as richly and genuinely as it does our own. It is most unfortunate that this text has been a contentious point in Jewish-Christian interpretation. It would be far better if it would be seen and cherished as a shared mystery, authorizing our several particularities, but particularities that have in common the rejection of self-sufficiency and despair, and the grace-filled wonder of life given away for others.

It is no wonder that in the narrative of Acts 8:26–40, Philip helps the Ethiopian to understand the text. Philip did so "starting with scripture" (v. 35) and ending with baptism (vv. 36–38), the access of an alternative life in the world. The poem surely intends, in its endless generativity, to be reread and reheard and reembraced, always with a concrete particularity, but always with a transformative inscrutability that changes everything. Perhaps it is not so surprising to have a lyrical outburst in 54:1. That outburst is what surely happens among us when we notice the God-impelled drama of humiliation and exaltation enacted in our behalf.

This servant is indeed "for others." We may notice how profoundly countercultural such an affirmation is. This model of life stands in deep contrast to the superman of Nietzsche that now dominates a world of macho military consumerism. Nietzsche presented the case in order to make this model "for others" a weak, timid, cowardly failure in the world. It is now clear, at the turn of the century, this most barbaric of centuries, that the Promethean superman of Nietzsche has run his course and leaves only a legacy of death. The alternative offered here is not a weak, second-rate proposal. It is rather a daring proposal that takes profound courage for its practice. A massive critique of our failed cultural values arises almost inescapably from the text. Its legitimacy is found, in the end, not in the rich imagery or the daring rhetoric, but in the practice, the only practice that here and there breaks the cycles of violence and makes life possible.

PROMISES OF NEWNESS
54:1–17

Through a variety of images, this poetry anticipates and celebrates Israel's new status as liberated, protected, embraced, and blessed by Yahweh.

A Wife Beloved and Blessed (54:1–8)

These verses use the metaphor of marriage in order to comment upon the relation between Yahweh and Israel. Inside the metaphor, Yahweh is husband and Israel is wife. The imagery permits the narrative of a vexed relationship that moves from alienation to restoration. It is now widely recognized that prophetic use of the imagery of marriage is profoundly sexist in that it is always the woman (Israel) who is treated as problematic, whereas the man (Yahweh) is always beyond question, even when the actions of the husband seem unthinking or brutalizing. Given that recognition, however, it is the case that the imagery permits an articulation of the intensity and complexity of the relationship, the reality of pain and affront and the wonder of reconciliation that can perhaps be voiced in no other figure.

54:1 **Sing, O barren one who did not bear;**
    burst into song and shout,
    you who have not been in labor!
  For the children of the desolate woman will be more
    than the children of her that is married, says the LORD.

² Enlarge the site of your tent,
    and let the curtains of your habitations be stretched out;
  do not hold back; lengthen your cords
    and strengthen your stakes.
³ For you will spread out to the right and to the left,
    and your descendants will possess the nations
    and will settle the desolate towns.

These verses assure a "barren" one that she is about to be blessed with children. The imagery appeals in a most direct way to the stories of Genesis, so that the one addressed is mother Sarah of the ancestral narratives. In the book of Genesis, it is mother Sarah who is barren and without hope and then, by the goodness of God, is given a child and heir (Gen. 21:1–7). In our context, however, the imagery of Sarah refers to exilic Israel, whose barrenness signifies the hopelessness of exile. The anticipated birth of children, the subject of these verses, signifies in turn the hope-filled future of Israel now about to be initiated by Yahweh, the giver of all children and the giver of all futures. Thus the imagery of barrenness-birth in context concerns the despair of exile and the happy prospect of restoration.

The verses are organized in two series of imperatives, inviting Sarah-Israel to new, joyous hope (vv. 1a, 2). In each series, the imperative summons is supported by reasons that concern Yahweh's promise (vv. 1b, 3). The first sequence of verse 1, addressed to a woman who has not yet been in labor, consists of three imperatives: "sing, burst, shout." The poetry anticipates shrieking, unrestrained joy at birth long expected and too long delayed. The reason, introduced by "for," is the promise that "desolate" Israel will be more than those of "married" Babylon, who in truth has no joyous future in prospect.

The second sequence employs a different image (vv. 2–3). The five imperatives of verse 2 envision a Bedouin tent. (On the nomadic linkage to Abraham, see Genesis 18:1.) There is need to get a bigger tent and to make it more secure by cords and stakes. The reason is that the tent is going to be crawling with an abundance of children, so many that they will climb all over the tent, which, if not reinforced, will fall down. Moreover, the particular phrasing of verse 3, "your descendants will possess the nations," especially recalls the book of Genesis and its promises (Gen. 22:17). In the return from exile, the ancient promises and memories of Genesis are coming to dramatic and abundant fruition.

54:4 **Do not fear, for you will not be ashamed;**
    do not be discouraged, for you will not suffer disgrace;

> for you will forget the shame of your youth,
>   and the disgrace of your widowhood you will remember no more.
> ⁵For your Maker is your husband,
>   the LORD of hosts is his name;
> the Holy One of Israel is your Redeemer,
>   the God of the whole earth he is called.
> ⁶For the LORD has called you
>   like a wife forsaken and grieved in spirit,
> like the wife of a man's youth when she is cast off,
>   says your God.

In these verses, the imagery is slightly altered, though the poem continues to speak of a bereft woman as a figure for Israel bereft in exile. Here the image concerns a widow rather than a barren woman. However, the force of the metaphor is nearly the same, because in a patriarchal society, both barren women and widows are endlessly in jeopardy; they have no male guarantee in social transactions.

This vulnerable woman (Sarah = Israel) is here addressed by a salvation oracle, a rhetorical form we have reviewed in 41:8–13. Here speaks the husband with an assurance in a twofold "do not fear." The assurance is that the one addressed will no longer be ashamed or disregarded, as she was sure to be in a patriarchal society when her husband had deserted her and cast her out. In that patriarchal context, a woman barren or widowed is a woman abandoned. Indeed, in the society of honor, such a woman is shamed and humiliated, an object of scorn and social rejection, most likely to be exploited and excluded. Israel in exile, like that woman, is mocked and scorned because her God-husband has abandoned her.

The assurance that supports the "do not fear" is given with three occurrences of "for" as an introductory practice: (1) In verse 4b it is announced that all the humiliation Israel has suffered will be overcome, whether the shame of a young barren woman or the shame of an old, abandoned widow. (2) In verse 5 Yahweh is identified as the husband, an agent of importance and force, Lord of hosts, Holy One, Creator. Perhaps the most poignant title is "Redeemer," the kinsman who "redeems" the kinswoman from the shame of social abandonment. The theme of "redeemer" may be a common one in exilic Isaiah, but here the metaphor is peculiarly appropriate to the imagery. (3) Yahweh, the husband, has summoned the woman, summoned her back to relationship, summoned her like a saddened widow, summoned her like a woman expelled (v. 6). The patriarchal quality of the imagery is evident. It is husband-Yahweh who has been free to reject and now is free to restore (see Deut. 24:1–4). In context, however, the summons is nonetheless immense. It assures the woman of restoration to dignity, to security, and to well-being. Thus, although the imagery of verses 4–6 is somewhat different from that of verses 1–3, the two units together make poignant use of a most intimate metaphor that has huge social implications. The metaphor in itself may be affirmative, but the use to which it is put here is a stunning assurance of rehabilitation when the barren woman-widow-Israel must have no longer expected any gesture of support from the husband who had scorned her.

54:7 **For a brief moment I abandoned you,**
    but with great compassion I will gather you.
  [8] **In overflowing wrath for a moment**
    I hid my face from you,
  but with everlasting love I will have compassion on you,
    says the LORD, your Redeemer.

These verses are among the most remarkable in scripture. They continue to play on the themes of verses 1–6 concerning Israel's rejection by Yahweh (in exile) and Israel's promised restoration by a summoning husband. What is astonishing is the candid admission on the part of Yahweh, twice uttered in verses 7a and 8a, that Yahweh did indeed abandon Israel. To be sure, it was "for a brief moment," for only an instant. But it was a genuine abandonment; not an apparent one—a real one. God's own testimony here is that *God did abandon Israel in exile*. It is not claimed, moreover, that this abandonment is punishment or that wife-Israel has sinned. If we stay within the imagery of verses 1–6, it is suggested that Yahweh "bailed out" of the marriage, perhaps because Yahweh could not tolerate the humiliation of a barren wife. It is important to note that in this remarkable admission, Yahweh offers no explanation or justification. We are given only a bare acknowledgment. It is possible, without excessive overreading, to think that the poet leaves Yahweh "for a moment" exposed and undefended, so that Israel (and the listener) may observe Yahweh coming as close to an expression of regret or apology for exile as is possible.

It is not surprising that such a portrayal of Yahweh is awkward for "high Christian theology" that will entertain no such dimension of Yahweh. Commentators must be agile indeed to overcome what seems to be acknowledged in this text. Calvin is an example of the footwork required by the text to have it conform to an otherwise less troubled theology:

When he says that he *forsook* his people, it is a sort of admission of the fact. We are adopted by God in such a manner that we cannot be rejected by him on account of the treachery of men; for he is faithful, so that he will not cast off or abandon his people. What the Prophet says in this passage must therefore refer to our feelings and to outward appearance, because we seem to be rejected by God when we do not perceive his presence and protection. And it is necessary that we should thus feel God's wrath, even as a wife divorced by her husband deplores her condition, that we may know that we are justly chastised. But we must also perceive his mercy. . . . At the same time it ought to be observed, that what was said was actually true as to the whole body of the people, who had been divorced on account of their wickedness (*Isaiah IV*, 140).

A strategy less daring than that of Calvin simply insists that the huge assurance of compassion completely overrides the "moment" of abandonment. The two lines of Yahweh's acknowledgment are, in each case, immediately countered and overcome by verses 7b and 8b, an adversative through which Yahweh-husband reverses field and now embraces the rejected wife. The recovery of the relationship—the reembrace of Israel, the homecoming and welcoming of Israel—is grounded in Yahweh's "great compassion," in Yahweh's "everlasting love." Here speaks the redeemer, the one who guards and guarantees the well-being and reputation of the wife. The relationship is fully restored.

This surprising twofold sequence of acknowledgment and assurance admits of more than one reading. If we are interested only in outcomes and see the primary message as one of homecoming—the "all's well that ends well"—Israel, at the end, is loved and Yahweh is loyal. That may be enough. If, however, we dwell on the poignancy of the imagery that continues from verse 1, our reading is different. On such reading, the abandonment may be "for a moment" and the reembrace everlasting. But there was an abandonment! There was a time of complete desolation when a woman in a patriarchal society must count on a man, and the man is one who abandons. In the exuberance of homecoming, perhaps the woman should move on and accept the belated gift of compassion and love. But surely a season of shame and humiliation is not so easily nullified. I would imagine it lingers, even if the poet leaves the question unacknowledged and unresolved. In the end, Yahweh is faithful, if not all the way through. In the Christian tradition, the spin-off of such an abandonment suggests taking the Friday-abandonment of the cross seriously and without toning it down. Something is given here that is not easily palatable in our common traditions of theological triumph.

Prosperity and Vindication
(54:9–17)

These verses also offer great assurances for about-to-be rehabilitated Israel, only now with sharply altered imagery.

> 54:9 **This is like the days of Noah to me:**
>   **Just as I swore that the waters of Noah**
>   **would never again go over the earth,**
>   **so I have sworn that I will not be angry with you**
>   **and will not rebuke you.**
> 10 **For the mountains may depart**
>   **and the hills be removed,**
>   **but my steadfast love shall not depart from you,**
>   **and my covenant of peace shall not be removed,**
>   **says the LORD, who has compassion on you.**

In a remarkable and daring use of images, the poem suggests that "this" (= the Exile) is like the Flood recalled in the book of Genesis. Thus the ancient memory of the Flood narrative is invoked in yet another portrayal of the transformation about to be worked for Israel. The Exile is like the Flood (a) in that it is a season of deep chaos, (b) it is caused by and authorized by Yahweh, and (c) it is about to end.

It is this last point that concerns our poetry. Yahweh acknowledges having caused the Flood; this is a means whereby the Exile is acknowledged as Yahweh's own work in verses 7–8. Eventually, after enough water and enough destruction, Yahweh has made a solemn vow, sealed by the rainbow, that the Flood would not happen *ever again* (Gen. 9:11). In parallel, Yahweh has given a solemn oath that exile would not happen *ever again*. Never again would Israel be abandoned and left exposed. Never again will Yahweh give Israel over to exile. The relationship is now on a new basis, not unlike the new basis of the marriage in verses 7–8.

Indeed, the new assurance of Yahweh's fidelity to Israel is more reliable than is creation itself (v. 10). It is assumed in that ancient world that the creation is durable and reliable. But for purpose of contrast, the poem entertains a scenario in which even mountains and hills may become unstable (see 51:6; Psalm 46:2–3; and Jer. 31:35–36). The use of creation in this way is parallel to that of 49:15, in which mothering love, surely counted as stable, is imagined to be unstable for purposes of contrast. Yahweh's promise is more durable and more reliable than is creation itself. The assurance makes use of Israel's best covenantal vocabulary: "steadfast love, covenant of peace, compassion." This is the most extreme claim that can be made for Yahweh. Israel's future, unlike its precarious past, is utterly assured, grounded in Yahweh's good intention.

> 54:11 O afflicted one, storm-tossed, and not comforted,
>   I am about to set your stones in antimony,
>   and lay your foundations with sapphires.
>   ¹² I will make your pinnacles of rubies,
>   your gates of jewels,
>   and all your wall of precious stones.
>   ¹³ All your children shall be taught by the LORD,
>   and great shall be the prosperity of your children.

Although these verses take up a very different set of images, the beginning of verse 11 is connected to the flood imagery of verses 9–10. Jerusalem is addressed as "storm-tossed," whereby we imagine the chaotic threat of the Flood, and by extrapolation, the extreme jeopardy of the Exile. Jerusalem in exile, moreover, is "not comforted," not yet assured, not yet brought home to safety and well-being. Thus, "storm-tossed" shares the negative force of "barren" (v. 1) and "ashamed" (v. 4). But as with those images, here the condition of "not comforted" is now to be powerfully and extravagantly overcome.

The poetry imagines the rebuilding of the devastated city of Jerusalem (vv. 11b–12). The elements of a city under construction are named: "stones, foundations, pinnacles, gates, wall." In each case, however, the rebuilt element is matched to a precious gem. The new city will be utterly dazzling in wealth and beauty. The whole of the new city will be "fit for a king." The rhetoric envisions a complete reversal of international economics, whereby all the wealth of the nations will be given over to Jerusalem, so that the last will indeed become first. (See a concrete case in 23:17–18.)

As a result, the children of returning Jews, the ones assured in verses 1–6, will live in complete splendor. They will be the special object of Yahweh's own teaching, and they will luxuriate in extravagant well-being. (The term "prosperity" in verse 13 renders *shalom*.) The reversal is complete: barren . . . birth; flood . . . peaceableness; displacement . . . rebuilt royal splendor!

> 54:14 In righteousness you shall be established;
>   you shall be far from oppression, for you shall not fear;
>   and from terror, for it shall not come near you.

¹⁵ If anyone stirs up strife,
    it is not from me;
  whoever stirs up strife with you
    shall fall because of you.
¹⁶ See it is I who have created the smith
    who blows the fire of coals,
    and produces a weapon fit for its purpose;
  I have also created the ravager to destroy.
¹⁷   No weapon that is fashioned against you shall prosper,
    and you shall confute every tongue that rises against you in
      judgment.
This is the heritage of the servants of the LORD
  and their vindication from me, says the LORD.

This long recital of guarantees concludes with yet one more assurance of the guaranteed well-being of Jerusalem in time to come. One could understand if the returning exiles were still unsure, still felt threatened, still doubted. Their oppressive situation was a bad dream that must have kept recurring like a nightmare. In the imagination of Israel, the ominous possibility of oppression and terror must have been endlessly close at hand. In verse 14, the threat of oppression is countered by an assurance of "righteousness," Yahweh's resolve to establish a governance that is fair, just, durable, and reliable.

The poem entertains a hypothetical case of a troublemaker against Jerusalem, perhaps a new power or perhaps revivified Babylon, who was never far from the bad dreams of Judaism (v. 15). But such a troublemaker cannot succeed. It will fail "because of you," that is, because of Yahweh's commitment and guarantee to Jerusalem. The powers of chaos have no chance, for Yahweh has decreed "never again." In more detail, verses 16–17 seek to underscore the assurance given in verse 15. Yahweh is the one who controls the production and distribution of arms. Yahweh, moreover, is the one who has in the past dispatched destructive powers. Those powers do not act on their own (10:5–19; 45:1; 47:6a); any power that takes an initiative with whatever arms they may have, moreover, cannot succeed. No adversary will have a chance against restored Israel, either in the courtroom or on the battlefield.

The final lines of verse 17 offer a summary assurance, gathering together the previous assurances offered in a rich field of images. "This" refers to all of the assurances of Israel's future well-being. *This* is Israel's inheritance. What Israel now possesses is a secure future—so unlike its past. That secure future rests on a vindication given by Yahweh.

The language of "vindication" refers back to the "righteousness" of verse 14 (the same Hebrew word). Yahweh has made the case for Israel's well-being, and that is now ground on which to stake the future. The use of judicial language was taken up by Paul in his notion of sure "justification" (= vindication) in the gospel. That same assurance belonged to Judaism before Paul wrote. Christians are belated heirs of that which is perennially bequeathed to Judaism. In both cases—Judaism and Christianity—God has decreed a safe, prosperous well-being into the future against every threat, every jeopardy, every adversary. For the exiles, the future is utterly unlike the past. Yahweh has made it so; Israel's future stands under Yahweh's sovereign "never again."

"GO OUT IN JOY AND PEACE"
55:1–13

This final unit of exilic Isaiah completes the authorization and anticipation of a joyous, secure homecoming for the exiles.

55:1 **Ho, everyone who thirsts,**
  come to the waters;
 and you that have no money,
  come, buy and eat!
 Come, buy wine and milk
  without money and without price.
 2 **Why do you spend your money for that which is not bread,**
  and your labor for that which does not satisfy?
 Listen carefully to me, and eat what is good,
  and delight yourselves in rich food.
 3 **Incline your ear, and come to me;**
  listen, so that you may live.
 I will make with you an everlasting covenant,
  my steadfast, sure love for David.
 4 **See, I made him a witness to the peoples,**
  a leader and commander for the peoples.
 5 **See, you shall call nations that you do not know,**
  and nations that do not know you shall run to you,
 because of the LORD your God, the Holy One of Israel,
  for he has glorified you.

In these verses, the poet makes a sharp contrast between old modes of life under Babylonian authority and the new offer of life with Yahweh. The initial verse, perhaps in the summoning mode of a street vendor, offers to passersby free water, free wine, and free milk. This of course is in contrast to the life resources offered by the empire that are always expensive, grudging, and unsatisfying. Israel is invited to choose the free, alternative nourishment offered by Yahweh. Thus, although we may ponder the metaphor of free food, the underlying urging is the sharp contrast between the way of life given in Babylon that leads to death and the way of Yahweh that leads to joyous homecoming. This is the central theme of the entire poetic unit.

With the offer of the free food of covenantal emancipation, the poem contrasts that offer with the bread of the empire (vv. 2–3). The rhetorical questions ask, incredulously, why Jews in exile would invest so much in forms of life that cannot work—why work so hard and so long in ways that give no satisfaction; why give life over to the demands and rewards of the empire that yield nothing of value in return. As an alternative to Babylonian junk food, Israel is summoned to listen, as was ancient Israel, to the offer of the rich food of the gospel of Yahweh (see Deut. 6:4).

In the middle of verse 3, the poetry departs the imagery of *food* and speaks directly of the deep promise of *fidelity* made long ago to David, a promise now enlarged and extended and reiterated for the entire community of Israel (reference is to 2 Sam. 7:11–16; Psalm 89:19–37). The language of covenant here is Israel's best rhetoric for fidelity, this in parallel to the assurances given in 54:10. This *offer of fidelity* is sharply contrasted with *the Babylonian offer of exploitative, coercive, oppressive life* that denies dignity, freedom, and security, and never yields abundance or joy. Indeed, the regime of the empire is profoundly opposed to the very notions of well-being fostered by Yahweh.

The Davidic reference in verse 3 appeals to the old covenant promises of Yahweh; at the same time, however, it also permits an awareness of royal prowess and domination, so that David is conjured in exile, after the dynasty had ended, as a political force that would guarantee Israel. Combining the offer of *covenantal fidelity* with *political force*, Israel will be powerful and prominent; nations will rely upon Israel and eagerly bring gifts, tributes, and payments that will make Jerusalem secure and prosperous. The Davidic agent is offered as an important vehicle for Jerusalem's new well-being. In the end, however, it is no Davidic agent, but the Holy One of Israel who will be decisive. Israel's new well-being will enhance Yahweh in the eyes of the nations (v. 5). Israel has a wondrous choice to make: either the *new future* now offered by Yahweh or *more submissiveness* to Babylon that yields nothing of well-being. The choice seems clear enough.

⟨55:6 **Seek the** LORD **while he may be found,**
      call upon him while he is near;
   7**let the wicked forsake their way,**
      and the unrighteous their thoughts;
    let them return to the LORD, **that he may have mercy on them,**
      and to our God, for he will abundantly pardon.
   8**For my thoughts are not your thoughts,**
      nor are your ways my ways, says the LORD.
   9**For as the heavens are higher than the earth,**
      so are my ways higher than your ways
      and my thoughts than your thoughts.

These verses are a quite familiar call to worship and a stylized summons to repentance. It is important, nonetheless, not to settle for a general understanding of the summons but to appreciate its intent in a quite concrete context. Israel is summoned to "seek Yahweh," to draw near to Yahweh, to come to terms with Yahweh, to respond to Yahweh's offer, to rely upon Yahweh for an alternative future.

"The wicked," I suggest, are not disobedient people in general. In context, they are those who are so settled in Babylon and so accommodated to imperial ways that they have no intention of making a positive response to Yahweh's invitation to homecoming. That is, they have no "thought" of enacting Jewish passion for Jerusalem. To "return" to Yahweh here means to embrace fully the future that Yahweh is now offering. This "return" is not simply a spiritual resolve but the embrace of a new hope and a new historical possibility that entails a dramatic reorientation of life in political, public categories. Those who have excessively accommodated the empire are indeed to be pardoned. But pardon requires serious resolve for a re-ordered life commitment.

Yahweh's ways and plans are contrasted with the *ways and plans* of some of the Jews in exile. Yahweh's intention is for a wholly new future in Jerusalem. Perhaps the *ways and plans* rejected are the plans to refuse Jerusalem and remain in Babylon, either because it is comfortable and too good to leave or because leaving does not seem to be an actual possibility. That is, remaining under Babylon may be an outcome of either complacency or despair. Either way, the exiles do not believe that Yahweh has a clear resolve that they can really choose. They can fall into this despair only if they do not believe the massive rhetoric of assurance and empowerment heretofore offered in exilic Isaiah. The news of Yahweh is that Yahweh does indeed have an independent, sovereign purpose that is not an echo of anything else in the world (40:9; 52:7). For the exiles, as for ancient Abraham, "faith" is acceptance of a radical promise and summons to alternative life (Gen. 15:6; Heb. 11:8–12).

55:10 **For as the rain and the snow come down from heaven,**
      and do not return there until they have watered the earth,
    making it bring forth and sprout,
      giving seed to the sower and bread to the eater,
  ¹¹ **so shall my word be that goes out from my mouth;**
      it shall not return to me empty,
    but it shall accomplish that which I purpose,
      and succeed in the thing for which I sent it.

The verification of Yahweh's resolve is the assertion that Yahweh's word of promise is indeed consequential and produces real outcomes in public life. This *word of promise and summons* has already been celebrated in 40:8 at the outset of this exilic writing. And now it is reasserted at the conclusion of the writing. Everything exilic Isaiah has to say to exiles is grounded in Yahweh's reliable resolve that is uttered in the faith of Israel.

The consequential power of Yahweh is here likened to rain and snow. Rain and snow are not phantoms but are real, forceful powers that produce something tangible in the earth, that is, growth and life and future. They water the earth, and the result, regularly and reliably, is that the earth is nourished, creation is sustained, and the food chain is maintained.

Yahweh's word of promise and summons is like that. It is not idle chatter or religious fantasy. It is substantive utterance carrying with it the full weight of Yahweh's majestic rule. Snow and rain are not ineffective. Yahweh's word is not empty verbiage; it will work! It will guarantee! It will produce! Rain and snow cause food. Yahweh's decree causes a new future for exilic Israel. This word of summons and promise thus is contrasted both with the empty nourishment of the empire (vv. 1–3) and with the fearful refusal of some in Israel who rely on their own banal thoughts and ways.

55:12 **For you shall go out in joy,**
      and be led back in peace;
    the mountains and the hills before you
      shall burst into song,
      and all the trees of the field shall clap their hands.
  ¹³ **Instead of the thorn shall come up the cypress;**
      instead of the brier shall come up the myrtle;
    and it shall be to the LORD for a memorial,
      for an everlasting sign that shall not be cut off.

The outcome offered in exilic Isaiah, and the outcome anticipated for exilic Jews, is joyous homecoming. The term "go out," as in 52:11, is an Exodus term. This is the new Exodus undertaken, not in fear or in haste as the first Exodus, but in joy and peace, in well-being and calmness. The poetry, since the vision of the processional highway (35:8; 40:3–5; 49:11), anticipates that there will be a triumphant parade of Jews headed home, with Yahweh at the head in exuberant well-being.

The departure is here offered as a dramatic geographic transfer back to Zion. And ultimately, in context, it is indeed geographical. If, however, one takes the rhetoric of exilic Isaiah seriously, it is unmistakable that before there can be any geographical departure from the empire, there must be a liturgical, emotional, imaginative departure. Israel in exile must be able to think and feel and imagine its life out beyond Babylonian administration. Israel must so trust the rhetoric of assurance and victory that it can flex its muscles of faith and sense that the cadences of faith are more compelling than the slogans of the empire. This lyrical conclusion to the exilic poetry proceeds as if this point is well made and fully accepted. Israel, in the lyrical rhetoric of the poet, is on its way under new governance, moving to a wondrous new future.

The processional parade here imagined is a visible, cosmic event. It was already expected in 40:5 that "all people" would witness the return, so wondrous and noteworthy is it. Here the poet imagines all the creatures gathered along the highway in order to see the spectacle. Even hills and mountains and trees have gathered to watch, so marvelous is the sight that vouches for the new start of all of creation and a decisive defeat of violating, destructive, imperial tyranny. All the creatures applaud the victory embodied in the homecoming of Israel. Perhaps they salute Israel for its courageous, determined faith; more likely they join the cosmic salute of Yahweh, because this manifest defeat of Babylon bespeaks the evident defeat of all of the powers of chaos. The mountains, hills, and trees have a deep stake in the defeat of such military powers as represented by Babylon, because empires such as Babylon are notorious for the irreversible damage done to nonhuman creation. Back in the old temple liturgy of Psalm 96:10–13, the creatures ecstatically welcome Yahweh's new rule. Here they take Yahweh's rescue of Israel as a sign and guarantee that all of creation—Israel and the others, human and nonhuman—now will be safe and well in Yahweh's protective governance.

The cosmic significance of this emancipation is evident in verses 12–13. "Thorn and brier" have been a tag word in the Isaiah tradition for life diminished by God's judgment (5:6; 7:23–25; 27:4; 32:13). But now these prickly evidences of negativity are dismissed and overcome. They are not needed and are no longer appropriate. In place of these gestures of nullity come now signs of growth and life and beauty—cypress and myrtle. The homecoming of Israel bespeaks the healing of all creation. These beautiful growths—and all such loveliness—are signs and witnesses and reminders of Yahweh's new rule. The creator God now prevails. Life is possible for all creatures. No wonder these large creatures clap and sing! No wonder Israel dances in joy! No wonder the mood is of *shalom!* All are now at home, safe, beloved, free, free at last. Thank God Almighty, free at last!

8. "Maintain Justice, and Do What Is Right"
Isaiah 56:1–66:24

For over a century, these chapters have been treated by scholars as a distinct literary section in the book of Isaiah. With the scholarly judgment that Isaiah, the prophet of the eighth century B.C.E., is linked to chapters 1—39 and a subsequent exilic poet is responsible for chapters 40—55, scholars have designated these present chapters "Third Isaiah," naming a third wave of texts that rearticulate the core of Isaianic theology in yet another situation of faith.

It is the common assumption of scholars that this material, although it has close connections to chapters 40—55, is to be dated somewhat later and reflects subsequent theological concerns. The literature seems to reflect the theological crisis of the formative years of Judaism, just after the return to and restoration of the community in Jerusalem after the Exile. It may well be that there was no void of a worshiping community in Jerusalem during the Exile, and no dramatic return from exile; but that is the telling of the tale of Judaism by the dominant voices of the reconstructed community. That is, this "canonical" account of emerging Judaism is in some part "social construction." That social construction, in any case, is the assumption of this literature. This literature is likely situated somewhere between (a) the rebuilding of the temple and the revival of temple worship in the years 520–516, a crisis to which Haggai and Zechariah are related, and (b) the restoration of the torah community under the leadership of Ezra and Nehemiah (444 B.C.E.). It is more likely, according to current scholarly opinion, that these chapters are to be located in the earlier part of this period, thus soon after 520.

We may identify two principal accents dominating this literature, accents that reflect an advocacy position in emerging Judaism. First, this literature comes in the wake of the visioning promises of chapters 40—55, with their exultant notion of a triumphant return of the Jews to Jerusalem under the protection of the Persians. That literature envisioned a triumph in which the glad power of Yahweh would make everything wondrous for the returning exiles. Third Isaiah is much influenced by this vision, particularly in the eloquent anticipations of chapters 60—62 and 65:17–5. That is, this literature, which continues to affirm the most sweeping promises of Yahweh, believes that Yahweh's faithful intention will override every debilitating circumstance.

Second, the returnees from exile did not find Jerusalem to be "empty space." Therefore major disputes arose about how to shape and order the refounding of Jewish faith. Otto Plöger, in *Theocracy and Eschatology*, and Paul D. Hanson, in *The Dawn of Apocalyptic: The Historical and Sociological Roots of Jewish Apocalyptic Eschatology*, have made a strong case for viewing this literature as emerging to represent a partisan position in the midst of sectarian conflict. In Third Isaiah, then, we have one side of the quarrel that dominated emerging Judaism, one advocacy in the face of which other advocacies must be imagined or reconstructed, perhaps from Haggai and Zechariah or perhaps from Ezekiel. In any case, these materials are profoundly disputatious, much more so than in Isaiah 40—55.

For purposes of convenience, it will be useful to see this material in three distinct units, though it is surely more complex than such an ordering may suggest. At the center of the material, there can be no doubt, are chapters 60—62. These poems have most in common with Isaiah 40—55 and issue sweeping, glorious promises about those happy intentions that Yahweh will soon work in behalf of the needful community of emerging Judaism.

The chapters before these, that is, chapters 56—59, give evidence for the emerging disputes that will dominate the shaping of Judaism. In these chapters, we may identify remarkable ethical claims, an insistence that Judaism must practice a torah obedience that transcends self-protective punctiliousness. Specifically, 56:3–8 seeks to enact the imperative for justice in 56:1–2 by an insistence on a large *inclusiveness* in the community, presumably an attempt to counter and resist any narrow exclusivism. And in 58:6–8, the text makes an argument for faith that is focused on *neighborly needs* in a generous and concrete way, clearly an advocacy to counter self-indulgent worship. The advocacy of both *inclusiveness* and *neighborly needs* is an important ethical passion in emerging Judaism. Along with these specific issues, we notice the general affirmation of the "humble and contrite" (57:15; see 66:2) and the urging of justice (57:8, 11, 14, 15), echoing the mandate of 56:1–2. This accent anticipates a faithful community fully engaged in the large human questions of the day.

Along with ambitious ethical mandates, these chapters also reflect the partisan terms of dispute that will subsequently grow more shrill. In 57:1–13, 20, and 59:1–8, it is clear that there are adversaries in the community who hold a very different vision of the community, seemingly not passionately engaged in covenantal requirements that are indispensable for Yahwistic faith.

The third element of this material, chapters 63—66, is somewhat more miscellaneous and randomly ordered. But we can see the themes of *vision and dispute* being more sharply focused in these later texts. The hymn and complaint of chapters 63—64 may not yet be partisan, but there is an awareness of an adversary (63:18). It is not clear yet that the adversaries are members of the community. The dispute is more clearly evident in the polemic of 65:1–7; 66:3–4, 14c–17, and the division of the community into distinct contrasting elements is unmistakable in 65:13–14. This conflictual pattern is matched in 65:17–25 by a vision of newness that contextualizes and perhaps overrides the conflict. The concluding verses of the book of Isaiah indicate an unresolved dispute that is already rooted in the advocacy of 56:1–2. The problem of a community of discipline that is open and accepting of outsiders is a vexation to the Jewish community. Subsequently, the same trouble emerged in the early church and was settled on Pauline terms in Acts 15. It takes no great imagination, however, to see that this vexing issue has continued to haunt and disturb the church even until our own day.

It is clear in current scholarship that chapters 56—66 are not simply late, "Judaic" add-ons to the book of Isaiah. Rather, they reflect an integral engagement with the central themes of the Isaiah tradition, of which I mention two.

First, we have seen in 9:1 and much thereafter in exilic Isaiah a reflection on former things and latter things. I have suggested, following others, that the dialectic of former–latter pertains to early Isaiah and later Isaiah, to judgment and grace, to exile and homecoming. The theme shows up in Isaiah 56—66 in a pivotal way in 65:16–17:

> because the *former troubles* are forgotten
>   and are hidden from my sight.
> For I am about to create new heavens
>   and a new earth;
> the *former things* shall not be remembered
>   or come to mind.

The former things—judgment and exile—are now over and done. The focus now is completely upon new things about to be wrought by Yahweh. That theme of course generates both buoyant hope and sharp dispute. The trust and the passion of the community are engaged in rightly receiving the newness that Yahweh will now give.

Second, like the rest of the book, Isaiah 56—66 is primally concerned with the future of Jerusalem. It is urgent to determine if the new Jerusalem, which epitomizes new heaven and new earth, will or will not be a place of inclusion, will or will not be a practice of neighbor ethic, will or will not manifest a passion for justice. Yahweh will create a new Jerusalem, will send his glory there (60), will enact jubilee there (61), will break the silence so that the city can be renamed and recharacterized (62). This is the very city that had to be terminated in the earlier traditions, but now is to be the focus of Yahweh's positive zeal.

But the city cannot just be received from Yahweh. It must be ordered, administered, and managed, and therein lies the trouble. It is clear in the conclusion to Isaiah 56—66 that this beloved city, which is the pivotal point of Yahweh on earth, is both a *wondrous gift* of all of Yahweh's possibilities and a *place of deep dispute* wherein profound fears, angers, and hates are to be evoked in the name of the God of Zion.

Nothing really has changed. A current study of Jerusalem—of Israelis and Palestinians—yields the same great hope and deep conflict. In our own way, of course, it is not different with Christians. Current shapes for these family disputes are now fumblingly termed "conservative" and "liberal." But only the labels have changed to keep matters contemporary. The disputants about the shape of "Zion" are, without exception, serious in faith, eager to receive God's gift rightly. The text, for all its visionary power, may suggest that there is no way around the dispute. As in the book of Isaiah, a last word has not yet been spoken.

LIFE WITH THE GOD WHO GATHERS
56:1–12

Isaiah 55:12–13 has promised a glorious, wondrous, exuberant homecoming on the royal road of triumph anticipated in 40:3–5. The move from 55:12–13 (the conclusion of exilic Isaiah) to 56:1–2 is a major leap in imagination. For now, by 56:1–2, the initial venture of homecoming has already been undertaken. If 55:12–13 is spoken with reference to 540 B.C.E. and the anticipated emancipation of exiles by Cyrus the Persian, 56:1–2 begins a new literature, perhaps dated to 520 B.C.E. The gap between 55:12–13 and 56:1–2 is perhaps only twenty years in the life of Israel. Ten years after 55:12–13, however, the circumstance of the community is abruptly changed. Now the text places us back in Jerusalem, in the shambles of the still ruined city.

In the context that the text invites us to imagine, severe questions and heavy demands awaited the faithful. It was a time for rebuilding the city. It was a time for reshaping the faith of Israel that was now to become Judaism. As is characteristic in emerging Judaism, a time of rebuilding and reshaping calls for disputation among competing visions of the future.

This text is one voice that makes a particular advocacy about the future shape of Judaism in that high-stakes dispute. This text begins with an assertion of a primal vision for coming Judaism (vv. 1–2), a concrete enactment of that vision (vv. 3–8), and what appears to be a deep dispute with competitors who do not share that vision (vv. 9–12).

56:1 **Thus says the LORD:**
>   **Maintain justice, and do what is right,**
> **for soon my salvation will come,**
>   **and my deliverance be revealed.**

> [2] **Happy is the mortal who does this,**
>   **the one who holds it fast,**
> **who keeps the sabbath, not profaning it,**
>   **and refrains from doing any evil.**

These verses state the primary theme that is to guide the vision of coming Judaism as expressed in postexilic Isaiah. They begin with "Thus says Yahweh," offering this remarkable utterance from the presiding God of the divine council, thus paralleling the negative decree of 6:9–10. Structurally, this utterance functions not unlike the visionary utterance of 6:1–13, which epitomizes early Isaiah, and 40:1–11, which thematizes exilic Isaiah. Now speaks the God who will shape coming Judaism in a particular and intentional way.

This verse contains two defining word pairs that stand in a delicate relationship to each other. The first word pair is an imperative address by Yahweh to the community of faith: "Maintain *justice*, and do what is *right*" (v. 1). The terms "justice . . . right" (*mišpat-ṣedeqāh*) have been a conventional pair in Israel's prophetic faith from the outset. In Isaiah 5:7, Israel is severely judged because it failed in justice and righteousness (see Amos 5:7, 24; 6:12). In Isaiah 9:7, echoing Psalm 72:1, it is anticipated and insisted that Davidic power will be devoted to justice and righteousness for the poor and needy. The two terms together bespeak a radical torah obligation to order the community of covenant so as to bind in mutuality the strong and the weak, the rich and the poor. The intent is to assure every member of the community security, dignity, and well-being. In the tradition of Isaiah, this is the primal ethical obligation of recovering Judaism.

The second word pair is a promise from Yahweh: *salvation-deliverance.* It is important that the second word, "deliverance," is also *sedeqāh*, the term rendered "right" in the first word pair. That is, Yahweh is about to establish, by unilateral act, the very well-being commanded in the first word pair. Yahweh will bring this community to the well-being that Yahweh has intended from the outset. Thus, *imperative* and *promise* locate both Yahweh and the community of Jews as contributors to coming well-being.

Verse 2 states the consequence of *enacting* justice and righteousness and *receiving* Yahweh's salvation and deliverance. The first line of this verse is a wisdom saying reminiscent of Psalm 1:1. Good fortune (happiness) results from enacting the mandate of 56:1. Here the substance of the mandate of verse 1 is stated in a different way. Positively, the ground of good fortune is sabbath observance, an observance that becomes definitional and urgent in the postexilic period as a distinctive mark of serious Judaism. Negatively, good fortune arises from the avoidance of evil (see Job 28:28; Psalm 1:1; Prov. 3:7).

These two verses together envision a community that is intensely and intentionally committed to the practice of torah. The Torah brings every phase of life under obedience to Yahweh; it states the distinctive ethics of Jewishness that in the end consists in attentiveness to and enhancement of the neighborly community. It is for good reason that this poetry is most recently connected to the strenuous reforms of Ezra and Nehemiah, who were intent on reconstituting a community of vigorous torah obedience.

56:3 **Do not let the foreigner joined to the LORD say,**
    "The LORD will surely separate me from his people";
  and do not let the eunuch say,
    "I am just a dry tree."
    ⁴For thus says the LORD:
  To the eunuchs who keep my sabbaths,
    who choose the things that please me
    and hold fast my covenant,
    ⁵I will give, in my house and within my walls,
    a monument and a name
    better than sons and daughters;
  I will give them an everlasting name
    that shall not be cut off.

The ethical insistence of verses 1–2 is here brought to a particular issue: Who should be included in the reconstituted community of Judaism? Although the torah accent of verses 1–2 agrees with the insistence of Ezra the Reformer, these verses move in a surprising direction. Whereas Ezra insists on communal purity that some regard as severe as "ethnic cleansing" (see Ezra 9:1–4), these verses move in a very different, inclusive direction. Apparently the debate turned on the inclusion of foreigners and eunuchs who applied for membership in Judaism but feared rejection. The key verb "separate" is stated in an intense form and is the key word in emerging Judaism for the kind of ordering that will get everything and everyone sorted out, to avoid disorder, confusion, or impurity. (The same term is used, presumably in the same context, in Genesis 1:4, 6, 14 to signify properly separated elements of creation so that there is no cosmic disorder.) The verb moves strongly in an exclusivist direction. In verse 3, it is suggested that both foreigners and eunuchs anticipated rejection from the community.

The ground of such rejection could be found in the apparently old torah provision excluding both those with mutilated sexual organs and those from "illicit" marriages (Deut. 23:1–2). The old Torah had envisioned a quite exclusive community of purity, and some in the late sixth century proposed to continue that mandate. What is remarkable is that our text voices a counterurging that directly, perhaps intentionally, flies in the face of the old torah provisions. Indeed, Herbert Donner ("Jesaja lvi 1–7") takes these verses as an "abrogation" of the torah teaching in these two particular uses. The visionary act of this poet radically and deliberately flies in the face of the old torah provision.

The first case concerns eunuchs (vv. 4–5). The eunuch appears to be expressly excluded from the community of Israel in Deuteronomy 23:1: "No one whose testicles are crushed or whose penis is cut off shall be admitted to the assembly of the LORD." Isaiah 56:3 anticipates an exclusion that renders such persons hopeless, without a future in Israel.

The oracle of verses 4–5, however, overrides both the old torah commandment of Deuteronomy 23:1 and the despairing assumption of verse 3. The oracle is inclusive and permits the entry into community of eunuchs who keep covenant (see v. 2) and who practice sabbath (see 58:13–14). That is, the specific torah teaching of Deuteronomy 23:1 is nullified on the ground that eunuchs should in general be adherents to torah covenant. The only specific requirement is that the eunuch should practice sabbath, a provision required of every Jew and an intensely important discipline in the postexilic community, which marked obedient Jews as distinctive. To those who meet these requirements, Yahweh promises a monument, a name, an everlasting name, an assurance of not being cut off. The four provisions of promise in verse 5 are rough equivalents. They all four promise that the eunuch will be received, honored, and remembered. It is clear that the eunuch will have no children to continue his family identity. Here the community is placed under obligation to remember in a way that is "better" than children. The community of Judaism is to be a community that remembers, cherishes, and preserves the name and identity of those otherwise nullified in an uncaring world.

The eunuch obviously was a point of contention in this debate over the character of emerging Judaism. It may be that the eunuch is anyone with genitals mutilated for whatever reason, rendering him less than "whole." But it is more likely that the eunuch is one who was mutilated in order to *qualify for imperial service*, that is, one who had compromised faith and identity in order to advance in the alien empire. (See 39:7 on the anticipation that Davidic heirs would be forced into such imperial service.) Frederick Gaiser, in "A New Word on Homosexuality?" has noticed that 39:7 and our verse are the only two mentions of eunuchs in the book of Isaiah. The first of these, 39:7, concludes First Isaiah and our verse opens Third Isaiah, thus together bracketing Second Isaiah. We may suspect that the claim of 56:3–5 is to readmit those tragic figures destined for the role of eunuch in 39:7.

Moreover, the final verse of Nehemiah (13:31) may refer to Nehemiah, who was a cup-bearer in the imperial court and may have been a eunuch, for there it is presumed that Nehemiah will not be forgotten, which may happen if there are no children. If it is the case that the dispute concerns compromisers, this is a remarkable provision with a willingness to embrace even such compromisers. It is evident in this oracle and in the mandate for "justice and righteousness" in 56:1 that this tradition *resists exclusion*. In the contemporary life of the church, it may be worth noting that the principle of inclusion applies primarily to those who are viewed by others as ritually unacceptable. In contemporary interpretation, therefore, we must at least ponder whether our counterpart to those ancient eunuchs are homosexuals, now the object of great exclusionary energy.

56:6 **And the foreigners who join themselves to the LORD,**
to minister to him, to love the name of the LORD,
and to be his servants,
all who keep the sabbath, and do not profane it,
and hold fast my covenant—

> ⁷these I will bring to my holy mountain,
>   and make them joyful in my house of prayer;
>   their burnt offerings and their sacrifices
>   will be accepted on my altar;
>   for my house shall be called a house of prayer
>   for all peoples.
> ⁸Thus says the Lord GOD,
>   who gathers the outcasts of Israel,
>   I will gather others to them
>   besides those already gathered.

As the eunuchs in verses 3–5 are a contested category for inclusion in this emerging community of torah obedience, so now foreigners are a second parallel category. In the initial statement of anticipated exclusion in verse 5, foreigners are treated in a fashion parallel to eunuchs, as candidates for exclusion. And indeed, the same torah traditions that exclude eunuchs insist that at least some foreigners must be excluded (Deut. 23:2–8). As the community of Jews became more attentive to its *ethnic* constitution, the likelihood of excluding "outsiders" is sure to grow. (In another context, notice now the secular drive in the United States to "gain control of our borders" and to exclude "illegal aliens.")

The oracle, however, will no more give in to such exclusion of foreigners than it will concerning eunuchs. Thus the oracle for a second time resists what must have been the easier, more popular option. The inclusiveness pertains not randomly to any foreigner but to those with deep Yahwistic intention. The two requirements of eunuchs in verse 5—covenant keeping and sabbath practice—are here reiterated (v. 6a). But prior to those criteria, verse 6a identifies four terms that suggest an effective commitment to Yahweh more elemental than political affiliation. These are they who "*join . . . to minister . . . to love the name . . . to be servants.*" The foreigners, with a whole and full heart, are drawn to Yahweh.

And they are welcome (v. 7; see Eph. 2:12–13)! As Yahweh is the agent of the active verbs pertaining to the eunuchs in verse 5—"I will give . . . I will give"—so here Yahweh is the subject of the active verbs—"I will bring . . . I will make joyful." This is Yahweh's doing. Yahweh is the recruiter and the welcome committee. As a consequence, the foreigners are inducted into the full life of the worshiping community, participating in both prayer and sacrifice. *They are welcome!* They are welcome because Yahweh intends that "my holy mountain . . . my house of prayer" (v. 7) will be for all people who want to join, all who love, all who obey. (See Matt. 21:13; Mark 11:17; Rom. 8:15; Gal. 4:6.) The oracle intends to overcome every fearful limitation that is thinkable, that constitutes a human response of defensiveness and fearfulness, every fearful limitation that is not grounded in Yahweh's own purposes and commands. This is a mandate to open faith to "Gentiles."

The ground for such radical inclusiveness is given in the summary oracle of verse 8, now introduced with a special formula, so that the urging is heard as from Yahweh's own mouth. Three times in this verse, the verb *gather* is sounded: "who gathers . . . I will gather . . . those already gathered." The term refers to an end of exile and addresses the "outcasts," the ones expelled. The verb, in context, is Yahweh's most defining verb, Yahweh's most characteristic activity. Yahweh is an *exile-ender* who intends homecoming for all peoples, a homecoming to torah, to community, to communion with Yahweh. The oracle is a remarkable assurance in that ancient world of displaced persons.

It is, moreover, a remarkable evangelical disclosure of Yahweh in our contemporary world, saturated as it is with refugees. Only the most visible of refugees make our television coverage, but they are present among us every day. Indeed, the production of fugitives is not, in ancient times or now, happenstance. It is rather a sure by-product of large, imperial combines of money and power. Yahweh's self-disclosure is set against such a systemic production of exiles. The God who gathers intends homecoming for all. The old gospel hymn is addressed everywhere to the displaced: "Softly and tenderly, Jesus is calling: 'Come home, come home.'"

56:9 **All you wild animals,**
    all you wild animals in the forest, come to devour!
¹⁰ **Israel's sentinels are blind,**
    they are all without knowledge;
  they are all silent dogs
    that cannot bark;
  dreaming, lying down,
    loving to slumber.
¹¹ **The dogs have a mighty appetite;** — *by power*
    they never have enough.
  The shepherds also have no understanding;
    they have all turned to their own way,
    to their own gain, one and all.
¹² **"Come," they say, "let us get wine;**
    let us fill ourselves with strong drink.
  And tomorrow will be like today,
    great beyond measure."

These verses of fierce threat are an abrupt surprise after the wondrous consolation and assurance of the preceding. Perhaps they do not belong in any intimate way to the preceding. But if their placement here is intentional, then we may conclude that the insistence upon inclusiveness we have just observed in the foregoing is not uncontested.

These verses are an attack upon the leaders of the community ("sentinels, shepherds") cast in the traditional language of prophetic speech of judgment. The oracle begins with a most threatening sentence (v. 9). It summons "wild animals . . . wild animals," occupants of the untamed to come into the community and devour. The invited invader is unnamed, but it is conventional that the one who "devours" is an occupying army. In this assertion, Yahweh is willing to hand over the community to an outside threat, so degenerate and unbearable has it become. This, of course, is a replication of the earlier "handovers" in the Isaiah tradition to Assyria (10:5–6) and Babylon (47:6a).

The indictment—as ground for the preceding sentence—consists in the remaining verses of the oracle (vv. 10–12). The sentinels are those expected to be alert and on guard in order to warn and protect and instruct (vv. 10–11a). But those who lead in Judaism are ineffective. They are blind and do not see danger. They are silent and do not speak a warning or sound an alarm. They are dumb and neglectful and have abdicated, putting the entire community at risk. The sentinels are portrayed in the figure of "dogs": who are silent and do not bark to sound alarm; who sleep excessively and are inattentive to danger; who eat voraciously, looking after their own appetites while neglecting the community.

The indictment continues in verses 11b–12 with reference to "shepherds." This also is a reference to leadership in a parallel to "sentinels" and has close parallels to the self-serving shepherds of Ezekiel 34. Here the metaphor is not as suggestive as is "dogs" for sentinels. The shepherds are self-serving and self-indulgent. They look only after themselves; thus they are public officials who use their public trust for private advantage and amass personal wealth. (The phrasing could hardly be more contemporary!)

The self-promotion of verse 11b is matched by the self-indulgence of verse 12 that concerns pursuit of alcohol, which functions here as an image for a self-indulgent, neglectful, uncaring life. The quotation attributed to the shepherds is something like a drinking song (See Amos 4:1f.). But the closer parallel to rhetoric of self-indulgence is in Amos 6:4–6:

> Alas for those who lie on beds of ivory,
>   and lounge on their couches,

> and eat lambs from the flock,
>> and calves from the stall;
> who sing idle songs to the sound of the harp,
>> and like David improvise on instruments of music;
> who drink wine from bowls,
>> and anoint themselves with the finest oils,
>> but are not grieved over the ruin of Joseph!

The leaders do not care and do not notice. They imagine that nothing is at stake today, so why bother!

The community of Judaism is an odd community endlessly at risk. It will not be sustained over time unless there are attentive leaders who value the odd identity and the sustaining practices to be done daily. It is not different in the church that always suffers through self-promoting, self-indulgent leadership.

The force of these verses is intense. Such intensity is evident in the odd juxtaposition to verses 3–8. The community there is affirmed in its oddity; here it is at risk because God will not preserve a community of indifference. This intensity is reinforced by the much reiterated "all" to make everything sweeping and comprehensive:

> Thus in the sentence:
>> *all* you wild animals, *all* you wild animals (v. 9).
> And in the indictment:
>> *all* without knowledge;
>> *all* silent dogs;
>> *all* turned to their own way (vv. 10–11).

All are summoned; all have failed. No exceptions! And therefore no hope. The urgent demand for inclusiveness is cynically nullified by a leadership deeply flawed and failed.

CHOOSING FOR PEACE
OR AGAINST YAHWEH
57:1–13

This difficult passage reflects the deep and defining division in the community of emerging Judaism, with its clear contrast between "the righteous," who are intensely committed to Yahweh, and their negative counterparts, who readily compromise faith in Yahweh. Or at least that is the way the contrast is set up by "the righteous" who are given voice in this poem. This poem is not clear in its meaning at many points. We can, in any case, observe the structural arrangement of the whole; the large central section of this poem is occupied with a condemnation of the wicked, a condemnation cast as a characteristic speech of judgment (vv. 3–13a). This long poetic unit is bracketed by two affirmations of the loyal element in the community that trusts Yahweh (vv. 1–2, 13b).

57:1 **The righteous perish,**
   and no one takes it to heart;
the devout are taken away,
   while no one understands.
For the righteous are taken away from calamity,
 2   **and they enter into peace;**
those who walk uprightly
   will rest on their couches.

These verses articulate a benediction upon the righteous, the God-fearers who cleave to Yahweh but who are in deep jeopardy, presumably under assault by others in the community who ruthlessly destroy. Paul Hanson may be correct to term these verses a "requiem" (*Isaiah 40–66*, 198). Although the righteous may die, they are carried to peace and to rest. The poetry surely has no notion of life-after-death but only offers an assurance that the righteous are kept peaceably and safely, even though large threats are operative. Calvin, using Luther's "fortuitous" death as an example, suggests that God may "snatch" the righteous to death just to save them from impending trouble (*Isaiah* IV, 197). In any case, the lament that grieves for the righteous expresses an assurance as well. The faith of the righteous does not go unnoticed or unvalued.

57:3 **But as for you, come here,**
   you children of a sorceress,
   you offspring of an adulterer and a whore.
 4 **Whom are you mocking?**
   Against whom do you open your mouth wide
   and stick out your tongue?
 Are you not children of transgression,
   the offspring of deceit—
 5 **you that burn with lust among the oaks,**
   under every green tree;
 you that slaughter your children in the valleys,
   under the clefts of the rocks?
 6 **Among the smooth stones of the valley is your portion;**

they, they, are your lot;
   to them you have poured out a drink offering,
     you have brought a grain offering.
     Shall I be appeased for these things?
7 Upon a high and lofty mountain
     you have set your bed,
     and there you went up to offer sacrifice.
8 Behind the door and the doorpost
     you have set up your symbol;
   for, in deserting me, you have uncovered your bed,
     you have gone up to it,
     you have made it wide;
   and you have made a bargain for yourself with them,
     you have loved their bed,
     you have gazed on their nakedness.
9 You journeyed to Molech with oil,
     and multiplied your perfumes;
   you sent your envoys far away,
     and sent down even to Sheol.
10 You grew weary from your many wanderings,
     but you did not say, "It is useless."
   You found your desire rekindled,
     and so you did not weaken.

11 Whom did you dread and fear
     so that you lied,
   and did not remember me
     or give me a thought?
   Have I not kept silent and closed my eyes,
     and so you do not fear me?
12 I will concede your righteousness and your works,
     but they will not help you.
13a When you cry out, let your collection of idols deliver you!
     The wind will carry them off,
     a breath will take them away.

This long poetic section abruptly changes the subject. Whereas verses 1–2 concerned the righteous, now the address is disjunctive: "But you," an address to the unrighteous. What follows is a long accusation against that element of the community for whom this poet (and his party) have no sympathy. Although we are not able to identify every facet of this sweeping indictment, suffice it to say that this group is accused of idolatry and religious disloyalty that compromise loyalty to Yahweh. Paul

Hanson characterizes the situation as it would have been viewed by the poet, who saw

> a chaotic situation in which people, in their drift away from the God of compassion, hate justice, are indiscriminately attaching themselves to degrading cults that promise immediate satisfaction free of moral obligations.

This element of the community, whom we may take as "the wicked," is summoned by a triad of polemical terms: children of a sorceress, offspring of adulterers, a whore (v. 3). The language is intense and extreme. The rhetorical question of verse 4a takes as its answer, *Yahweh*. It is Yahweh who has been mocked. The second question of verses 4b–5 suggests a series of unorthodox cultic activities. This is followed by verses 6–7a, which identify a number of cultic practices bespeaking allegiances to loyalties other than Yahweh. The question of verse 6a asks if Yahweh should be comforted by these gestures or perhaps moved by them. The indictment continues in verses 7–9 with a series of religious activities that are unacceptable in standard Yahwism.

We are not able to be precise about these alleged activities, even though the commentaries provide thorough exposition. For our purposes, it is enough to suggest a rich array of alternative religious practices, all of which are here assessed as departures from the tried and true, already mandated ways of Yahwism. Clearly, the particularities of these ancient practices are not important to us. What matters is the normative faith of this community as Yahweh is known in the covenantal requirements of Moses. This "religion of requirements" is clear, conventional, well-known, and not very novel. The lack of novelty plus its rigor no doubt invited people to seek alternatives. In our time, the alternatives to demanding, rigorous Yahwism may be evidenced in a variety of new gnosticisms, some forms of careless mysticism, and "new age" options that lack the summons to discipline so central to covenantal torah faith.

The practices themselves are roundly condemned. Worse than that, however, is the recognition that such religious adventurism is exhausting and unsatisfying (v. 10). Having tried such alternatives, Israel had an opportunity to reject them. But the desire for the illicit is endlessly evocative, and so Israel remained stubbornly with the unorthodox practices, even when they clearly produced nothing positive.

The rhetoric of this strident denunciation moves toward its climax in verses 11–13a. Verse 11 confronts "the wicked" with two probing questions: "Whom did you dread and fear . . . ? Have I not kept silent . . . ?"

But the questions are in fact weighty, accusatory conclusions: You dreaded the idols and not Yahweh. Yahweh has not been silent and does not deserve such rejection. Nevertheless, Yahweh has been endlessly rejected: "You lied and did not remember me or give me a thought. . . . You do not fear me."

This series of negatives indicates in a backhanded way what serious faith in Yahweh would look like. The question is in fact a probe into the curious religious conduct of the wicked. The wicked must have been much impressed by or much intimidated by someone or something to cause such a profound, futile, mindless rejection of Yahweh. Such a theological decision to reject Yahweh is absurd, but the wicked have made just that choice. No doubt, the double question of verse 11 is not in the interest of securing information. Indeed, there is nobody else available who could impress and intimidate those who seek Yahweh. The question is asked only to make unmistakably clear the absurdity of what the wicked have decided.

The question of verse 11 receives no serious answer. In place of an answer, verse 12 proceeds with sharp irony. Yahweh will concede the righteousness of the wicked; but such righteousness, a thin, phony righteousness lacking in substance, will be of no help. Compared with the genuinely righteous of verses 1–2, there is no loyalty to Yahweh and no ethical substance that will yield any future. But if the "works of righteousness" fail because they are thin and unreliable, then the alternative is to petition the idols, the ones who constitute the religious efforts of verses 3–10. The wicked must turn to their idols because they are, for the wicked, the last resort. But their actions are to no avail! The idols are nothing and have no power to save. The poet culminates the argument with two terms to characterize the vacuousness of this alternative hope: The idols are carried by wind; the idols are taken by vanity. The point of the rhetoric is to portray the situation of the wicked as completely hopeless, without access or ground for appeal to Yahweh. Yahweh has been rejected by this party in the community, and now the consequence is unavoidable.

**57:13b But whoever takes refuge in me shall possess the land
        and inherit my holy mountain.**

This verse returns to the accents of verses 1–2 and is an abrupt contrast to the harshness of verses 3–13a. Those who rely upon Yahweh are the righteous, unlike the wicked who rely on everything except Yahweh. The promises of Yahweh are made to the righteous, who are to be the recipients of all of Yahweh's good gifts, here especially the land and all the well-being implicit in it. Thus this community has hopes congruent with the oldest promises made to Abraham.

The abrupt movement from *affirmation* (vv. 1–2) to *denunciation* (vv. 3–13a) then to *affirmation* (v. 13b) makes clear in the literature the abrasion that must have been intense in the actual community itself. We may imagine the poet as a serious party to the deep conflicts within the community. Thus postexilic Isaiah voices and reflects a certain perspective on the future of Judaism that is deeply contested. This poetry has no doubt that an unorthodox community uncommitted to the Torah of Yahweh cannot succeed.

Whether the wicked are in fact addressed in this poetry is an important question. It is difficult to imagine "the wicked" coming around for such a reprimand. It may be possible, alternatively, to suggest that the poetry is in fact aimed precisely at the righteous community. One strategy for embracing and enhancing the torah-based community is to imagine the destiny of the religiously careless and indifferent. Thus, if this speech is not *real speech*, it may have as its audience the righteous who are thereby confirmed in their position of faith. If the poetry is "over the heads" of the present "wicked," then the future of the poem is not unlike speeches of disjunction in exilic Isaiah that eventually summon the faithful to fresh trust. If such a rhetorical function is credible, then we can prepare for the promissory notice in verses 14–21. In any case, the speech of judgment (vv. 3–13a) and the speech of affirmation (vv. 1–2, 13b) constitute two sides of a common insistence that Judaism must cleave only to Yahweh. Such a commitment begets life. Any other propensity begets deep distortion and misery.

ONCE MORE THE GIFT OF COMFORT
57:14–21

After the abrasive assault on transgressors in verses 3–13a, the tone of address changes abruptly in verses 14–21, the kind of abrupt change that is characteristic of the Isaiah tradition. Indeed, the juxtaposition of *judgment* (vv. 3–13a) and *assurance* (vv. 14–19) is structurally decisive in the tradition that takes judgment with great seriousness but repeatedly asserts hope-after-judgment.

57:14 **It shall be said,**
    "Build up, build up, prepare the way,
      remove every obstruction from my people's way."

This one verse of assertion reiterates the metaphor of "highway" as an image for homecoming (see 35:8; 40:3; 49:11). Because it is likely that this chapter is no longer concerned with the actual return from exile, it is probable that the reused imagery here pertains to the path of torah that will have no "obstructions" that hinder full obedience. In any case, the imagery bespeaks glad restoration of the community at the behest of Yahweh.

57:15 **For thus says the high and lofty one**
      who inhabits eternity, whose name is Holy:
   I dwell in the high and holy place,
      and also with those who are contrite and humble in spirit.
   to revive the spirit of the humble,
      and to revive the heart of the contrite.

This simple, familiar verse asserts the character and identity of Yahweh in a peculiarly nuanced way. Here speaks the one who is *high* and *holy*, who is elevated in regal splendor beyond circumstance. The imagery recalls the vision of 6:1–8, a vision of massive, unapproachable sovereignty. The wonder of this proclamation, pertinent to the larger horizon of biblical faith, is that this one *high and holy* is the one who "dwells" with the *lowly and crushed*. These latter terms do not refer to guilt, penitence, or remorse over sin or "theological" humility. They refer, rather, to those abused and exploited, who are endlessly taken advantage of and rendered powerless. In context, the phrasing surely refers to the marginalized Jews for whom and from whom the poet speaks.

The juxtaposition of *high-holy* and *lowly-crushed* is at the core of Yahweh's self-disclosure, the mystery of God who is the subject of biblical faith. The juxtaposition is not to be reduced to speculative categories like "transcendence" and "immanence," but is a royal metaphor for the great sovereign who from the exalted throne room extends the royal presence and the royal concern to the most lowly and undeserving of subjects. It is this characteristic move that dominates Yahweh's way with Israel. Thus, already in the Exodus narrative, this same God says to the slaves, that is, to the lowly and crushed:

"I have observed the misery of my people who are in Egypt; I have heard their cry on account of their taskmasters. Indeed, I know their sufferings, and I have come down to deliver them from the Egyptians, and to bring them up out of that land to a good and broad land, a land flowing with milk and honey" (Exod. 3:7–8).

The "coming down" marks Yahweh as one who is engaged for, in solidarity with, subjected to the circumstance of the lowly and crushed.

This same juxtaposition, moreover, is the story line of Jesus of Nazareth, who characteristically was in the presence of the broken and the powerless. In Christian interpretation, it is the cross that is the full epitome of Jesus' solidarity with the powerless when he "emptied himself" in an obedience unto death (Phil. 2:7–8). The point is well said in Luther's carol:

> From heaven above to earth I come
> To bear good news to every home;
> Glad tidings of great joy I bring,
> Whereof I now will say and sing.

This juxtaposition, in the end, is articulated in classic Christian orthodoxy wherein the creed confesses Jesus to be "truly God" (= high-holy) and "truly human" (= lowly-crushed), a formulation that insists that Jesus' (and therefore God's) sojourn with the lowly in no way detracts from or compromises the claim of high and holy.

The conclusion of verse 15, however, not only characterizes the capacity of Yahweh to be with the lowly in complete sovereign splendor, but also moves beyond such a self-announcement to assert the purpose of such solidarity. It is to *revive*. The term is used twice, a causative form of the term "life"—thus, "to enliven," "to cause life." The object of this verb is peculiarly the *lowly-crushed* of the preceding phrase. This high-holy one acts to give life to those who have had their life squeezed out of them. Thus the creator God so celebrated in exilic Isaiah now does the work of revitalization among the returnees from exile who just barely have energy for life.

57:16 **For I will not continually accuse,**
      nor will I always be angry;
    for then the spirits would grow faint before me,
      even the souls that I have made.
   [17] **Because of their wicked covetousness I was angry;**
      I struck them, I hid and was angry;
      but they kept turning back to their own ways.
   [18] **I have seen their ways, but I will heal them;**
      I will lead them and repay them with comfort,
      creating for their mourners the fruit of the lips.
   [19] **Peace, peace, to the far and the near, says the LORD;**
      and I will heal them.

These verses develop the marvelous announcement of verse 15. They provide a theological account of the entire sequence of Yahweh's dealing with Israel in the grid of the Isaiah tradition. The *good news*, as basis for what follows, is the assurance that Yahweh, who has been angry with Israel, will not stay angry (v. 16). This verse has close parallels to Psalm 103:9–10 where it is asserted:

> He will not always accuse,
> 　　nor will he keep his anger forever.
> He does not deal with us according to our sins,
> 　　nor repay us according to our iniquities.

Yahweh's anger is limited by Yahweh's identity as merciful and gracious (Psalm 103:8), inclined toward compassion (Psalm 103:13). Verse 16 is likely an old, familiar liturgical formula that in our present passage is brought close to the bereft community of returnees. It is candidly admitted that Yahweh has been angry and that the anger took the form of litigation against Israel—that is, accusation in court that Israel has violated covenant and deserves to be severely punished. The imagery of litigation is already present in 1:2, 18–20 and elsewhere in the tradition. But the *high-holy* one makes it clear that enduring anger on Yahweh's part will cause a diminishment of God's way in creation. Thus, in the interest of "the souls that I have made," Yahweh's anger is curbed.

In verses 17–19 we may identify a three-step sequence of Yahweh with Israel, a sequence that follows the interpretive inclination of the Isaiah tradition (as in 47:6):

1. "I was angry" . . . the judgment of preexilic Isaiah (v. 17);
2. "I will heal" . . . the rescue of exilic Isaiah (v. 18);
3. "Peace, peace" . . . the presence to contemporary postexilic Isaiah (v. 19).

We may consider the three moments in turn:

1. The destructive anger of Yahweh that caused exile is presented as fully justified (v. 17). Yahweh, who insists on torah obedience, had to deal with a people bent on destructive acquisitiveness, that is, violent pursuit of gain. Such a way of living is deeply opposed to Yahweh's intention, sure to evoke Yahweh's hostility. The response of Yahweh was anger (a term used twice), plus hiddenness (absence), plus striking (violent punishment at the hands of Babylon). The point of verse 17 is to indicate that Yahweh was

completely justified in destructive action, a justification reinforced by the fact that Israel kept going in its autonomous, headstrong way. Israel refused Yahweh, and Yahweh will not tolerate such recalcitrance.

2. The utterance of Yahweh pivots on the adversative conjunction "but": I will heal; I will lead; I will restore with comfort (v. 18).

The ground for the "but" that reverses field is perhaps given as awareness already available in verse 16. More anger will destroy. But behind such a pragmatic reason, the larger reason is Yahweh's own inner life. In the end, Yahweh is not a God who punishes and destroys but a God who wills life for the people of God:

> I will not execute my fierce anger;
>   I will not again destroy Ephraim;
> for I am God and no mortal,
>   the Holy One in your midst,
>   and I will not come in wrath. (Hos. 11:9; see Ezek. 18:32)

The turn of verse 18 speaks the character of Yahweh and Yahweh's own disposition toward Judah.

The three verbs concern full restoration. Yahweh is a healer and has been so for Israel since Exodus 15:26. Yahweh wills and empowers well-being. The verb "lead" recalls the ancient protection of Israel in the wilderness (see Deut. 1:31; 8:3–4) and the more immediate protection and sustenance of returning exiles (see Isa. 40:11). The three verbs reiterate the gift of "comfort," the theme term of exilic Isaiah (40:1). The cumulative effect of the three terms is a fully guaranteed well-being because of the attentive presence and powerful resolve of Yahweh. The cluster of terms calls to mind the complete reliance upon Yahweh voiced in Psalm 23, wherein a vulnerable sojourn is completely safe, protected, fed, nurtured, led, and guarded.

The contrast between the anger of verse 17 and the attentiveness of verse 18 nicely summarizes the self-understanding of Judaism, a people oppressed in exile and now given well-being at home. The juxtaposition, however, tells more than Judaism's journey. It reports Yahweh's own character, already voiced to Moses in Exodus 34:6–7, a God "merciful and gracious" but one who "visits iniquity." In our poem, iniquity is visited upon the community through exile (v. 17), but now it is a time of "mercy and grace."

3. The move from anger (v. 17) to healing (v. 18) leads to a condition of wholeness now promised and yearned for in the postexilic community

(v. 19). The double use of *shalom* ("peace, peace") is a complete contrast to *lowly-crushed* for the Jews and a total contrast to anger from Yahweh. *Shalom* is not only desired by Judaism but it is assured by Yahweh. It is, moreover, assured to those "far and near," that is, the Jews already gathered home from exile (see 58:9), but also those Jews still scattered in the diaspora. *Shalom* is now Yahweh's unqualified intention for all of Yahweh's people, a state of well-being that is the result of heal-lead-repay with comfort. It is a new gift given by the one *high and holy*, who aims at revival of a *lowly-crushed* community.

57:20 **But the wicked are like the tossing sea**
      that cannot keep still;
      its waters toss up mire and mud.
    ²¹ **There is no peace, says my God, for the wicked.**

For all of that, the deep conflict in the community promised *shalom* is never far from the horizon of the poet. The gift of *shalom* from Yahweh is not cheap or easy or automatic. As a result, it is not for everyone, but for those who no longer "keep turning back to their own ways" (v. 17). There were still those, evidently, who acted in resistant autonomy, who mocked the disciplines of torah, of covenant, and of sabbath (see 56:4, 6). Those are outside the offer of *shalom*. Thus, as the heavy indictment of transgressors in verses 3–13a offers a glance at the "righteous" "who take refuge" in Yahweh (vv. 1–2, 13b), so here the exuberant celebration of *shalom* for the lowly and crushed who are revived offers an acknowledgment of those excluded. In each case, the dominant theme requires an understated counterpart of the opposite number. We must not imagine that *shalom* is an easy, free, unconditional offer. Like everything else in emerging Judaism, the gift of *shalom* is powerfully contested and disputatious. "The wicked," the ones catalogued in verses 3–13a, are like the endlessly churning waters of chaos—ruthless, disordered, defiant, and destructive. They keep unsettling and disturbing and threatening what tenuous order there is. Thus, even the gift of *shalom* is a gift that takes into account a profoundly divided community.

If we take the declaration of *shalom* together with the image of surging, defiant, and recalcitrant waters, we may connect this marvelous text to the narrative of Jesus in Mark 4:35–41. In that parabolic narrative, Jesus and his disciples are "swamped" by the surging waters of the chaotic sea. Jesus addresses the waters: "*Shalom!*" And the waters subside in obedience to Jesus. But the *shalom* enacted is only for the sake of the disciples who are in the same boat with Jesus. The narrative may be a suggestive parallel to our text. The lordly assurance of *shalom* given in our text provides a place of safety and well-being for the community of the faithful. All around are the surging waters of destruction. Only Yahweh's promise makes safe!

FAITH IN ITS DEMAND
58:1–14

This poem is a long, insistent, concrete advocacy addressed to a community in deep conflict. The poet urges a strong vision of the future of the community that is ethically demanding, that requires policies and actions of a neighborly kind that are congruent with its profession of Yahweh.

58:1 **Shout out, do not hold back!**
   Lift up your voice like a trumpet!
 Announce to my people their rebellion,
   to the house of Jacob their sins.
 ² **Yet day after day they seek me**
   and delight to know my ways,
 as if they were a nation that practiced righteousness
   and did not forsake the ordinance of their God;
 they ask of me righteous judgments,
   they delight to draw near to God.

These two verses establish the core problem of the community, namely, a hypocritical gap between the *actual conduct of the community* and the *intention of the community expressed in worship*. There is, asserts the poem, a deep, dishonest variance between the two, a variance that must be overcome if there is to be well-being in the community.

   In the first two lines of the poem, a speaker—presumably the poet as messenger—is summoned and authorized to speak. Although this may be only a rhetorical flourish, the imperative coupled with the image of the trumpet indicates that what is to be said is a life-or-death matter, or at least so the poet intends (see Hos. 8:1).

   The primal announcement that is urged upon the speaker is a declaration of the sin of the community expressed in two characteristic terms—"rebellion" and "sin," or "transgression"—that is, life organized in resistance to the purposes of Yahweh. We are given no particulars in this verse about Israel's affront against Yahweh. It becomes clear in later verses that the violation of Yahweh's intent concerns a lack of a neighborly economics.

The issue of hypocrisy only becomes clear in verse 2, which is stated as a disjunction from verse 1: "Yet." Though there is sin and rebellion, this community of faith *delights* in worship. The term "delight" is used twice in this verse, matched with the verbs "seek" and "draw near," both signifying worship. In an echo of Amos 4:4–5, the poet chides his contemporaries who have turned worship into an act of self-indulgence void of ethical content. They "enjoy" worship! Worship, if faithful to Yahweh, is a focus upon Yahweh's concerns known in the Torah. This present worship, however, only mouths a concern for Yahweh but in fact is a fakery untouched by the true character of Yahweh. We may imagine this is feel-good worship that violates the true intention of Yahweh.

58:3 **"Why do we fast, but you do not see?**
    Why humble ourselves, but you do not notice?"
  Look, you serve your own interest on your fast day,
    and oppress all your workers.
 4 **Look, you fast only to quarrel and to fight**
    and to strike with a wicked fist.
  Such fasting as you do today
    will not make your voice heard on high.
 5 **Is such the fast that I choose,**
    a day to humble oneself?
  Is it to bow down the head like a bulrush,
    and to lie in sackcloth and ashes?
  Will you call this a fast,
    a day acceptable to the LORD?

With the statement of the basic contradiction, these verses now spell out the fraudulent liturgy of the community. These verses attribute a complaint to Israel (v. 3a), a double summons to "notice" (vv. 3b–4a), and a conclusion (v. 4b). The lament placed in the mouth of worshiping Judaism is in fact an ironic statement that mocks. The complaint attributed to contemporary worshipers is that they dutifully fast and humble themselves, but their acts of devotion are unnoticed by Yahweh. The notice of Yahweh, however, is the only reason they do such acts. That is, worship is to call Yahweh's attention to themselves. Implicit in this alleged prayer is the accusation—here indirectly admitted—that the purpose of worship is to gain advantage. That is, worship has become instrumental, as a means to an end, no longer an end in itself. Yahweh is thus *useful* for advantage. The alleged prayer that is in fact accusation plays upon the great question asked of Job: "Does Job fear God for nothing?" that is, without hope of gain (Job

1:9). Whatever may be said of the figure of Job, here worship is seen to be calculated and manipulative, that is, no worship at all. Moreover, it does not work to produce the intended effect. Of course, such calculating worship never "works" with God!

The alleged protest against Yahweh for not noticing is followed by two indictments introduced by the command "Look." The religious act of fasting, which can indeed be a serious act of faith, is here only a calculation. Moreover, even while this public piety is practiced (even as we speak!), laborers are oppressed. The final line of verse 3 lets us see both the general argument of the poem and the actual substance of the "rebellion," the "transgression," of verse 1. This is worship without *public ethics* that pertains to *economics*. Worship not congruent with humane economic practice is bad worship! Calvin explicates with more precision:

> Not only do many people fast in order to atone for their cheating and robberies, and to plunder more freely, but even that, during the time of the fast, they may have greater leisure for examining their accounts, perusing documents, and calculating usury, and contriving methods by which they may lay hold on the property of their debtors.

More than that, those who worship are quarrelsome and contentious precisely because they are focused on themselves, assuring that there will be no self-transcending generosity. The verdict of verse 4b derives from the foregoing. Such worship gives no access to God, because the God of Judaism is not open to instrumental, calculated manipulation. This worship embodies a complete distortion of Yahweh and eventuates in a complete distortion of social relationships.

58:6 **Is not this the fast that I choose;**
       to loose the bonds of injustice,
       to undo the thongs of the yoke,
     to let the oppressed go free,
       and to break every yoke?
     ⁷**Is it not to share your bread with the hungry,**
       and bring the homeless poor into your house;
     when you see the naked, to cover them,
       and not to hide yourself from your own kin?
     ⁸**Then your light shall break forth like the dawn,**
       and your healing shall spring up quickly;
     your vindicator shall go before you,
       the glory of the LORD shall be your rear guard.

⁹ᵃ **Then you shall call, and the LORD will answer;**
    you shall cry for help, and he will say, Here I am.

If such calculated, manipulative, self-serving religious discipline as that of verses 3–4 does not "work," what will? The answer is given in these verses. The poet plays on the word "fast," but transposes the notion of *disciplined piety* into an act of *neighborly affirmation*. These verses present a clear, radical statement of social ethics that is at the heart of Judaism, derivative from older covenantal-prophetic tradition. The God of Judaism is not a God who likes to be flattered in a more or less passive routine of worship; this God is out working the neighborhood and wants all adherents doing the same.

The "fast" concerns *injustice*, that is, socioeconomic practices that deny some members of the community access to resources necessary for life. The lead term "injustice," echoing the theme of 56:1–2, refers to all distorted social relations and is developed in more detail in verses 6b–7. The action commended here is a "true fast"; it requires doing without, denying self, and giving things up in obedience. The neighborly actions urged here require a decision against self-indulgence, thus a mode of fasting. The double use of the term "yoke" likely refers to disproportionate indebtedness that placed some members of the community "in hock" to others. To "undo" and "let go free" means to cancel paralyzing debts, thus anticipating the allusion to the practice of Jubilee in 61:1–4.

Verse 7 becomes more specific in the requirements of this neighborly fast: (a) shared bread, (b) shared houses, and (c) shared clothing. That is, share the elemental resources necessary to life. (In Matthew 6:25, these same elements are the fundamental references for anxiety.) This neighborly fast is in the gift of the community to share these resources with all members. The final phrase of verse 7 is especially compelling. It refers to the hungry and needy as "your own kin," that is, a part of one's family with whom one inalienably belongs. The devotion Yahweh desires is solidarity that troubles with the elemental requirements of economic life for every member of the community.

It may of course be asked if this imperative intends face-to-face charity or refers to public policy. To raise that question, however, is to miss the urgency of the mandate. The triad of requirements speaks against a selfish preoccupation with one's own needs and passions; that is, the imperatives speak against individualism in order to assert that we are "members one of another." My own judgment is that the imperatives challenge our current passion for "privatization," a social ideology and strategy that denies our mutual obligation to all members of the community. If this mandate be taken seriously, then it concerns all kinds of acts of solidarity, both charity and public policy. It is to be noticed, moreover, that in our own time, the most zealous adherents of privatization also tend to exhibit loud devotion to "religion," but it is a religion that completely misconstrues the social solidarity implicit in covenantal faith. As this text deeply contradicts such social practice in that ancient time, so it deeply challenges the temptations of an affluent, postindustrial society short on neighborliness.

Verses 6–7 state the nonnegotiable ethical mandates that belong to worship of this God of Israel. The mandates of these verses are the condition for what follows; an implicit "if" is followed in verses 8–9 by a double, explicit "then." Thus the "if" of bread-housing-clothing is connected to the double "then," as *condition* to *consequence*. The first "then" of verse 8 anticipates immense well-being, here identified as "light" (see 61:6ff.), healing, protection ("vindication"), and safety. Everything good will be given that is hoped for from Yahweh. Here reference should be made back to the alleged prayer of verse 3. What the worshipers hoped for was to be seen by Yahweh, to be noticed. The "then" of verse 8 is an assurance of being seen, noticed, cared for by Yahweh. Yahweh will be the protector who guarantees well-being and safety (see 52:12). But notice, it is a "then" linked to an "if." Unless there is an undoing of injustice, unless there is neighborly sharing, there will be no light or healing from Yahweh.

We may take this conditionality of "if-then" as a hard-nosed, "legalistic" requirement, that is, as a "work." But we may also regard this conditionality as a shrewd assessment about how "social security" really works. Well-being comes only in a community of neighbors. The alternative here implicitly warned against is selfishness, greed, indifference, and exploitation that are anticommunity. These latter practices are never the bases for a viable life in the world, and can never be.

A second "then" of consequence is offered in verse 9, reinforcing the ethical conditionality of verses 6–7. Again the "if" is implied for these verses. The "then" is full communion with Yahweh based on Yahweh's attentiveness and availability. Yahweh's presence, attentiveness, and availability are exactly what is hoped for in verse 3 but are not given there. The poem recognizes that the deepest religious need and craving is the reassuring presence of Yahweh, an assurance that in risk and danger we are not alone. This assurance here is a "then" premised on the threefold "if" of bread-housing-clothing in verses 6–7. This "then" is on the way to the hope-filled assurance of Isaiah 65:25. In that wondrous statement of extremity, it is asserted that Yahweh hears *before Israel calls*, so attentive is

Yahweh. But that is not yet given here. What is affirmed here is that communion with Yahweh is linked to *neighborly attentiveness*. In his instruction to his disciples, Jesus makes the same linkage:

> So when you are offering your gift at the altar, if you remember that your brother or sister has something against you, leave your gift there before the altar and go; first be reconciled to your brother or sister, and then come and offer your gift (Matt. 5:23–24).

The linkage is missed by the voices in verse 3 who both *worship* and *oppress.* Here in verse 9, however, is a genuine alternative—authentic communion.

58:9b **If you remove the yoke from among you,**
> **the pointing of the finger, the speaking of evil,**
> [10] **if you offer your food to the hungry**
> > **and satisfy the needs of the afflicted,**
> **then your light shall rise in the darkness**
> > **and your gloom be like the noonday.**
> [11] **The LORD will guide you continually,**
> > **and satisfy your needs in parched places,**
> > **and make your bones strong;**
> **and you shall be like a watered garden,**
> > **like a spring of water,**
> > **whose waters never fail.**
> [12] **Your ancient ruins shall be rebuilt;**
> > **you shall raise up the foundations of many generations;**
> **you shall be called the repairer of the breach,**
> > **the restorer of streets to live in.**

In these verses we have a complete "if-then" statement of conditional assurance. The *condition* ("if") in verses 9b–10 is twofold. The first "if" consists of three elements. The first is removal of the yoke, which probably refers to heavy economic requirements hinted at in verse 3 and made explicit in verse 6. The basis of genuine communion and well-being is in the practice of a just, compassionate economics that is to be contrasted with the "yoke" of exploitation. The "pointing of the finger" and "speaking of evil" are less specific conditions to be avoided but perhaps refer to social recriminations, accusations, slander, and gossip that make neighborliness impossible. The *condition* of verse 10a, the second "if," also looks back to verses 6–7. It is that the ones addressed shall attend to the "afflicted," those humiliated, exploited, and demeaned by social practice. The offer of food is likely a broad-based offer of social resources in order to make a viable life possible. The two "ifs" here envision a social practice that is built upon genuine sharing of social power and social goods.

The "then" of verses 10b–12, which is the gift of Yahweh given in response to or on the basis of genuine sharing, begins with reference back to the "then" of verse 8. "Light" probably means communal *shalom* marked by internal prosperity and harmony and freedom from external coercion. In the context of the Isaiah tradition, it perhaps refers to freedom from imperial intervention. Reference here may usefully be made to the familiar cadences of 9:2, where "darkness" (see v. 1) refers to Assyrian oppression and "light" is the coming of a new, just, and glorious rule of David.

Light will be given by Yahweh to a community of justice and compassion. The imagery of verse 11 offers figures of *safe leadership* by Yahweh and *ample water* in an arid climate. The convergence of these two themes perhaps recalls the faithful, generous, protective leadership of Yahweh in the ancient wilderness traditions (see Exod. 17:1–7). Or closer at hand, it reflects the imagery of exilic Isaiah in the return across the desert from Babylon (Isa. 35:6–7; 41:17–20). Or, more familiarly, it echoes the assurances of Psalm 23, of a good shepherd who leads "by still waters" and who guards "in the valley of the shadow of death." Yahweh is guarantee of safe passage and an antidote to every threat.

The imagery is changed in verse 12, apparently to reflect more concretely the situation of early Judaism when, in the time of Haggai and Zechariah (520–516) or more likely the time of Ezra and Nehemiah (444?), the rebuilding of the city is required. Although the first verb may be passive ("be rebuilt"), the second verb is active: "You shall raise." The community addressed will have the energy, fortitude, and resources to rebuild—energy, fortitude, and resources that arise from genuine neighborly investment in the community. The community, as a consequence, will be renamed and reidentified as "repairer, restorer," the one who makes a new, viable community possible.

The tight structure of these verses is important. The promise of verses 10b–12 looks to complete restoration of a devastated community. But the *promise* derives from the *condition*. Restored community is not rooted primarily in bureaucracy or technology or high finance or ingenuity. It begins, rather, in noticing the neighbor in public ways—from which arises a public future.

58:13 **If you refrain from trampling the sabbath,
     from pursuing your own interests on my holy day;**

if you call the sabbath a delight
    and the holy day of the LORD honorable;
if you honor it, not going your own ways,
    serving your own interests, or pursuing your own affairs;
14 then you shall take delight in the LORD,
    and I will make you ride upon the heights of the earth;
I will feed you with the heritage of your ancestor Jacob,
    for the mouth of the LORD has spoken.

Key the
sabbath.

The implied "if-then" of verses 6–9a and the expressed "if-then" of verses 9b–12 are echoed once more in verses 13–14. The "if" of verse 13 is a summons to the focal point of obedience that expresses the quintessential identity of the community of Judaism. The public sign of a faithful identity is *sabbath*, a practice of uncommon importance in emerging Judaism. (Notice that in 56:4, 6 sabbath is the primary specific marker for admitting eunuchs and foreigners into the community.) Sabbath is the alternative to a restless, aggressive, unbridled acquisitiveness that exploits neighbor for self-gain. The ancient command provided rest for the members of the community and for all the household of the members, including workers (Deut. 5:12–15). All will rest and enjoy the abundance of creation (Exod. 20:8–11). Sabbath is a cessation of feverish anxiety and control. But the people addressed here are strangers to the sabbath. They "oppress all your workers" (v. 3) and impose a cycle of exploitation (vv. 6, 9b). That is, the disciplined act of finding life outside feverish acquisitiveness is rejected by serving one's own interests. The term "interest" concerns that in which one takes pleasure, thus self-indulgence. Sabbath is a curb on self-indulgence for the sake of the community. This "if" calls exploiters away from self to notice the needs of the community.

The "then" of verse 14 is a wonderful promise. Yahweh assures that an alternative community will delight in Yahweh. The term "delight" bespeaks a deep, erotic sense of well-being that is completely unencumbered by greed or oppressiveness and that takes Yahweh directly as true subject of well-being. This "delight" is of a piece with the anticipated community of verse 9 but goes further than the wish to be heard. As a consequence, Judah will be *successful* ("upon the heights") and *cared for* ("I will feed you"), the very things hoped for by aggressive exploiters but finally only available through obedient neighborliness. What is most desired by the folk in verses 1–4 can only be secured by the alternative practice of Yahweh's neighborliness.

The threefold "if-then" structure of this poem (vv. 5–9a, 9b–12, and

13–14) is astonishing. It introduces a *communal conditionality* into the future of Judaism that is important to notice. Such *communal conditionality* is a crucial protest against two common misperceptions. First, the rhetoric of "free grace" beguiles us into imagining that God's good presence is easily available; against this notion, the God of covenantal vision is not so easily accessible but has neighborliness as a precondition to access. Second, individual autonomy, especially in the marketplace, seems in our society to be a viable way to well-being. Against such a presupposition, this poem asserts that nothing we finally desire as human beings can be had through individual autonomy. The neighbor is not a detraction or an inconvenience but is the currency through which community with Yahweh is on offer. The lyrical quality of the poetry does not conceal the abrasive advocacy against every easy self-indulgence. The *true delight* (v. 14) does not follow from *our interests* (v. 13). Judaism is invited to give up *little interests* for the sake of *large delights.*

WAITING FOR JUSTICE
59:1–21

This long poem is filled with disjunctions and reversals of field; moreover, the subject (often given as a pronoun without a clear antecedent) is not always evident. Thus our reading is filled with ambiguity. Nonetheless, the poem reflects the conflictual situation of the community of early Judaism and the readiness of the poet to enter into severe disputation with others in the community. The disputatious style is reflective of earlier, preexilic prophets and shares with them an overriding concern for the practice of justice. The general advocacy of the poem thus is congruent with the accent on *inclusiveness* in chapter 56 and *economic justice* in chapter 58.

Israel's Failure (59:1–8)

59:1 **See, the LORD's hand is not too short to save,**
      nor his ear too dull to hear.
  ² **Rather, your iniquities have been barriers**
      between you and your God,
    and your sins have hidden his face from you
      so that he does not hear.
  ³ **For your hands are defiled with blood,**
      and your fingers with iniquity;

your lips have spoken lies,
    your tongue mutters wickedness.
4 No one brings suit justly,
    no one goes to law honestly;
they rely on empty pleas, they speak lies,
    conceiving mischief and begetting iniquity.
5 They hatch adders' eggs,
    and weave the spider's web;
whoever eats their eggs dies,
    and the crushed egg hatches out a viper.
6 Their web cannot serve as clothing;
    they cannot cover themselves with what they make.
Their works are works of iniquity,
    and deeds of violence are in their hands.
7 Their feet run to evil,
    and they rush to shed innocent blood;
their thoughts are thoughts of iniquity,
    desolation and destruction are in their highways.
8 The way of peace they do not know,
    and there is no justice in their paths.
Their roads they have made crooked;
    no one who walks in them knows peace.

Something is deeply amiss in the community of faith. The covenant agreement between Yahweh and the community is not working. Such a breakdown evokes a *speech of judgment*, whereby it is to be determined whether Yahweh or Israel is responsible for the breakdown. Apparently it occurred to some to fault Yahweh for this dysfunction of covenant, an attitude characteristically expressed in Israel's psalms of complaint. Here we do not have such a complaint against Yahweh; what we have, rather, is a brusque dismissal of any such a charge against Yahweh (v. 1). It takes only one verse to refute the charge against Yahweh, a bold, direct assertion that Yahweh's hand is not shortened; that is, Yahweh's power is not weakened or curtailed. It is Yahweh's hand (power) that saves, and that capacity is undiminished. In 50:2, Yahweh had answered the same charge that must have been on the mind of exilic Israel. Some thought the trouble was Yahweh's failure. The verse asserts: No way!

Predictably, the argument is reversed in verses 2–8 to make the countercase that it is Israel, not Yahweh, who has defaulted on covenant. The indictment of Israel is relentless and intense, without any great rhetorical development. In verse 2, the indictment is general, concerning "iniquities"

and "sins" that preclude access to Yahweh. The charge becomes more specific in verses 3–4. The hands of Israel are "defiled" by blood. The imagery
refers to murder, but phrasing need not refer directly to murder but to any
action that diminishes or harms other members of the community. Calvin
comments on the comprehensive possibilities intended:

> By mentioning *blood*, he does not mean that murders have been everywhere
> committed; but by this word he describes the cruelty, extortions, violence,
> and enormities, which were perpetrated by hypocrites against the poor and
> defenseless; for they had not to deal with robbers and assassins, but with the
> king and the nobles, who were highly respected and honoured. He calls
> them manslayers, because they cruelly harassed the innocent, and seized by
> force and violence the property of others; and so, immediately afterwards,
> he uses the word "iniquity" instead of "blood" (*Isaiah* IV, 247–248).

The inventory of the verse refers to hands, fingers, lips, and tongue, thus
contending that all parts of these actors are negative. The four bodily parts
are in two pairs, two concerning action and two concerning speech. Both
action and speech are ways of violating Yahweh; both action and speech
are ways of hurting others.

But the indictment does not simply concern interpersonal relations.
Verse 4 shows that the violations of Yahweh that bring trouble are public
actions, specifically in the court. In the end, it is the court upon which reliable public social relations depend. It is to the court that members of the
community can appeal as a last resort for fair, equitable treatment. The
urging of the ninth commandment is clear: "You shall not bear false witness against your neighbor" (Exod. 20:16). When the courtroom is distorted by lies and misrepresentation, no one is safe. The outcome of such
courts, the last defense of truthfulness, is sure to be "iniquity," the very acts
that in verse 2 are barriers to God. Thus the linkage between *reliable social
relations*, *communal well-being*, and *access to Yahweh* are all interrelated aspects for the community of Judaism.

The specific indictment of verse 4 is shrewdly extrapolated by the stunning double metaphor of verses 5–6, "eggs and webs." The eggs being
hatched by Israel in its social distortion are adder's eggs, that is, the birth
of more poison in the community. The eggs, hatched in skewed court pro-
ceedings, are as poisonous as the snakes that produced them. They are
killer eggs! And they in turn produce more poisonous snakes, vipers! The
image is of a "hatching operation" that in itself looks innocuous enough.
However, the eggs of distortion come from poison and produce more poison for the very long term, thus releasing into the community fresh di-

mensions of deathly distortion. The metaphor exposes a deathliness loosed in the community by seemingly modest court maneuvers that have immense, long-term destructive effects.

The second metaphor is a spider web whereby "food" is "caught," so that those "caught" may expect to be devoured and destroyed. Calvin understood the figure of web to mean "utterly pervasive":

> The wicked do mischief in all places, at all times, and in all transactions, and . . . they never do anything good; and . . . every person who has anything to do with them will find them to be venomous and destructive (*Isaiah* IV, 251).

This image of "web" is not as powerful as that of eggs and appears to be turned in verse 6b to become a cover or cloth that is inadequate. It is not clear, in the end, what the metaphor signifies. If we extrapolate from "eggs" to "web," the image is in any case negative.

Verses 6b–7 move away from the metaphor and return to the more concrete indictment of verses 3–4. The term "iniquity" is now sounded a third time (see vv. 2, 4) and this time is matched by the term "violence," already implied in verse 3. Again in verse 7, there are "blood" and plans for "iniquity" (a fourth time). The result is "desolation and destruction." Clearly, Yahweh is not at fault in the breakdown of covenant. We may suggest that this indictment moves symmetrically in the following way:

(a) general indictment: iniquities and sins (v. 2);
    (b) specific indictment: blood (vv. 3–4);
        (c) metaphors: eggs and web (vv. 5–6a);
    (b′) specific indictment: blood (vv. 6b–7);
(a′) general indictment: desolation and destruction (v. 7b).

Israel is portrayed as a community of hopeless recalcitrance and destructiveness. Although the iniquity is a violation of Yahweh, what is also presented is an anarchic social situation in which none is safe.

Verse 8 draws a general conclusion: No peace—no justice—no peace. This is a community totally lacking in *shalom*. The reason is that the elemental requirements of human community are absent. The determined practice of exploitative injustice is widespread—rooted, it is suggested, in the court. Israel is indeed poisoned!

Israel's Need (59:9–15a)

59:9 **Therefore justice is far from us,**
        and righteousness does not reach us;

we wait for light, and lo! there is darkness;
　　and for brightness, but we walk in gloom.
10 We grope like the blind along a wall,
　　groping like those who have no eyes;
we stumble at noon as in the twilight,
　　among the vigorous as though we were dead.
11 We all growl like bears;
　　like doves we moan mournfully.
We wait for justice, but there is none;
　　for salvation, but it is far from us.
12 For our transgressions before you are many,
　　and our sins testify against us.
Our transgressions indeed are with us,
　　and we know our iniquities:
13 transgressing, and denying the LORD,
　　and turning away from following our God,
talking oppression and revolt,
　　conceiving lying words and uttering them from the heart.
14 Justice is turned back,
　　and righteousness stands at a distance;
for truth stumbles in the public square,
　　and uprightness cannot enter.
15a Truth is lacking,
　　and whoever turns from evil is despoiled.

The severe indictment of verses 2–8 evokes a prayer of complaint that is in part a confession of Israel, affirming the charges. The word pair "justice and righteousness" in verse 9 is a characteristic prophetic requirement, one we have seen most recently in 56:1. Here, however, the terms seem to refer not to Israel's obligation but to Israel's expectation of what Yahweh will give. The gift of justice and righteousness, not yet given, bespeaks an ordered, prosperous community. The two terms are in parallel to *light-brightness* (v. 9b) and to *justice-salvation* (v. 11). Indeed, "justice-righteousness," "light-brightness," and "justice-salvation" form something of a rhetorical conclusion. The six terms together summarize that for which Israel hopes from Yahweh.

But it is not given! Instead, the community only experiences darkness and gloom, such darkness that it is like being blind, without eyes, stumbling, like being dead. The language of need and grief is highly imaginative. Nothing is specific. The community lacks everything it must have from Yahweh in order to live a viable, joyous life. As a result, Israel engages in mourning, a low growl like a bear, a soft coo like a dove, subdued voices of hurt, need, and loss perhaps expressed liturgically. Characteristically, complaint in Israel serves to voice a loss but also hopes to move Yahweh to give what is needed. Here the complaint is a statement of deep need, but there is no imperative or petition addressed to Yahweh. Judah is in such a sorry state that it does not ask from Yahweh.

In verses 12–13 the statement of need is turned to a confession that responds to and accepts the charges of verses 2–8. These verses are pervaded with admissions of failure: "transgressions, sins, transgressions, iniquities; transgressing, denying, turning away; talking oppression and revolt; conceiving lying words." It is difficult to imagine a more wholesale admission of failure! The charge has been that Israel has failed to obey Yahweh. Now Israel admits the charge. The point asserted in verse 1 is here confirmed. The problem is not any default by Yahweh. It is all caused by Israel's recalcitrance whereby the entire fabric of society is flawed.

This unit of text ends in verses 14–15a in a statement of verdict not unlike verse 8. Here speaks a different voice, no longer the utterance of failed, guilty Israel. This voice—the voice of the poet?—is more objectively descriptive in identifying the deficiencies that are so obvious in Israel. The summary is developed around five terms: justice, righteousness, truth, uprightness, and truth—all rough synonyms for the practices that make a community viable. The first two terms are reiterated from verse 9. "Truth" here perhaps looks back to the courtroom distortion in verse 4 as well as verse 13. The setting in "the public square" is equivalent to the courtroom; here distortion is referred to as a public practice. The last two terms echo the preceding two: "uprightness," a synonym for righteousness, and "truth" reiterated. The five terms together constitute covenantal practice that makes clear that public life depends upon an intentional ethic of accountability. All of that, however, is absent in this community. The phrases "turned back" (see v. 13) and "at a distance" (see v. 9) indicate how pitifully the community has deteriorated. Thus, both indictment (vv. 2–8) and confession (vv. 9–13), as well as the reprise of verses 14–15a, are agreed. There is a total failure. And it is all the failure of Israel. Postexilic Isaiah had asserted at the outset the nonnegotiable requirements of justice and righteousness as the condition of new community (56:1–2). Now it is apparent—no justice and righteousness—no viable community life.

Yahweh's Response (59:15b–21)

Only now does Yahweh, absent since verse 1, become explicitly engaged in the poem. To be sure, Yahweh is everywhere implied in the indictment of verses 2–8 and the complaint-confession of verses 9–15a. But now Yah-weh moves directly.

59:15b **The LORD saw it, and it displeased him**
>   **that there was no justice.**
> 16a **He saw that there was no one,**
>   **and was appalled that there was no one to intervene;**

Not only is there *no justice*, a point asserted in verse 8 and admitted in verses 9, 13, and 14, but there is *no one* available, *no one* at work, *no one* engaged. All of this absence Yahweh has noticed. Yahweh had assumed that some in Israel would accept responsibility for justice, which is Israel's great *raison d'être*. But no, none! Nobody cared; nobody bothered. Nobody took the trouble. The community is in a deeply sorry state.

59:16b **so his own arm brought him victory,**
>   **and his righteousness upheld him.**
> 17 **He put on righteousness like a breastplate,**
>   **and a helmet of salvation on his head;**
>   **he put on garments of vengeance for clothing,**
>   **and wrapped himself in fury as in a mantle.**
> 18 **According to their deeds, so will he repay;**
>   **wrath to his adversaries, requital to his enemies;**
>   **to the coastlands he will render requital.**
> 19 **So those in the west shall fear the name of the LORD,**
>   **and those in the east, his glory;**
>   **for he will come like a pent-up stream**
>   **that the wind of the LORD drives on.**

As a consequence, Yahweh must undertake the mission of justice for Yah-weh's own self. Yahweh had learned as long ago as Ezekiel 34:11–16 that if one wants something done right, one must do it for one's self. In that text, Yahweh accepts the role of shepherd (= ruler) because all the other rulers and regents for Yahweh had failed. Here, in a different image, Yah-weh takes the role of warrior precisely to establish the proper rule of jus-tice. Yahweh is now on the move to create a realm of justice and righteousness and truth and peace for which nobody else has been at work.

The poetry portrays Yahweh being dressed and armed for the mission of "victory" and "righteousness"—that is, the full establishment of Yah-weh's proper governance. Yahweh dons a breastplate, a helmet, garments of war, a mantle—the full uniform of a warrior. The language, which anticipates Ephesians 6:11–17, shows Yahweh prepared with the military equipment of righteousness and salvation in order to enact vengeance and fury against all who resist that governance. This is no benign God but a forceful agent who will powerfully defeat all those organized and mobilized against a right ordering of the world. The metaphor of warrior's equipment permits the substance of Yahweh's rule to be articulated. The outcome of this "invasion" by Yahweh is sure to be righteousness and salvation, wherein "salvation" in verse 17 is the same verb as "victory" in verse 16. The term refers to Yahweh's good rule.

But the actual implementation of Yahweh's rule is first of all negative—vengeance and fury. Yahweh sets out to defeat and destroy all those who resist Yahweh's intention, that is, those who oppose the righteousness and liberation that Yahweh's rule guarantees. The language of verses 17a–18 presents a warrior who is on the loose with all the energy, adrenalin, and bravado of an excited, highly motivated marauder turned loose on hapless, helpless enemies. It is Yahweh's resolve to destroy on a worldwide scale.

Westermann, however, has noticed the oddity of this language in this context. There is no doubt that the rhetoric is military and characteristically refers to Yahweh's foes outside Israel, that is, on the international horizon. In our period of emerging Judaism, however, the community faced no such external threat, being relatively peaceable in the more or less benign context of Persian rule. Rather, the troubles in Judaism were all internal, a dispute among Jews for control of the community, a dispute reflected in both the crisis of 520–516 (Haggai and Zechariah) and that of 444? (Ezra and Nehemiah). Thus it is plausible to suggest, as does Westermann, that the poem uses the old rhetoric of external threat for an internal dispute. This may sound odd to us; however, we may notice that in religious communities (the church!), some of the most extreme negative rhetoric occurs in internal disputes in which the most violent language is reserved for fellow members of the community. The rhetoric of ruthlessness often operates toward those closest at hand.

The threat of Yahweh, who will instill justice, is portrayed as an appearance of God in which Yahweh comes as a mighty, irresistible force (v. 19). Yahweh will come with all the violent power of a great surging river that will sweep all before it. The result is that all—west and east—will submit to Yahweh's rule. The language of Yahweh's cataclysmic coming is not easily applied to internal disputes. We may conclude that the poet engages in rhetorical overkill, no doubt a measure of how deeply felt were the issues contested. In any case, the poem is certain that resisters to Yahweh (and resistance to the "party" of Yahweh in the community for whom the poet speaks) will indeed be overcome, even violently overcome.

> 59:20 **And he will come to Zion as Redeemer,**
>   **to those in Jacob who turn from transgression, says the LORD.**
>   [21] **And as for me, this is my covenant with them, says the LORD: my spirit that is upon you, and my words that I have put in your mouth, shall not depart out of your mouth, or out of the mouths of your children, or out of the mouths of your children's children, says the LORD, from now on and forever.**

The violent, negative imagery of verses 16–19 is matched by the assurance of verses 20–21, which consist of two quite distinct elements. Verse 20 probably concludes the preceding poem, but may be treated separately because it is positive. Yahweh will act as *redeemer* of Zion. The promise echoes exilic Isaiah (see Isa. 43:1; 44:6). However, here the assurance of "Redeemer to Zion" is sharply qualified. In context, the promised restoration is not to Zion but to those in Zion "who turn." Thus, even the most characteristic promise of exilic Isaiah is submitted to the disputatious condition of the postexilic community so that the promise pertains only to some in the community. The assurance is to those who repent and return to torah, decisively excluding all those in Zion who continue to be "transgressors." The starchiness of this vision greatly tones down the sweeping gospel of Yahweh in order to serve the belated battle for control and definition of the community. Those excluded are not far away as foreigners but are those near at hand as dissenters (see "far" and "near" in 57:19).

Verse 21 is an addition that further qualifies and substantiates the claim of the separatist community within the larger world of Judaism. "This" at the beginning of the verse has no clear antecedent, except perhaps to refer to "turn from transgression" in verse 20. That is, turning from transgression is the entry point into covenant. In context, the term "my covenant" surely refers to the Torah, which must be kept; the substance of covenant is ready, willing, complete obedience whereby Judaism is defined as a people of the Torah.

The term "my covenant" is further explicated with "my spirit" and "my words." We may imagine that "my words" refer to a written torah tradition to which the community assents, as in Nehemiah 8:1–8. "My spirit" is less clear but perhaps refers to the energy and will of Yahweh given to the community of obedience that now has a vibrant resolve to keep torah. The triad of "my covenant, my spirit, my words" are in "your mouth," ready for endless speaking and hearing, reciting, learning, and embracing.

This is a community that meditates on the Torah day and night, and will continue to do so for all thinkable generations to come (see Psalm 1:2). The intent is to identify the *true Israel* as the *Torah-keepers* who are visibly and easily contrasted with "the transgressors" who do not care about torah obedience.

The positive torah affirmation of verses 20–21 gives a curious turn to the entire chapter and draws the chapter into the close and deep disputes of a community preoccupied with doing God's will. The huge *indictment* for iniquity (vv. 1–8) and the pathos-filled *complaint* that is partly confession (vv. 9–15a) receive a vigorous positive *assurance* from Yahweh (vv. 15b–19). In the end, however, the well-being of the community is only initiated by Yahweh's ready intervention. It is sustained by torah resolve. That profound determination for torah is the glorious mark of Judaism. It is also, in context, a mark of an endless and intense dispute that readily excludes "the other."

"THE LORD, YOUR EVERLASTING
LIGHT AND GLORY"
60:1–22

We have seen that chapters 56—59 are deeply disputatious, reflecting serious and deep divisions in the community of recovering exiles. The mood and tone of chapters 60—62, however, are quite different, reflecting an unqualified and undisputed buoyancy about the future. It is commonly thought that chapters 60—62 are closely linked, in attitude and perspective, to chapters 40—55 and are not impinged upon by the disputatious inclination of the surrounding chapters.

This relatively long chapter is a sustained offer of good news to the reconstituted community of Jerusalem. The poem appears to be a divine oracle, an assertion of promise in Yahweh's own mouth, even though at times Yahweh is spoken of in the third person. The oracle asserts Yahweh's unmitigated resolve to work goodness for Jerusalem that will feature safety, well-being, prosperity, abundance, and preeminence among the nations. The poem easily and without any awkwardness holds together *divine resolve*, making it a foundational theological-evangelical announcement and material well-being that will be highly visible in the world. Although the poem is a sustained affirmation, it will be helpful and convenient to deal with smaller elements of the poem, even though the larger theme dominates the whole.

60:1 **Arise, shine; for your light has come,**
      and the glory of the LORD has risen upon you.
   2 **For darkness shall cover the earth,**
      and thick darkness the peoples;
    but the LORD will arise upon you,
      and his glory will appear over you.
   3 **Nations shall come to your light,**
      and kings to the brightness of your dawn.

These verses dramatically announce the primary theme that is to follow. Though the grammar at the outset is a double imperative summoning Jerusalem to arise out of despair and lethargy into hope and buoyancy, in fact the imperative is an assurance from Yahweh. The double imperative "arise, shine" is grounded in the assertion that "your light, the glory of Yahweh" has arisen. Jerusalem shall arise because Yahweh has arisen to power. It is Yahweh who is "your light," an identity made evident in verse 2. It is Yahweh who is Jerusalem's best hope in the world. The gospel announcement of Yahweh's arousal in behalf of Jerusalem has, as always in the tradition of Isaiah, the other nations on its horizon. In the past, Jerusalem has been subordinate to the nations. Now, because of Yahweh's fresh resolve, we are about to witness a great inversion. "The peoples" will be beset by negativity ("darkness"; v. 2). Jerusalem by contrast is recipient of Yahweh's positive attentiveness. As a consequence, "nations and kings" will be drawn to Jerusalem. Thus the oracle asserts Jerusalem's favor from Yahweh and Jerusalem's specialness vis-à-vis the nations, a specialness for a long time not visible.

The great reversal in geopolitics is good news for Jerusalem. As long ago as 2:2–4, the Isaiah tradition imagined the nations streaming to Jerusalem. In that promissory oracle, however, the purpose was to receive torah, and the nations were on a par with Judah before the Torah. Here, as we will see, the purpose of the influx of the nations is very different, less "theological" and more economic and political. The news for Jerusalem is good indeed!

60:4 **Lift up your eyes and look around;**
      they all gather together, they come to you;
    your sons shall come from far away,
      and your daughters shall be carried on their nurses' arms.
   5 **Then you shall see and be radiant;**
      your heart shall thrill and rejoice,
    because the abundance of the sea shall be brought to you,

> the wealth of the nations shall come to you.
> ⁶A multitude of camels shall cover you,
>   the young camels of Midian and Ephah;
>   all those from Sheba shall come.
> They shall bring gold and frankincense,
>   and shall proclaim the praise of the LORD.
> ⁷All the flocks of Kedar shall be gathered to you,
>   the rams of Nebaioth shall minister to you;
> they shall be acceptable on my altar,
>   and I will glorify my glorious house.

Now we are told why the nations are drawn to Jerusalem like insects to a light. Again this unit (as in verse 1) begins with a double imperative, again functioning as a promise. When Jerusalem looks around, what it sees is a great caravan of the nations, all coming to the recovering city. The nations have heavy cargo for Jerusalem. First, the nations bring "your sons, your daughters." That is, they willingly and gently bring the last of the scattered, exiled Jews from all parts of the world. This is the great ingathering of the faithful "from the north and the south, from the east and the west."

But the nations not only bring exiled Jews home. Jerusalem will see and rejoice (v. 5a), because other cargo includes all the "wealth and abundance" of the nations (v. 5b). This is tribute or tax money the other nations now will bring to Jerusalem. We are not told if they bring it gladly or under coercion. What matters is that this vision is a hugely important inversion of geopolitics. For as long as anyone can remember, Israel had paid imperial tribute to others—the Assyrians, the Babylonians, the Persians—all money going out. Now the process is reversed.

Verses 6–7 add particularity to the general assurance of verse 5b. The "wealth and abundance" will consist in everything the nations can offer, their best produce, thus enacting submission to the preeminence of Jerusalem. The poet imagines the great camel caravans of the desert loaded with the most exotic produce. (The reference to Sheba recalls 1 Kings 10:10 in which the queen of Sheba brought exotic tribute in order to enhance the splendor of Solomon. Indeed, the encounter of 1 Kings 10:1–13 is a narrative anticipation of what is envisioned here.)

The wealth and abundance of the desert caravans includes gold and frankincense, flocks and rams, all a tribute to this now-dominant power. Christian readers will not fail to notice the phrase "gold and frankincense" and make a connection to Matthew 2:11, wherein representatives of the Gentile world bring their best gifts to the Christ child in order to acknowledge his messianic identity. There can be no doubt that the Matthew narrative alludes not only to the specific commodities brought but to the dramatic theme of the submission of the nations in our poem.

All of this wealth shall be referred to "my altar, my glorious house" (v. 7b). Thus the submission is a liturgical, *theological* submission to Yahweh. There can be no doubt, however, that *theological* submission to Yahweh entails *political* submission to Jerusalem. The well-being and preeminence of Yahweh in this poem is intimately linked to the well-being and preeminence of the realm of Jerusalem. The poet envisions a wondrous capitulation of the nations who have for very long been superior to Israel in exploitative ways.

> 60:8 Who are these that fly like a cloud,
>   and like doves to their windows?
>   ⁹For the coastlands shall wait for me,
>   the ships of Tarshish first,
>   to bring your children from far away,
>   their silver and gold with them,
>   for the name of the LORD your God,
>   and for the Holy One of Israel,
>   because he has glorified you.
>   ¹⁰ Foreigners shall build up your walls,
>   and their kings shall minister to you;
>   for in my wrath I struck you down,
>   but in my favor I have had mercy on you.
>   ¹¹ Your gates shall always be open;
>   day and night they shall not be shut,
>   so that nations shall bring you their wealth,
>   with their kings led in procession.
>   ¹² For the nation and kingdom
>   that will not serve you shall perish;
>   those nations shall be utterly laid waste.
>   ¹³ The glory of Lebanon shall come to you,
>   the cypress, the plane, and the pine,
>   to beautify the place of my sanctuary;
>   and I will glorify where my feet rest.
>   ¹⁴ The descendants of those who oppressed you
>   shall come bending low to you,
>   and all who despised you
>   shall bow down at your feet;
>   they shall call you the City of the LORD,
>   the Zion of the Holy One of Israel.
>   ¹⁵ Whereas you have been forsaken and hated,

with no one passing through,
   I will make you majestic forever,
      a joy from age to age.
16 You shall suck the milk of nations
      you shall suck the breasts of kings;
   and you shall know that I, the LORD, am your Savior
      and your Redeemer, the Mighty One of Jacob.

17 Instead of bronze I will bring gold,
      instead of iron I will bring silver;
   instead of wood, bronze,
      instead of stones, iron.
   I will appoint Peace as your overseer
      and Righteousness as your taskmaster.
18 Violence shall no more be heard in your land,
      devastation or destruction within your borders;
   you shall call your walls Salvation,
      and your gates Praise.

These verses continue the announcement that Yahweh has reversed field to the great benefit of Jerusalem. The poetic lines are fully aware, and have no wish to deny, that recent suffering and dislocation of Zion have been willed by Yahweh. But now everything is changed. The God who has scattered is the God who will now gather. The gathering consists of (a) the return of "your children," Jews scattered all around the Fertile Crescent (v. 9), but also (b) the vast wealth of the nations who have heretofore exploited and abused Jerusalem but who now will submit to that same city in generosity and extravagance. This long section of poetry is a meditation on this double theme of restoration.

The vision of restoration in these verses begins with a homecoming from the Mediterranean world of sailing and shipping (vv. 8–9). The reference to the coastlands and Tarshish refers to the shipping fleets that work the entire Mediterranean and signify enormous wealth generated by commerce (see 2:12–17). But before the ships of Tarshish become fully visible, they are like a mere cloud and doves on the horizon. They are not immediately recognizable. As they come into fuller view, they are seen as cargo vessels. And the cargo is "your children" plus "silver and gold," people and wealth all gladly brought to Jerusalem. As elsewhere in this long poem, the expectation of *national well-being* is kept intimately connected to the *theological authorization* of Yahweh. It is "Yahweh your God" who sponsors this wondrous restoration (v. 9). The verse marks a momentary climax in the poetry and does so by appealing to the preferred Isaianic title for Yahweh, "The Holy One of Israel" who has power to reverse the public process.

The next section of poetry also concludes with "the Holy One of Israel" (vv. 10–14). In these verses, foreigners and kings are willing vehicles for the coming well-being of Israel (v. 10a). But the dominant imagery is of Yahweh. It is Yahweh who previously acted in *anger* who now acts in *mercy* to effect a reversal of fortunes. This two-step presentation of Israel's life with Yahweh replicates the rhetoric of 54:7–8 that acknowledges Yahweh as both the perpetrator of exile and the one who now moves gloriously beyond exile (v. 10b).

As a consequence of Yahweh's new, positive resolve toward Jerusalem, the city will be kept open day and night in order to receive the constant and unending influx of restored Jews and accumulated goods. International commerce will be undivided in its shipment of produce and manufactured goods for the benefit of Jerusalem. The imagery is of busy ports, endless loading docks, crowded scales, and shipping agents who are preoccupied with recording and receiving and storing. The cargo that will enhance the city includes the material wealth of Lebanon and its vast lumber trade (v. 13). It may be recalled that in ancient memory, Hiram from Lebanon was the primary builder of Solomon's temple (1 Kings 5:1), and now the same Lebanese merchants will enhance the rebuilt temple.

The vision of luxury, extravagance, and unqualified prosperity is not without its concrete bite of warning and threat. In verse 12, the nations are on notice that submission to Jerusalem is an offer that cannot be refused. The only alternative for the nations is destruction. The only way for a nation to prosper, or even to survive, is to be deeply involved in the enhancement of Jerusalem. And in verse 14, the poet recalls that these busy, ostensibly willing subjects were those who oppressed Israel in former times. Those who oppressed are now the ones who must submit in humiliation and subordination. This is indeed "the humbled being exalted and the exalted being humbled" (Luke 14:11; 18:14), all becuase of the will and purpose of Yahweh, whose purposes will surely prevail.

The reversal is celebrated specifically in verses 15–16. The "forsaken" will be made majestic, a complete reversal of fortunes. The nations and their kings will be completely submissive to Zion and will give themselves over, even their bodies, to enhance the city. The imagery of Jews sucking at the breasts of Gentile kings serves both the vision of well-being for Judah but also the humiliation and reduction of erstwhile powers to nursemaids (see 49:26)—and all of this by "the Mighty One of Jacob" (v. 16).

A different mode of rhetoric is used in verses 17–18 to continue the theme of drastic reversal. Verse 17 consists of a fourfold "instead" that is surely an intentional counterpoint to the fivefold negative "instead" in 3:24. Whereas the earlier negative sequence had anticipated complete humiliation and reduction to slavery for Judah, now the replacement is all in the direction of strength and preeminence. Everything in the city will be upgraded, as can now be afforded because of the import of international wealth. Westermann comments on this upgrade:

> Sorry times are kept sorry because of the sorry stuff that men are obliged to make use of if they want to stay alive. It must be substitutes all along the line, a life vexatious, constricted and wretched, when the finer stuffs, which are not to be had, take on an importance that is more than material because they become symbols of a freer and fairer life (*Isaiah 40–66*, 362).

The verse continues by a formidable personification of *shalom* and *ṣedeqāh* (peace and righteousness) as agents and powers who will superintend for well-being. Such a forcible embodiment of these themes is paralleled in Psalm 85:10–13, where the same terms are treated as actual characters in the life of the world. The overseers and taskmasters of Israel in exile were harsh, ruthless, and demanding (see Exod. 5:10–14). But they are now displaced by the most gracious, magnanimous, gentle of agents. As a consequence of the new overseers, all of the old negativities—violence, dislocation, destruction—are voided. Now the city is marked by "Salvation" that leads to unending doxology (praise). The term "salvation" is *yš'*, the term expressed in the name "Isaiah" and eventually in the name "Jesus" (see Matt. 1:21). The poet clearly employs the most extreme imagery imaginable through which to present a newness that is totally discontinuous from the past and totally unqualified by any previous negativity of any kind.

60:19 **The sun shall no longer be your light by day,**
    nor for brightness shall the moon
      give light to you by night;
    but the LORD will be your everlasting light,
      and your God will be your glory.
  20 **Your sun shall no more go down,**
    or your moon withdraw itself;
    for the LORD will be your everlasting light,
      and your days of mourning shall be ended.
  21 **Your people shall all be righteous;**

> they shall possess the land forever.
> They are the shoot that I planted, the work of my hands,
>   so that I might be glorified.
> ²² The least of them shall become a clan,
>   and the smallest one a mighty nation;
> I am the LORD;
>   in its time I will accomplish it quickly.

The poem employs yet more daring imagery to continue the stupendous announcement of well-being. Whereas the poem thus far has used political and economic categories of reversal, now the poem pushes toward the more comprehensive reach of creation. The ordered life of the new creation clearly counts on the regularity of sun and moon. But now, in a marvelous rhetorical extremity, even sun and moon are displaced by Yahweh, who will be the light and the glory, the guarantor and assurance, of Israel. Indeed, Yahweh will be "light perpetual," so that there will be no darkness, no night, no threat, no danger, no loss of control (see Psalm 139:11–12; Rev. 22:5).

But the sweeping cosmic imagery is quickly brought back to the lived reality of Jerusalem (v. 21). Jerusalem will have no more exile. The term "forever" (everlasting) has been used twice for Yahweh as light. Now the term is used a third time, this time to refer to Zion's land, which will be held to perpetuity, utterly safe and guaranteed, never again to be lost by displacement. Zion is the planting through which Yahweh will be glorified.

The concluding verse asserts that the very least among the families and clans of Jerusalem will prosper. All the assurances of creation will generate newness; all the ancestral promises of Genesis will come to fulfillment. Israel will multiply and spread throughout the land unimpeded, utterly safe, utterly prosperous, utterly guaranteed. The long poem ends with one more self-announcement of Yahweh: "I am Yahweh." This sovereign claim is reinforced by a terse resolve that Yahweh will act quickly. This last phrase anticipates apocalyptic rhetoric that subsequently assures that Yahweh acts promptly and decisively to bring a new world to fruition. Such a radical anticipation of a new world is already implicitly present in this poem.

This poem is a most extraordinary practice of hope. It is a hope addressed to a most needy (despairing?) community and appeals to the primal commitment and resolve of Yahweh, who is powerfully cited throughout the poem (vv. 9, 14, 16, 22). We may observe four daring theological claims that persist in the practice of the faith of the church:

1. The reversal is total, without qualification. The newness now to be given is in no way derived from what is previous. It is a pure gift of newness. There is something deeply prerational about such hope that offers no explanations or human reasons. In Christian parlance, this rhetoric, by being subsequently tagged as "new heaven and new earth" (Isa. 65:17; Rev. 21:1), is about the full coming of God's rule on earth that does not come by incremental developments but that comes in an instant, by the power of God.

2. The vision is powerfully theocentric. This is God's doing and depends upon no human agency, nor even upon Zion's qualification for newness. This is singularly the work of the creator, who has power to make all things new (Rev. 21:5).

3. The drastic depth of newness and the unqualified theocentric character of the vision attest to the practice of hope in situations of deepest despair. It is a peculiar mark of Christian faith, completely learned and inherited from Judaism, that tribulation produces hope and hope does not lead to despair (see Rom. 5:3). When circumstances are unbearable, then the faith of this community moves beyond circumstance to the God who governs all circumstance and who is not a prisoner or victim of any circumstance. It is this faith in a God beyond circumstance that is the ground for faith in every circumstance, not excluding the reality of death. It is for this reason of faith that the church characteristically grows Yahwistically lyrical precisely in the face of death:

> In all these things we are more than conquerors through him who loved us. For I am convinced that neither death, nor life, nor angels, nor rulers, nor things present, nor things to come, nor powers, nor height, nor depth, nor anything else in all creation, will be able to separate us from the love of God in Christ Jesus our Lord (Rom. 8:37–39).

Synagogue and church count so on the God of newness that praise in this guaranteed city is not silenced or even deterred by circumstance.

4. This long poem is shot through with a latent imperialism that imagines not only theological and evangelical guarantees but also political, economic, and material advantage. I suggest that the church's best hope also lives at the seductive edge of such claims that invite arrogance beyond joy. There is no sure protection against such a posture. It is kept in check, surely, only by the continuing awareness that it is the God of mercy who gives the newness and appoints *shalom* as taskmaster. When the primacy and initiative of Yahweh are neglected, self-aggrandizement is surely close

at hand. It is precisely praise that keeps *shalom* as gift and precludes its being regarded as possession.

In this poem, Israel is invited well beyond the old story of oppression and despair to a moment of waiting. At its best, Israel knows that the newness is *soon.* There is no doubt that the promised future will be an enhancement of Zion, presumably in the splendor of an anticipated temple:

> I will glorify my glorious house (v. 7);
> He has glorified you (v. 9);
> I will glorify where my feet rest (v. 13);
> I will make you majestic forever (v. 15).

All of that, however, in the end is penultimate. In the end, it is all "so that I may be glorified" (v. 21). Zion is able, at its best, to refer all of its enhancement beyond itself to the ultimate enhancement of Yahweh. It is this that keeps in check the imperialistic temptation intrinsic to the promise.

"I WILL MAKE AN EVERLASTING COVENANT" 61:1–11

This poetic unit continues the primary accents of chapter 60 concerning the coming reversal of the fortunes of Jerusalem, the coming abundance and prosperity of Jerusalem, and the corresponding subservience of the nations. This poem, however, includes one element quite different from that of chapter 60, namely, the cruciality of a human agent (presumably the poet who speaks) who will undertake and enact the intention of Yahweh. This first-person human agent speaks in verses 1–7 and verses 10–11. In the center of the chapter, however, there is an oracle that has Yahweh speak in the first person (vv. 8–9). The variation of speakers (human speaker—Yahweh—human speaker) indicates how intimately connected are Yahwistic resolve and human vocation.

61:1 **The spirit of the Lord GOD is upon me,**
     because the LORD has anointed me;
  he has sent me to bring good news to the oppressed,
     to bind up the brokenhearted,
  to proclaim liberty to the captives,
     and release to the prisoners;
  ²to proclaim the year of the LORD's favor,

> and the day of vengeance of our God;
> to comfort all who mourn;
> ³to provide for those who mourn in Zion—
> to give them a garland instead of ashes,
> the oil of gladness instead of mourning,
> the mantle of praise instead of a faint spirit.
> They will be called oaks of righteousness,
> the planting of the LORD, to display his glory.
> ⁴They shall build up the ancient ruins,
> they shall raise up the former devastations;
> they shall repair the ruined cities,
> the devastations of many generations.

Here speaks a human agent who is authorized and energized to do Yahweh's deeply transformative work in the community of Yahweh's people. We do not know the identity of the speaker; we may assume it is a poetic figure who exercises immense theological authority, enough authority to transform in decisive ways the circumstance of the community of emerging Judaism. The instigator of the human vocation here undertaken is Yahweh: Yahweh moves, summons, and authorizes what is to follow. Two figures are used for this authorization: (1) *Yahweh's spirit*, Yahweh's authorizing force that has the capacity to work a radical newness, the same spirit that blew back the power of chaos (Gen. 1:2) and the waters of the Exodus (Exod. 14:21) now blows upon this human agent (see 42:1). (2) *Yahweh's anointing* dramatically, sacramentally designates the human agent by a public gesture of authorization. It could be that the "spirit anointing" is a concrete liturgical act in the community or simply a metaphorical claim of authority. Either way, the juxtaposition of "spirit" and "anoint" is bound to recall in Israel the old narrative of the authorization of David with the same two features: "Then Samuel took the horn of oil, and *anointed* him in the presence of his brothers; and the *spirit* of the LORD came mightily upon David from that day forward" (1 Sam. 16:13; see 2 Sam. 23:1–2). As David was a massive *newness* in Israel, so now this speaker is to effect a deep social newness.

The authorization is followed in verses 1b–4 by three rhetorical uses. First there is a series of infinitive verbs to inventory what this empowered human agent will do: "to bring, to bind up, to proclaim, to release, to proclaim, to comfort, to provide, to give" (vv. 1b–3). All of these actions are powerful ministries to the weak, the powerless, and the marginalized to restore them to full function in a community of well-being and joy. We may especially notice two features of this series of transformative verbs.

First, the lead verb "to bring good news" is the verbal form of "gospel," which we have already seen in 40:9; 41:27; and 52:7. This is a dramatic announcement of Yahweh's newly gained power that is a harbinger of the reorganization of public life according to the will of Yahweh. This is "evangelism" that has concrete, public effect. The one anointed is to "gospel" the world of Judaism. The second observation is that the series of transformative verbs culminates in the double formula "the year of the Lord's favor, and the day of vengeance." Scholars in general agree that this is a reference to the practice of the jubilee year authorized in Leviticus 25, when all properties lost in economic transactions will be restored and returned in order to permit a stable, functioning community. Thus the series of verbs is taken to be an announcement of the jubilee.

In the context of emerging Judaism, the point may be the restoration of land, security, stability, and well-being to *the community as a whole* of Jews too long in jeopardy, that is, a community-wide restoration. Or if postexilic Isaiah should be drawn toward the economic circumstance of the community reflected in Nehemiah 5, then perhaps we may anticipate a reordering of *the internal economics of the community*, an adjudication of the social relationships between haves and have-nots. Either way, the announcement and evocation of jubilee are good news—Yahwistically based—about the rehabilitation of life out of impoverishment, powerlessness, and despair.

These verses are of special interest because they are quoted by Jesus, according to Luke 4:18–19, as the inaugural vision of his ministry. In that Lucan narrative, it is reported that the radicality of the proclamation evoked such hostility among listeners that they sought to kill him (vv. 29–30). There is no doubt that a vision of jubilee—that is, a profound hope for the disadvantaged—is shockingly devastating to those who value and benefit from the status quo. Sharon Ringe, in *Jesus, Liberation, and the Biblical Jubilee: Images for Ethics and Christology*, has forcefully suggested that this announcement is a clue and signal for the entire ministry of Jesus, a radical undertaking of the reordering of human community.

Thus our verses seem to be situated between Leviticus 25 (a torah vision of jubilee) and Luke 4:18–19, where the vision is taken up in the ministry of Jesus. Isaiah 61:1–4, however, is not directly an anticipation of Jesus. Rather, it concerns the concrete issues of a community in trouble, and it proposes a transformative response out of Yahweh's resolve. The proclamation is something of a test case for the way in which the Old Testament holds together *theological vision* and *concrete economic practice*.

The second rhetorical device is a series of three "insteads" in verse 3, thus using the same pattern of speech we have seen negatively in 3:24 and positively in 60:17. The terse series of "insteads" is a radical transformation of communal attitude and condition, made possible by the proclamation and enactment of jubilee: "garland . . . ashes; gladness . . . mourning; praise . . . faint spirit." The three are parallel moves from negating grief and despair to jubilant celebration. In context, the transformation is from powerless indebtedness to the restoration of dignity and viability. In Christian extrapolation, the transformation is given the shape of crucifixion and resurrection whereby "your pain will turn into joy" (John 16:20).

The third rhetorical feature is a series of "theys" in verses 3b–4. "They" are those who are addressed by the gospel of jubilee and so are restored to fullness of life and joy. The outcome of the actions that produce an "instead" is that "they"—presumably participants in emerging Judaism now fully empowered—will have energy, vision, and resolve. They will be "oaks," an image of sturdiness, durability, and resilience. The term is likely connected to the same term in 1:30, where the failed Zion of preexilic Isaiah is an oak that withers and is without strength or vitality. When seen in relation to 1:30, the image is of radical restoration to full strength. As a consequence of such restoration, the emerging community that benefits from the gospel of jubilee will have the capacity and resolve to rebuild, restore, and repair the ruins of Jerusalem. Thus in the end, the gospel powered by the spirit is a restoration of a viable economic community in a reorganized city, the redemption of public life. It may be that the actual recalcitrant city of Ezra and Nehemiah is more modest than this exuberant vision, but the vision, large as it is, is an evocation of the later concrete public practice that gives Judaism its staying power.

> 61:5 **Strangers shall stand and feed your flocks,**
>   **foreigners shall till your land and dress your vines;**
>   **⁶but you shall be called priests of the LORD,**
>   **you shall be named ministers of our God;**
>   **you shall enjoy the wealth of the nations,**
>   **and in their riches you shall glory.**
>   **⁷Because their shame was double,**
>   **and dishonor was proclaimed as their lot,**
>   **therefore they shall possess a double portion;**
>   **everlasting joy shall be theirs.**

The oracle continues now to contrast the coming well-being of Jerusalem with the client nations around about. In verses 1–4, the nations were not even mentioned. In these verses, the poet is aware that the old relationship of Jerusalem and the nations is now to be radically inverted. Whereas Judah had been lowly and abused at the hands of the nations, now the nations will be subordinated and cast in the role of menial servants who will do the chores necessary to maintain the city. These verses of contrast resume themes from chapter 60 concerning the subservience of the nations.

Whereas the nations do menial chores of agriculture, "you"—the restored inhabitants and heirs of the Zion promise—will have a special, honored, privileged vocation as priests and ministers. The rhetoric seems to refer back to the distinctive vocation of Israel in Exodus 19:5–6, which contrasts Israel and the nations (see 1 Pet. 2:9–10). Israel is to engage in no more menial work but is to be preoccupied with "holy things." Although this responsibility is a weighty one, the priestly office is also one of great privilege, enjoying the produce of the work of the nations. This rhetoric is surely triumphalist and reflects resentment for having been too long subjected; it evidences the easy, oft-repeated movement from sacramental specialness to economic privilege at the expense of others.

The poem returns to the theme of radical reversal, another stunning "instead" (v. 7). The twice-used motif of "double" probably appeals back to 40:2. Israel in exile had been doubly humiliated in the eyes of the nations, had suffered doubly, disproportionately, in exile. Now this rehabilitated Judaism is to enjoy a double portion of well-being, surely at the expense of the nations. The notion of "double portion" is apparently a characteristic way in that ancient rhetoric to express privilege, special well-being, and abundance (see Deut. 21:15–17; 1 Sam. 1:5; though both of these texts are somewhat problematic). The coming time will be one of immense inversion when Israel, Yahweh's sacramental people in the world, will luxuriate in gifts produced by erstwhile oppressors.

61:8 **For I the LORD love justice,**
> **I hate robbery and wrongdoing;**
> **I will faithfully give them their recompense,**
>> **and I will make an everlasting covenant with them.**
> ⁹**Their descendants shall be known among the nations,**
>> **and their offspring among the peoples;**
> **all who see them shall acknowledge**
>> **that they are a people whom the LORD has blessed.**

Here the utterance of the human voice is interrupted by an oracle of Yahweh. It is as though Yahweh must now speak to provide grounding for the remarkable anticipations offered by the human voice. In the end, the good possibilities for rehabilitated Judaism are thoroughly Yahweh-based. Although human effort is important, it is Yahweh's resolve that gives assurance for these promises that fly in the face of circumstance.

It is Yahweh who speaks. It is Yahweh who is completely committed to justice. Yahweh is already known in the liturgy as a "lover of justice" (Psalm 99:4). Here that liturgical formula is concretely related to circumstance. The injustice that Yahweh "hates" is not simply general and pervasive. Yahweh hates the injustice that Judaism has too long suffered at the hand of the nations. Therefore it is Yahweh's love of (devotion to) justice that now evokes the radical reversal here announced.

Because of Yahweh's deep propensity, Yahweh will now reward Israel accordingly. But the "recompense" is not according to Israel's merit. It is rather according to Yahweh's long-term, unbreakable commitment to Israel, to "an everlasting covenant." It was easy, perhaps inevitable, to conclude that the exile was a termination of Yahweh's covenantal fidelity to Israel. In exile and thereafter, however, the most daring theological voices in the community were able to assert that exile was not termination. And so now begin the recovery and the reassertion of the fundamental fidelity on which the life of Judaism is based. The tradition now must appeal to the ancient promises to Abraham and to David, that Yahweh's fidelity is not conditional but persists through all circumstances (see Gen. 17:7, 13, 19; 2 Sam. 23:5; 1 Chron. 16:17; Isa. 55:3; Jer. 32:40; Ezek. 16:60; 37:26). The future of Judaism, about to be enacted, is rooted in Yahweh's undisrupted resolve.

The oracle of Yahweh makes more specific allusion to the Abrahamic promises in verse 9. Now the nations will see, given the restoration, that the descendants of the promise are indeed the blessed people of Yahweh. The poetry plays with the theme of "nations/blessing" already set forth in Genesis 12:3. It is remarkable that this poet can appeal to and mobilize ancient promises as a ground for concrete faith in a later circumstance. The great "instead" of Judaism has ancient, reliable, Yahwistic foundation.

61:10 I will greatly rejoice in the LORD,
    my whole being shall exult in my God;
  for he has clothed me with the garments of salvation,
    he has covered me with the robe of righteousness,
  as a bridegroom decks himself with a garland,
    and as a bride adorns herself with her jewels.
   11 For as the earth brings forth its shoots,

> and as a garden causes what is sown in it to spring up,
> so the Lord GOD will cause righteousness and praise
> to spring up before all the nations.

The human speaker now speaks again. The opening lines of verse 10 are a characteristic hymn, stated with great intensity. The speaker is filled with joy. The phrase "greatly rejoice" is made intense in the Hebrew by a grammatical device that reiterates the verb, "joy, joy." While it is not reproduced in English, it is important to recognize it as a sweeping, extravagant statement. The anointed, authorized one is unreservedly exuberant. And the reason, again following hymnic form, is that Yahweh has fully outfitted the human agent in the apparel of salvation and righteousness (see Eph. 4:22–24). The language is rooted in liturgical garb and is here likely metaphorical. The rhetoric of dress, here all doxological, is contrasted with the military imagery of 59:17. The speaker is filled with the joy of a bridegroom, the delight of a bride, full of loveliness, of expectation, of buoyancy, of confidence concerning all the newness that is about to happen (see Psalm 24:5).

The joy expressed in the end, however, does not concern the person or office of the speaker. Rather, it concerns the consequence for the community of Zion (v. 11). The speaker is of only instrumental importance. The object of Yahweh's salvation and righteousness is the community that will be filled with righteousness and praise. The vibrant reality of economic rehabilitation—expressed as jubilee year—is likened to the flourishing of a productive garden that will be fruitful and blossom and produce. The emerging community of Judaism will blossom and produce righteousness; that is, equitable, life-giving social relationships that can only be expressed in lyrical doxology.

This remarkable vision seeks to summon Judaism out of every temptation to despair. The hope-filled message is Yahweh-rooted but concerns restored community. And that restored community will be a spectacle for all the nations to observe. The nations had assumed that Judaism was hopeless and that Yahweh was an irrelevance. But now the great evangelical "instead" of Yahweh will be visible. The lyrical prospect of Judaism has a counterpoint in the Easter buoyancy of the church that anticipates a complete renovation of the world wrought in inexplicable ways by the power of God. But the vision offered here cannot be preempted by the Easter faith of the church. The poem concerns the wondrous future of the Jewish community, wrought in and through this human agent, whose jubilee work overcomes all anticommunity conditions. The everlasting covenant is to take a concrete, visible form in a reconstituted community.

"NO MORE FORSAKEN"
62:1–12

This poem continues the eloquent, exuberant promise of chapters 60—61 for a radical, joyous transformation of the life of Jerusalem. In general, these verses appear to be a first-person utterance of Yahweh. However, there are some rhetorical markers suggesting that the poet "quotes" Yahweh, who has already spoken elsewhere (as in vv. 8, 11).

62:1 **For Zion's sake I will not keep silent,**
    and for Jerusalem's sake I will not rest,
  until her vindication shines out like the dawn,
    and her salvation like a burning torch.
 ² **The nations shall see your vindication,**
    and all the kings your glory;
  and you shall be called by a new name
    that the mouth of the LORD will give.
 ³ **You shall be a crown of beauty in the hand of the LORD,**
    and a royal diadem in the hand of your God.
 ⁴ **You shall no more be termed Forsaken,**
    and your land shall no more be termed Desolate;
  but you shall be called My Delight Is in Her,
    and your land Married;
  for the LORD delights in you,
    and your land shall be married.
 ⁵ **For as a young man marries a young woman,**
    so shall your builder marry you,
  and as the bridegroom rejoices over the bride,
    so shall your God rejoice over you.

Yahweh decides to break the silence. It is as though Israel, Yahweh's people, has been exploited and abused. And all the while, Yahweh has observed silently, permitting the exploitation and abuse without any protest or intervention. Indeed, this community of faith, given the vagaries of its life, has often seemed to live in a world from which Yahweh has been absent, detached, and indifferent. In its characteristic prayers of complaint, Israel has implored Yahweh to speak in the midst of unbearable suffering:

> "Hear my prayer, O LORD,
>   and give ear to my cry;
>   do not hold your peace at my tears.

> For I am your passing guest,
> an alien, like all my forebears."
>   (Psalm 39:12)

But often Israel's appeal to Yahweh is to no avail. And for a long time in exile, it proves to no avail.

Finally, in exilic Isaiah, Yahweh broke the silence and spoke in behalf of Israel. Yahweh has actively, vigorously intervened to say to the exploiting nations, "Enough!"

> For a long time I have held my peace,
> I have kept still and restrained myself;
> now I will cry out like a woman in labor,
> I will gasp and pant.
>   (Isa. 42:14)

It is as though Yahweh has now gone public in solidarity with Israel, to let the nations know that abusive treatment of Israel will not be tolerated any longer. The nations will no longer have impunity for their treatment of Israel. Our poem in chapter 62 seems to derive from 42:14 with a resolve to speak and to act in ways that break the cycles of suffering imposed by the nations. Yahweh will not keep silent, will not rest, will not be restrained or reticent, but will intrude out of devotion to Israel. After such a long dormancy as Israel has experienced, Israel may have wondered how determined and reliable Yahweh might now be. The answer is given: "until . . . !" (v. 1b). Verses 1b–5 give substance to the "until"—until circumstance is inverted, until Jerusalem is secure and prosperous, until Israel is at peace and at ease. Or we might say more broadly, until the full rule of Yahweh is established and all rival governances are defeated.

The tag words of the new regime are "vindication-salvation" (v. 1), the same Hebrew terms as "salvation-righteousness" in 61:10. This poetry, as in 60:10–14 and 61:54, is always aware of the watching nations, the ones who have oppressed. Now the nations will watch and will witness the deep transformation to be wrought by Yahweh (v. 2). The well-being anticipated is characterized in a series of promissory "You's": "You shall be called by a new name; . . . You shall be a crown of beauty; . . . You shall no more be termed Forsaken; . . . You shall be called My Delight" (vv. 2b–4). Yahweh will now enact a wondrous new condition for Jerusalem, all of which is subsumed under a new name.

A change of name signals a new identity, a new relation, a new chance for life in the world. The old name for Jerusalem, uttered in contempt, had been "forsaken" (see Jer. 30:17). The nations could mock and tease Israel about the failure and ineffectiveness of Yahweh (see Isa. 37:4, 24). The term "forsaken" is especially poignant. In Psalm 22:1, the best known of Israel's complaints, the psalmist accuses Yahweh of abandonment. And in Isa. 54:7–8, Yahweh admits that Yahweh has abandoned, albeit briefly. Not without cause, Jerusalem is marked as a city abandoned and without any protective God (see Lam. 5:20).

But now, says the silence-breaking God, the season of abandonment is over. Yahweh now acts in a new resolve. If "abandon" be understood as divorce, then the positive alternative is "married" (v. 4). It is worth noting that the term rendered "married" is from the same root as Baal, the god of fertility; and the land that is "married" is a land "baaled," or literally in the Hebrew, *Be'ulah*, that is, "Buelah land." Thus the imagery of divorce or widowhood (see 54:4–6) is transposed into an agricultural term for a land barren and unproductive. Now this people is reloved and the city is restored; the land is recovered for fruitfulness and productivity. The relational aspect of covenant fidelity has as a counterpart the covenantal fruitfulness of the land. The imagery of "marriage" and "delight" is thus a dramatic counter to the sense of abandonment, forlornness, grief, shame, and despair—the markings of exile. The rhetoric concerns Yahweh's resolve to begin again with the life of reconstituted Israel.

It is no wonder that this subsection of poetry concludes with a lyrical assertion of joy that is like the unrestrained delight of bride and bridegroom (v. 5; cf. 61:10). The language is especially freighted, because marital metaphors in that ancient world include fruitfulness and generativity. Israel as a people will be reloved. Jerusalem as a city will be rebuilt. The people will be remarried and refructified as Yahweh's new creation.

The basic announcement of the reconstitution of Jerusalem is now developed in five brief poetic elements organized in two pairs (vv. 6–7 and 10; vv. 8–9 and 11) plus a conclusion (v. 12).

62:6 **Upon your walls, O Jerusalem,**
    I have posted sentinels;
  all day and all night
    they shall never be silent.
  You who remind the LORD,
    take no rest,
 7 **and give him no rest**
    until he establishes Jerusalem
    and makes it renowned throughout the earth.

The governing image is of a city rebuilt. The more specific imagery is of watchmen on the city walls of reconstituted Jerusalem. The rhetoric of verse 6 is reminiscent of 60:11 but to very different effect. In 60:11, the city is open day and night, because there is so much import that the customs officials must function round the clock in order to receive it all. Here by contrast, the incessant work of the sentinels does not concern the importing nations. Rather, it concerns Yahweh. It is their task to *remind* Yahweh, to keep *reminding* Yahweh, to *remind* Yahweh without ceasing, of Jerusalem's need and Yahweh's obligation. The sentinels are portrayed as complainers who simply keep after Yahweh and nag Yahweh until Yahweh acts. How long should the nagging last? The answer is "until," the same "until" as in verse 1, until Yahweh finishes the work of fully reconditioning the city in splendor.

The imagery of reminding Yahweh is poignant and telling. Quite literally it is "cause for Yahweh to remember." Notice, the language suggests that Yahweh needs to be reminded or Yahweh will forget. Indeed, the complaint prayers of Israel regularly entertain the thought that Yahweh is neglectful because Yahweh has forgotten (see Psalms 13:1; 42:9; 74:19). This nagging insistence suggests that Yahweh's loud resolve of verse 1 is not quite reliable and at least needs constant reinforcement. Thus the prayers of Israel are a serious, urgent exercise that mobilizes Yahweh to do what Yahweh intends but may neglect to do.

62:8 **The LORD has sworn by his right hand**
and by his mighty arm:
I will not again give your grain
to be food for your enemies,
and foreigners shall not drink the wine
for which you have labored;
⁹but those who garner it shall eat it
and praise the LORD,
and those who gather it shall drink it
in my holy courts.

These verses, in rather solemn fashion, announce Yahweh's sober oath to which Yahweh is fully committed. One may wonder, in light of verses 6–7, whether the reiteration of the oath is not only an assurance to needful Jerusalem but also a reminder to Yahweh, that is, to recall the oath for Yahweh.

The actual substance of the oath is an appeal to what scholars have termed "futility curses," that is, curses that make human effort futile because under the curse one does not get to enjoy the results of one's efforts; one's efforts are futile (see Eccles. 2:18–23). In Deuteronomy 28:30, we hear: "You shall become engaged to a woman, but another man shall lie with her. You shall build a house, but not live in it. You shall plant a vineyard, but not enjoy its fruit" (cf. Amos 5:11). But now, in the new arrangement of life guaranteed by Yahweh's good intention and powerful resolve, the old futility will end. There will be stability enough so that one's produce will not be usurped, but one will enjoy the results of one's work: "They shall plant vineyards and drink their wine, / and they shall make gardens and eat their fruit" (Amos 9:14).

The same pattern is articulated in Isaiah 65:21–22:

> They shall build houses and inhabit them;
>   they shall plant vineyards and eat their fruit.
> They shall not build and another inhabit;
>   they shall not plant and another eat.

In our verses, it is promised and guaranteed by divine oath that well-being will be enjoyed and not forfeited to another, as has been the case in much of Israel's past.

62:10 **Go through, go through the gates,**
        prepare the way for the people;
    build up, build up the highway,
        clear it of stones,
        lift up an ensign over the peoples.

This verse resonates with verses 6–7 and concerns the rebuilding that is now to be undertaken. The difference is that in those verses it is asserted that Yahweh will act decisively, but here it is the community enjoined to act. The summons to the community is stated in a series of seven imperatives, all summoning and authorizing and empowering restorative activity. The anticipation of verses 6–7 and verse 10 suggests a characteristic function of Israel's hope. The future depends, in various articulations, fully upon Yahweh's reliable resilience and fully upon Israel's committed engagement. Yahweh will give the future; Israel must enact the future. It will not do to boil down such rhetoric to "grace-works," for such a way of thinking is alien to these urgent promissory texts.

62:11 **The LORD has proclaimed**
        to the end of the earth:

> Say to daughter Zion,
>   "See, your salvation comes;
> his reward is with him,
>   and his recompense before him."

This verse reiterates a promise of Yahweh that is parallel to the oath of verses 8–9. Yahweh has promised to Zion the full gift of salvation that is reckoned as reward and recompense. The rhetoric echoes 61:8 and declares Yahweh's determination to give to Jerusalem the consequence of Yahweh's own full commitment. It is Yahweh's guarantee to Jerusalem of complete well-being.

Verses 6–11 alternate between two themes: restore Jerusalem (vv. 6–7) . . . Yahweh's resolve (vv. 8–9); restore Jerusalem (v. 10) . . . Yahweh's resolve (v. 11). The rhetorical movement of the poetry shows the single and direct way in which Israel's faith holds together Yahwistic resolve and material possibility. It is exactly the resolve of Yahweh that opens the future for Jerusalem as a rehabilitated city.

62:12 **They shall be called, "The Holy People,**
        The Redeemed of the LORD";
      and you shall be called, "Sought Out,
        A City Not Forsaken."

The poem concludes with a name change, a reprise on the theme of verse 2. The new name, given in a fourfold form, is all relational and Yahwistic. The defining issue in the life of Jerusalem is its relation to Yahweh. Thus a new name bespeaks a reconciled relationship:

Holy means singularly committed to Yahweh. The term here might be rendered "Holy People" (as in NRSV), but could be taken as a "people belonging to the holy (one)."

Redeemed of Yahweh refers to those brought out of bondage to the nations, for Yahweh has long since been the one who brought Israel out of bondage. This is perhaps an allusion to the economic transactions of jubilee. (On the notion of "redeem" and the work of Yahweh, see Exodus 6:6 and Isaiah 43:1–4.)

Sought Out refers to the one looked after and cared for and valued. See negatively Jeremiah 30:14, 17, where the same term is taken negatively as "not cared for."

Not Forsaken is the term used in verse 4, whereby the shamed, rejected, divorced one is now fully reembraced.

The primary point is a simple one. Jerusalem's life can begin anew after the onslaught of exile because of Yahweh's reliable, genuine, unfailing concern. But that primal point requires daring, rich expression, a poetic effort to permeate the despair of Jerusalem that knew itself too long abandoned by Yahweh. The news to Jerusalem is "not abandoned" (see Isa. 54:7–8).

"IT IS I, MIGHTY TO SAVE"
63:1–6

The marvelous poetry of chapters 60—62 anticipates the decisive intervention of Yahweh into the life of the world, whereby Jerusalem will be exalted and all its erstwhile enemies will become subservient, cast in menial roles. That same promissory note is voiced in this brief poetic unit. However, here the action is much more forceful and abrasive, and the treatment of former abusive enemies is much more brutal. Yahweh here intervenes not only actively but violently as a warrior. Yahweh is The Enforcer who has the resolve and the leverage to effect the inversion of world power more benignly expressed in the preceding chapters.

63:1 **"Who is this that comes from Edom,**
   from Bozrah in garments stained crimson?
   Who is this so splendidly robed,
   marching in his great might?"

   "It is I, announcing vindication,
   mighty to save."

This single verse consists of a dramatic exchange of question and answer. Westermann has suggested that the exchange is between an alert sentinel (see 21:11–12; 52:8; and 62:6) and one who approaches who is required to identify himself (*Isaiah 40–66*, 380–381). The question is an inquiry that has the force of an imperative: "Halt! Who goes there?" The question is intensified because the approaching stranger (who comes from Edom-Borzah) arrive in question-raising red dress (see 34:6). It is possible that "Edom" is identified as the point of origin in order to make a play on the Hebrew terms "Edom" and "red" (see Gen. 25:25). In any case, it is the answer that is important: "It is I." Here speaks the one who is known and need not be named in Israel. The approaching one is marked by Yahweh's

most characteristic terms, "vindication" (*ṣedeqāh*) and "salvation" (*yš'*).
(Notice the same word pair in 61:10; 62:2.) It is Yahweh who comes to
right the wrong and to create a viable condition for life.

63:2 **"Why are your robes red,**
     and your garments like theirs who tread the winepress?"

   [3] **"I have trodden the winepress alone,**
       and from the peoples no one was with me;
     I trod them in my anger
       and trampled them in my wrath;
     their juice spattered on my garments,
       and stained all my robes.
   [4] **For the day of vengeance was in my heart,**
       and the year for my redeeming work had come.
   [5] **I looked, but there was no helper;**
       I stared, but there was no one to sustain me;
     so my own arm brought me victory,
       and my wrath sustained me.
   [6] **I trampled down peoples in my anger,**
       I crushed them in my wrath,
       and I poured out their lifeblood on the earth."

The sequence of question-answer is reiterated. The question inquires
about the appearance of the one who approaches, who we already know is
dressed in "stained crimson" (v. 1). The term rendered "red" in verse 2 is
'adom, clearly a play on *'edom* in verse 1. The sentry recognizes that the approaching stranger has the appearance of one who is wine-stained from
trampling grapes.

The answer to the second question now consists of the remainder of the
poetic unit as a divine oracle (vv. 3–6). The name of the speaker is nowhere
given, but we are in no doubt about the identity of the speaker. Three motifs recur in this brief utterance:

1. The theme of "winepress" is continued from the reference to
"crimson/red" in verses 1–2. This metaphor characteristically is used to refer to judgment, so that the "red juice of the grape" is in fact the blood of
Yahweh's enemies spilled in Yahweh's vigorous activity. (See Lam. 1:15;
Joel 3:13; Rev. 14:19, 19:15.) This image of massive judgment, moreover,
is carried over in our own national lore in *The Battle Hymn of the Republic*:
"He is trampling out the vintage where the grapes of wrath are stored."

2. Yahweh acts alone, without accomplice, without any human agent;

that is, here without Cyrus, who otherwise is prominent in the inversion of Jewish prospects. Yahweh is willing and able, and acts decisively alone to effect this brutal judgment. It is Yahweh whose clothes are badly stained by the killing that Yahweh has perpetrated.

3. Yahweh has undertaken this deathly work, motivated by "anger and wrath." Nothing is said here about the basis of such rage; elsewhere that anger against oppressive power is rooted in Yahweh's deep commitment to Jerusalem, for whom Yahweh will not finally tolerate such abuse. That motivation here, however, must be inferred.

These motifs of winepress/blood, solo activity, and rage are all in the service of a dramatic portrayal of a warrior fresh from a brutal confrontation. The dramatic articulation is, in the end, a means whereby Israel's most elemental trust in Yahweh can be voiced. The substance of that faith is expressed as Yahweh's "day of vengeance" and "year for my redeeming work" (v. 4) that will bring victory (*yš'*; v. 5). At the heart of prophetic hope that here tilts toward apocalyptic expression is the deep conviction of Judaism that in due course—soon or late—there will be a time when Yahweh will act decisively to right the wrongs of the world and to establish a just, peaceable rule in the earth. That new rule, inevitably, will be a governance especially attentive to and protective of Jerusalem, and therefore aimed at elimination of the threat to Jerusalem embodied in other military powers. We have already seen in 61:2 the "day of vengeance" that is the anticipated moment of Yahweh's decisive intrusion.

The poetic imagery of this unit is forceful and concrete, to the point of violence. In characteristic fashion, the poet is able to make a theological claim in vivid language that voices the central passions that are the ground of Israelite hope. Two observations derive from that awareness. First, the theological point is that the God who comes in this violent mode is the God who will make things right in the midst of an abusive world. It is the final conviction of Jerusalem that Yahweh will not quit until the "victory" over all negations is secure. But second, such a massive hope, in the face of circumstances to the contrary, requires a God who is vigorous and forceful in the extreme. As a consequence, the extreme *theological conviction* cannot be extracted from the *imagery of violence* that we may find deeply offensive. It is precisely such a God of force who gives Jerusalem buoyancy in the face of great threat. This linkage between the violent capacity of Yahweh and the trust of Israel is already implicit in the pivotal Isaianic invitation to faith in 7:9. A "nicer" God or a happier God might be preferred, but Israel entertains no romantic illusions about the vexed context of its life. Here is voiced faith fully situated in the context of a community under threat. It is evident that this mode of faith has left a deeply problematic residue of violence for the continuing faith claims of Judaism and Christianity.

"YOU, O LORD, ARE OUR FATHER"
63:7–64:12

The victory hymn of 63:1–6 exudes complete confidence in the "victory" Yahweh is about to work for Yahweh's people. That *hymn* is characteristic of Israel's exuberant trust in Yahweh. The power of the hymn, however, is abruptly and completely countered in these verses, which are a classic *psalm of lament* that might well be found in the Psalter. In this utterance, Israel ponders its lamentable situation in the context of Yahweh's promises, and focuses upon the profound contradiction between faith and circumstance.

The poem exhibits all the characteristic elements of the communal lament (see Patrick D. Miller, *They Cried to the Lord*, 55–134). The immediate context of the poetry may be the Exile, when Israel is preoccupied with the loss of land and temple and is unable to see beyond present misery. Indeed, Muilenburg suggests a date of 560 or 550, in the heart of the Exile. In that context, the poem has most in common with the book of Lamentations and Psalms 74 and 79. But of course Israel's near despair over loss is not confined to the Exile, so the poem may also be understood in the postexilic period when the high promises of exilic Isaiah did not grandly come to fruition.

In any case, the poem in the context of the book of Isaiah is candid about its circumstance and bold in its address to Yahweh. The complaint of the poem affirms that Judaism counted heavily upon Yahweh's promises, but its real life in the world is deeply and endlessly marked by contradictions that become the matrix of both great confidence and abrasive petition.

"They Remembered the Days of Old"
(63:7–14)

The present urgency to be expressed as complaint and petition is situated against a backdrop of Yahweh's past graciousness, which has been the source of Israel's life. Israel's rich past, here recited, sets in stark contrast the remembered gracious governance of Yahweh and Israel's present acute need.

63:7 **I will recount the gracious deeds of the LORD,**
    the praiseworthy acts of the LORD,

because of all that the LORD has done for us,
    and the great favor to the house of Israel
that he has shown them according to his mercy,
    according to the abundance of his steadfast love.
⁸For he said, "Surely they are my people,
    children who will not deal falsely";
and he became their savior
⁹   in all their distress.
It was no messenger or angel
    but his presence that saved them;
in his love and in his pity he redeemed them;
    he lifted them up and carried them all the days of old.

These verses are a rather general doxological opening that lacks specificity. They are dominated by Israel's preferred vocabulary of covenantal fidelity, all attributed to Yahweh: gracious deeds, favor, mercy, steadfast love (the same Hebrew term as "gracious deeds" in verse 7), love, pity, redeemed. Indeed, Yahweh (wrongly) had complete confidence in Israel, and it is on the basis of that mistaken confidence that Yahweh lavished generosity upon Israel. Yahweh is inordinately self-giving to Israel in the past and is so remembered.

63:10 **But they rebelled**
    and grieved his holy spirit;
  therefore he became their enemy;
    he himself fought against them.

This single verse disrupts the historical retrospect that focuses on gracious deeds; it claims that Israel's own conduct was incongruent with Yahweh's generosity. The verse reflects a standard theological tradition in ancient Israel that asserted that Israel's entire life with Yahweh is one of recalcitrant disobedience (see Deuteronomy 32; Psalm 106; Nehemiah 9). No specifics are given, but there is ample data offered in the other recitals. From the outset, Israel has found it difficult (impossible?) to entrust its life to the governance of Yahweh.

The phrase "grieved his holy spirit" cannot be taken to host any developed theological sense that eventuated in a later Christian doctrine of the Trinity. Rather, the verse asserts simply that Israel's recalcitrance violated Yahweh's self-giving power (spirit) that was inscrutably rooted (holy) in Yahweh's own life and character. That is, Israel has violated Yahweh's own person. The sin is acute, and it permeates all of Israel's past life.

63:11 **Then they remembered the days of old,**
        of Moses his servant.
      Where is the one who brought them up out of the sea
        with the shepherds of his flock?
      Where is the one who put within them
        his holy spirit,
   12 **who caused his glorious arm**
        to march at the right hand of Moses,
      who divided the waters before them
        to make for himself an everlasting name,
   13 **who led them through the depths?**
      Like a horse in the desert,
        they did not stumble.
   14 **Like cattle that go down into the valley,**
        the spirit of the LORD gave them rest.
      Thus you led your people,
        to make for yourself a glorious name.

Verse 10, however, is only a brief disruption, for in the next verse the rhetoric returns to a recital of Yahweh's goodness. Even in the midst of rebellion, Israel recited Yahweh's great acts and continued to count on them. And when trouble came—trouble presumably based in rebellion—Israel counted on Yahweh enough to ask: *Where?* Where now is Yahweh, who in the past did so much for Israel? The "where question," which raises issues about Yahweh's reliability, provides an occasion to identify Yahweh fully in terms of how Yahweh has treated Israel. This is Yahweh: who caused exodus; who empowered Israel by Yahweh's own spirit of holiness; who divided the waters; who led Israel to enhance Yahweh's own reputation. Except for a brief acknowledgment in verse 10, this is a sustained review of Yahweh's past. The tone of the whole suggests that Israel has no awareness that recalcitrance may alienate Yahweh and cause a pause in gracious fidelity from Yahweh's side. As a consequence, the recital of past graciousness functions in part as an accusation of Yahweh. Yahweh is not now as Yahweh was then. And so the faithful must pose the great question of theodicy that dominates Israel's complaints. Where now is Yahweh? Where now is Yahweh when needed? Where now is Yahweh when circumstance demands fidelity and intervention? This is the shrill question of the faithful who expect much from God in any case. It is worth noting that three times in verses 10–14 Yahweh's spirit is mentioned. Yahweh's spirit is the energizing force rooted in God's own inscrutable life that energizes Israel's existence. And now, so they observed, that Force is not effective for Israel as in times past. And therefore crisis!

"Turn Back . . . Come Down" (63:15–64:12)

With 63:7–14 as backdrop focused on Yahweh's past goodness and a fleeting acknowledgment of Israel's rebellion, now the complaint begins in earnest. The poem is an interweaving of characteristic themes of complaint, petition, confession of sin, and confession of confidence in Yahweh. These assertions may occur in a variety of configurations. In whatever configuration they occur, the ultimate intention of such insistent prayer is to move Yahweh to act salvifically according to Israel's need, according to Yahweh's character, and according to Yahweh's past commitments to Israel.

> 63:15 **Look down from heaven and see,**
>> **from your holy and glorious habitation.**
>> **Where are your zeal and your might?**
>>> **The yearning of your heart and your compassion?**
>>> **They are withheld from me.**
>> 16 **For you are our father,**
>>> **though Abraham does not know us**
>>> **and Israel does not acknowledge us;**
>> **you, O LORD, are our father;**
>>> **our Redeemer from of old is your name.**
>> 17 **Why, O LORD, do you make us stray from your ways**
>>> **and harden our heart, so that we do not fear you?**
>> **Turn back for the sake of your servants,**
>>> **for the sake of the tribes that are your heritage.**
>> 18 **Your holy people took possession for a little while;**
>>> **but now our adversaries have trampled down your sanctuary.**
>> 19 **We have long been like those whom you do not rule,**
>>> **like those not called by your name.**

The prayer begins with a direct petition that assumes that Yahweh is remote in heaven (see 1 Kings 8:36, 39, 43, 45, 49) but can be motivated to look to the earth, to Israel's need (v. 15a). And if Yahweh looks and notices, Yahweh will act accordingly (see Exod. 2:24–25). The second part of verse 15 raises a question with Yahweh that functions both as motivation and as reprimand. The "where" of this verse echoes verse 11 and assumes that Yahweh's zeal and compassion for Jerusalem should be reliable and visible now. That they are not available hints at a failure on Yahweh's part. The motivation is offered in verse 16 that reminds Yahweh of the intimate and enduring connection between Yahweh and Israel. Nothing here need be made of masculine gender imagery, because the accent is not on masculinity or a patriarchal role but on the reality that Israel belongs to Yahweh and is dependent on Yahweh, and that Yahweh in an inalienable way is responsible for the well-being of Israel (see Exod. 4:22; Isa. 1:2). (The rhetoric of Jeremiah 31:20 may support the same intensity of connection, perhaps with Yahweh portrayed as a mother.)

The contrast made between Yahweh as our father and Abraham as our father is a curious one. Clearly, Abraham as ancient ancestor is not available as is the living God. Westermann suggests that the pathos of the lines indicates moving beyond tradition to a live relationship. In an attempt to relate to concrete communal conflict, Paul Hanson interprets "Abraham" as that priestly community that has preempted the tradition and is unresponsive to the plight of the speaking community. In any case, reference to Abraham is only a foil for the positive point insisted upon. Israel has "from of old" counted on Yahweh and has no other recourse. Thus Yahweh is petitioned to act "in role" as the proper guardian and protector of Israel.

The affirmation of verse 16 is followed in verse 17a by a return to the implied rebuke of verse 15b. The question "why" is characteristic of complaint (as is "where") and suggests something is awry that Israel does not understand and will not accept. These lines are stunning because they are causative, suggesting that even Israel's waywardness is Yahweh's fault. Hanson observes:

> It is *God* who has made them stray (cf. Ezek. 20:25–26). In what could seem like a cruel mockery of their religious epic, Israel finds itself merged into the character of its arch villain, with heart hardened like the Pharaoh and with God fighting against them (63:17) (*Isaiah 40–66*, 239).

The lines of the poem suggest that Yahweh has done a bad thing in causing Israel to sin, and therefore Yahweh is addressed by a second major imperative (the first in verse 15). Yahweh is urged to repent, to change, to move from a neglectful God to a faithful God full of attentive compassion. Israel's future depends on Yahweh's changed disposition. The urging of this petition is explicated in verses 18–19, which sharply contrast *then* and *now*. *Then*—briefly—your people, the ones for whom you bear responsibility, had a safe land. But *now* in this situation of crisis that generates lament, your sanctuary is scorned by enemies, and Israel is like a people that has no God. The complaint amounts to a charge that Yahweh is neglectful. And when Yahweh neglects, the powers of chaos and negation (in the form of human adversaries) will do their worst. Israel is hopeless without an attentive Yahweh. Yahweh must repent and become attentive. Israel's need is urgent; Yahweh's obligation is acute!

64:1 **O that you would tear open the heavens and come down,**
    so that the mountains would quake at your presence—
  ²**as when fire kindles brushwood**
    and the fire causes water to boil—
  to make your name known to your adversaries,
    so that the nations might tremble at your presence!
  ³**When you did awesome deeds that we did not expect,**
    you came down, the mountains quaked at your presence.
  ⁴**From ages past no one has heard,**
    no ear has perceived,
  no eye has seen any God besides you,
    who works for those who wait for him.
  ⁵**You meet those who gladly do right,**
    those who remember you in your ways.
  But you were angry, and we sinned;
    because you hid yourself we transgressed.
  ⁶**We have all become like one who is unclean,**
    and all our righteous deeds are like a filthy cloth.
  We all fade like a leaf,
    and our iniquities, like the wind, take us away.
  ⁷**There is no one who calls on your name,**
    or attempts to take hold of you;
  for you have hidden your face from us,
    and have delivered us into the hand of our iniquity.

This unit of the poem begins with an abrupt and very strong imperative. It is a bid that Yahweh should tear open the distancing cover between heaven (where Yahweh is) and earth (where Jerusalem is), and come down into the situation of need. This rhetoric is an advance beyond 63:15 that only asked Yahweh to look. Now the need is escalated. The rhetoric is a bid for a replication of the old theophanies, as at Sinai, when Yahweh would forcibly, cataclysmically become present in dangerous and overwhelming ways (see Judg. 5:4–5; Psalm 18:7ff.; Hab. 3:6). The poet appeals to an old rhetorical-liturgical tradition that is primitive in its expectation of the physical assault Yahweh may make against Yahweh's enemies. The petition asks for a visible show of decisive power that will impress Israel's enemies and therefore create life space for Israel. The rhetoric here is quite in contrast to the general petition of 63:15–19, showing that the prophetic-poetic tradition of

Israel is variegated and liberated in its imagination, and is confined to no single mode of utterance.

Verse 4 is something of a doxological interlude that celebrates Yahweh's incomparability. (See the same theme as an interlude in the context of the great epiphanic poem of Exodus 15:10–11.) Looking back from verse 4, it is clear that Yahweh's incomparability consists in Yahweh's unrivaled power and capacity to intimidate Yahweh's adversaries. But looking forward from verse 4, Yahweh's incomparability is very differently stated. Verses 5–7 as a confession of sin may also function in a complaint as a motivation in order to evoke Yahweh's caring response. This confession is remarkable because it contradicts verse 17, which holds Yahweh accountable for Israel's trouble. Here Israel accepts responsibility and acknowledges that Yahweh is indeed available to those who do rightly. The implication, of course, is that Yahweh is not available to those who disobey as Israel has done (so 63:10). These verses thus change the tone of the prayer and admit that the current trouble in Israel is deserved trouble. Israel has been ritually impure (unclean; see 6:5), and even Israel's best obedience is unacceptable. Israel is totally unworthy, and therefore it is an understandable consequence that Israel's very existence is deeply jeopardized. The culmination of the confession is an admission of total failure, so that Yahweh is for good reason hidden and unavailable (v. 7). The admission that "there is no one who calls on your name" is nicely parallel to 63:19, "like those not called by your name." The connection between Yahweh and Israel is voided, and Israel is left to the destructive vagaries of the historical process. It is plausible that the confession of verses 5–7 might be the end of the matter. The terrible displacement of loss and jeopardy in exile is fully accounted for. Yahweh is fully vindicated, and Israel is left without recourse, hopeless in a world where adversaries prevail. That is the logic of the prayer thus far.

But of course such a logic completely misses the depth, pathos, and insistence of Israel's faith. Such a prayer ending in futility is completely logical. But it is not and cannot be the way faithful Israel prays. Therefore, beyond such a logical outcome, the prayer continues with a mighty "yet," the yet that is at the bottom of the theological tradition of Isaiah, the yet that makes hope possible when logic and circumstance dictate a harsh ending (see a parallel usage in Hab. 3:18).

64:8 **Yet, O LORD, you are our Father;**
       we are the clay, and you are our potter;
       we are all the work of your hand.

⁹ Do not be exceedingly angry, O LORD,
   and do not remember iniquity forever.
   Now consider, we are all your people.
¹⁰ Your holy cities have become a wilderness,
   Zion has become a wilderness,
   Jerusalem a desolation.
¹¹ Our holy and beautiful house,
   where our ancestors praised you,
 has been burned by fire,
   and all our pleasant places have become ruins.
¹² After all this, will you restrain yourself, O LORD?
   Will you keep silent, and punish us so severely?

Verse 8 enacts a radical rhetorical turn in the prayer of Israel. In the preceding verse, Israel has confessed its sin. In verse 5a, Israel has conceded that Yahweh will deal positively with the righteous. As a consequence, iniquitous Israel has no claim of any kind to make upon Yahweh.

But verse 8 is quintessentially Israelite. After the full admission of verses 5–7, a new rhetorical thrust begins that is, in Hebrew, "But now Yahweh. . . . " The "but now" is a move to the present, urgent moment, leaving everything heretofore behind as an irrelevance. In the now, what counts is not anything of us; what counts now is wholly of Yahweh. Characteristically, the gospel faith of Israel shifts the subject radically away from "us" to Yahweh, who is now the only compelling subject. What is to be said in this hour of Yahweh, moreover, is nothing of the quid pro quo assumed in verse 5. What is to be said now concerns Yahweh's primordial relations and foundational commitments that are not at all qualified by circumstance or impinged upon by response. In spite of everything heretofore, Yahweh is cast inescapably as "our father." In spite of everything heretofore, Yahweh is cast inescapably as "our potter." The two metaphors, father and potter, affirm that in the end Yahweh has total responsibility for Israel and Israel is completely dependent upon and derivative from Yahweh's initiative. Yahweh's identity as father of course reiterates 63:16 but looks beyond that to the most elemental relation possible, that of begetter and begotten. The second image of potter also assigns to Yahweh complete initiative for the shape and life of Israel.

The two metaphors are employed together in 45:9–10 to bespeak Yahweh's complete authority in the relation and to deny Israel any voice in its own future. Indeed, we may say that our verse prays back to Yahweh the reprimanding utterance on the lips of Yahweh in 45:9–10. Beyond that, the potter image is much represented in exilic Isaiah through the verb "form" that lies behind the noun "potter" (see 43:1, 7, 21; 44:2, 21, 24). Yahweh is in complete charge of Israel's life, and now Yahweh must act accordingly. The third identifying mark of verse 8, "the work of your hand," reinforces the complete initiative of Yahweh in the relationship.

With verse 8 offered as a motivational basis, verse 9 voices a petition in three imperatives, two of which are negative. The first two imperatives ask Yahweh to move beyond anger in a petition that is rooted in older liturgical usage. One such liturgical assurance is in Psalm 103:9–10:

> He will not always accuse,
>   nor will he keep his anger forever.
> He does not deal with us according to our sins,
>   nor repay us according to our iniquities.

And the ground for such an assurance is the assertion of Yahweh's "steadfast love" before and after, in Psalm 103:8 and 11. That is, the appeal to Yahweh is not an *ad hoc* request, but it is a confident petition grounded in trusted affirmation. Israel has good reason to hope that Yahweh in steadfast love will move beyond anger. The third petition, "Now consider," reiterates the imperative of 63:15, "Look."

The characterization of verses 10–11 is a detailed account, for the benefit of Yahweh, of the sorry situation of Jerusalem and its environs. It is standard practice in lament to engage in hyperbolic characterization of trouble, apparently to move Yahweh to care and to act. In this description, the city is a desolation, the temple is burned by foreigners, and the loveliness of the city is in ruins. These lines are fairly conventional in such prayers.

The final verse of the prayer is a reflective reprise wondering how effective the petition will be (v. 12). Will the prayer move Yahweh to act? In a double question the wonderment is put directly to Yahweh. "After all this" perhaps refers to the devastation just reviewed or perhaps more immediately to the prayer. Will Yahweh yet remain passive, neglectful, and uninterested? The question that dares to raise the troubling possibility of Yahweh's unresponsiveness is odd but not without parallel. The poignant ending of the book of Lamentations, the most sustained utterance on our subject, voices a parallel wonderment:

> Renew our days as of old—
> unless you have utterly rejected us,
>   and are angry with us beyond measure.
>   (Lam. 5:22)

Israel does not flinch from asking this most elemental question of faith. Most remarkably, Israel dares to end its prayer on such a note of wonderment and uncertainty. Israel does not know the answer to its question, does not know if Yahweh will be driven into activity or not. Israel does not know, because Yahweh cannot be summoned automatically, and its prayers do not produce guaranteed outcomes. Israel does not know, moreover, because its history is ragged and unresolved. There are hopes in such prayers, but it is hope that has "not received what was promised" (Heb. 11:39).

This is a most astonishing prayer, because it enters into and dwells on the contradiction that marks this faith. This prayer knows and acknowledges guilt. It knows and acknowledges deep trouble. It dares to hint that Yahweh is implicated in the trouble through neglect. All of these might be grounds for the cessation of prayer and the abandonment of faith. Indeed, that is the modern propensity, given the visible failure of God.

But Israel's life and Israel's faith are of another sort. Everything turns on the "yet" ("but now") of verse 8. In the end, Israel must pray this way because there is no other alternative. Israel must, in the end, turn its life back to Yahweh, because it has nowhere else to turn and no one else whom it may address. There is nothing rational or orderly or explainable or logical about this prayer. It is much more visceral and elemental than any of our usual categories for faith. It is the ground of Israel's future, situated in hope, but without assurance or guarantee.

We may pause to consider together *the hymn* (63:1–6) and *the lament* (63:7–64:12). The two are very different in every way, and yet they are here placed back-to-back. These two rhetorical units are a response to or extrapolation from the enormous hopes of chapters 60—62. The promises linger over emerging Judaism, but surely are well short of fruition.

The hymn of 63:1–6 is utterly certain of Yahweh's "day of vengeance." In the meantime, however, things are not well. The unresolved quality of Israel's life in displacement requires incessant prayer that draws Yahweh into the trouble. Such a prayer is not informed by general notions of prayer. It is informed, rather, by the history of "gracious deeds" that form a backdrop for wonder and trust. Hanson, in his exposition, alludes to the parable of Luke 18:1–8 concerning the widow who nagged the judge sufficiently to receive a favorable ruling. It is important to notice the purpose of the prayer of the widow in the parable: "Then Jesus told them a parable about their need to pray always and not to lose heart" (Luke 18:1). Israel, remarkably, in its most devastating circumstance, does not lose heart. Prayer is a practice of faith that "keeps heart." When the church is honest and imaginative, this is what the church does every time it utters "Our Father." It cedes initiative for its life over to God, the only one who can give futures. The "Our Father" addressed in our most conventional Christian prayer is the "Father" to whom the exiles here may petition. It is confidence in this God that evokes the great "yet" of faith as the ground for all coming possibilities.

"HERE I AM, HERE I AM"
65:1–16

Everywhere in the Isaiah tradition Yahweh looms large. That large-looming God here speaks an oracle that is characteristic of the prophetic tradition and that insists that all parties to the covenant must come to terms with Yahweh. The assertion of Yahweh, characteristically two-sided, consists of both *a speech of judgment* and *a speech of assurance*. Both patterns of speech attest to Yahweh's sovereignty, but that awesome power may be voiced and experienced in two contrasting ways.

65:1 **I was ready to be sought out by those who did not ask,**
   to be found by those who did not seek me.
I said, "Here I am, here I am,"
   to a nation that did not call on my name.
²I held out my hands all day long
   to a rebellious people,
who walk in a way that is not good,
   following their own devices;
³a people who provoke me
   to my face continually,
sacrificing in gardens
   and offering incense on bricks;
⁴who sit inside tombs,
   and spend the night in secret places;
who eat swine's flesh,
   with broth of abominable things in their vessels;
⁵who say, "Keep to yourself,
   do not come near me, for I am too holy for you."
These are a smoke in my nostrils,
   a fire that burns all day long.
⁶See, it is written before me:
   I will not keep silent, but I will repay;
I will indeed repay into their laps

> [7] their iniquities and their ancestors' iniquities together,
>   says the LORD;
> because they offered incense on the mountains
>   and reviled me on the hills,
> I will measure into their laps
>   full payment for their actions.

As we have seen in 59:1, Israel's disputatious inclination was prepared to accuse Yahweh of malfeasance when things went wrong. In response, Yahweh is regularly prepared to offer a self-defense, asserting that a break-down in the relationship is no fault of Yahweh. Inevitably, such a self-defense on the part of Yahweh is regularly turned into a counteraccusation against Israel, providing evidence that the cause of trouble is the unresponsiveness and disobedience of Israel.

The self-defense of Yahweh is the assertion that Yahweh is indeed available, ready to be sought, ready to be found, ready to announce Yahweh's own presence, all the while extending hands of welcome, affection, and protection (vv. 1–2a). It is not true, so it is asserted, that Yahweh is hidden or absent, remote or unavailable. The word pair "seek and find" probably refers to serious worship activity, but in a larger sense it may indicate a readiness on Israel's part to be devoted actively to Yahweh. The crisis of exile raised acute questions about the availability and responsiveness of Yahweh, and some concluded that Yahweh had completely withdrawn from the exilic community. Exilic texts, however, assert Yahweh's readiness to be engaged with Israel:

> From there you will seek the LORD your God, and you will find him if you search after him with all your heart and soul. In your distress, when all these things have happened to you in time to come, you will return to the LORD your God and heed him (Deut. 4:29–30; see also Jer. 29:12–14).

Yahweh is completely available: "Here I am, here I am" (v. 1). Although the rhetoric is more or less conventional, it is worth noting that the same pattern of announcement is offered in 40:9, a text we have identified as quintessentially a "gospel" pronouncement: "Here is your God!" This is the God to be announced as present, the most profound piece of good news possible for exiles.

But as Yahweh is acquitted (by Yahweh's own testimony) of any charges of neglect, the speech turns aggressively to an indictment of Israel, who is the genuinely offending party in the relation (vv. 2b–5). Verse 2b provides a summary indictment: Israel refuses to walk in Yahweh's ways but walks in a different way, that is, obeys a different rule. Israel refuses to engage the plans ("devices") of Yahweh, but has its own plans (see 55:8–9 for the same term). That is, Israel refuses its proper identity as partner and subject to Yahweh, and acts autonomously or in response to would-be gods who are no gods at all. Of course, Yahweh will not be sought by such and surely will not be found. Yahweh is not seekable or findable among those who refuse to seek and find.

The summary indictment of verse 2b is detailed in verses 3–5 by a series of participial clauses, reproduced in English by "who . . . ". They are the ones who: (1) provoke Yahweh by engaging in rites and offerings to other gods; (2) seek messages from the dead, a clear violation of the *living* God; (3) ignore torah instructions regarding acceptable food and so render themselves ritually unclean and disqualified to "seek and find" in worship; (4) prattle about their own religiosity, all the while, by their vain and arrogant religious activity, cutting themselves off from Yahweh.

There can hardly be any doubt, given such evidence, who it is that is responsible for the deep alienation from Yahweh now experienced in exilic Israel. Israel is so unreflective and so obtuse that it cannot even recognize the heavy costs that come with its recalcitrant worship activity, which is no more than self-indulgent self-deception. Its much religious activity is an unpleasant smell and a distraction to Yahweh. Perhaps the last lines of verse 5 are reminiscent of Yahweh's complete repudiation of Israel's worship described in 1:12–15.

Inevitably, such an indictment (vv. 2b–5) is followed by a harsh judgment (vv. 6–7). The judgment is no *ad hoc* or arbitrary decision on Yahweh's part—no quixotic, emotional response. "It is written." It may be, by the time of the postexilic community, that such rhetoric refers to engraved royal decrees, unchanging decisions like "the law of the Medes and the Persians," so that even Yahweh must mete out what is prescribed. Or it may more generally refer to the old torah teachings whereby Israel has always known that violation of Yahweh will be punished. Either way, a response of punishment and harsh judgment is soon to flow. Yahweh will repay. Israel in its obstinance is sure to receive from Yahweh what is deserved in "full payment." It is no wonder that Israel in exile knows itself to be alienated from Yahweh!

65:8 **Thus says the LORD:**
> **As the wine is found in the cluster,**
> **and they say, "Do not destroy it,**
> **for there is a blessing in it,"**

so I will do for my servants' sake,
    and not destroy them all.
⁹I will bring forth descendants from Jacob,
    and from Judah inheritors of my mountains;
my chosen shall inherit it,
    and my servants shall settle there.
¹⁰ Sharon shall become a pasture for flocks,
    and the Valley of Achor a place for herds to lie down,
    for my people who have sought me.

The rhetoric of divine oracle turns abruptly in verse 8. What had been a speech of judgment now, inexplicably, becomes a speech of saving assurance. As wine is to be valued and not destroyed, so exilic Israel is labeled "Do not destroy." Yahweh, moreover, is fully prepared to respect the protective label. The poetry is arranged to accent the stark change of mood after verses 6–7, a change made without acknowledgment. Now Yahweh is the guarantor of the future existence and well-being of Israel.

The promises of verses 9–10 concern recovery of the land and so are peculiarly appropriate for displaced people who long for return to their land. The promise in verse 9 is saturated with the cadences of the land promises of Genesis, including the naming of Jacob and reference to "descendants" (seed), "inheritors" (possessors), and "settled." The old promises that have long lingered in Israel's imagination are still in force. Some no doubt had concluded that the Exile had disrupted and nullified such promises. But no; they are still in effect and about to be implemented.

The general rhetoric of promise in verse 9 is made quite specific in verse 10. "Sharon" is seldom mentioned in the Old Testament; it refers to the coastal plain along the Mediterranean and is perhaps an image of prosperity and agricultural abundance (see 35:2; Song of Sol. 2:1). "The Valley of Achor" is situated somewhere in the vicinity of Jericho, thus to the east of the land. Although it is remembered in Israel as a place of vexation wrought by Israel's self-destructive disobedience (Joshua 7—8), the poetry of Hosea also makes it an image of recovered well-being, restored covenant, and renewal of agricultural abundance (Hos. 2:14ff.). The two references together, Sharon and Achor, perhaps encompass the west and the east of the land, thus all of the land. Or more likely the imagery bespeaks rich fertility and productivity in a restored land of well-being. The lines in our verse envision a serene and secure pastoral vista (see Psalm 16:6).

The last line of verse 10 provides a pivotal interpretive clue for our passage. We have seen the sharp disjunction between judgment (vv. 1–7) and promise (vv. 8–10). The last line of verse 10 illuminates that disjunction greatly. The renewed land is for "my people who have sought me." The verb "seek me" is the same as the term in verse 1. There are those who "seek Yahweh," who worship Yahweh, who live in serious obedience to Yahweh, and who acknowledge their membership in Yahweh's covenant. The promise is for them. But there are those, evidently, who refuse to seek Yahweh. The latter are the subject of the harsh judgment of verses 6–7. Thus the oracle, which addresses the seekers and the nonseekers, is reflective of a community that is divided between seekers and nonseekers. It becomes clear that this text is generated in and for a community, likely postexilic, that is deeply divided between the Yahweh-purists and "others," and that the categories of division are determined and championed (and voiced here) by the former group that understood themselves as the true seekers after Yahweh. Thus, although the poetry is divine oracle and surely has serious torah substance ("Obedience matters!"), it is equally clear that the poem is a tendentious, ideological threat to claim Yahwistic legitimacy and therefore authority for one segment of the community over against another. That is, Yahweh is here made a party to a torah dispute that is narratively reflected in the texts concerning Ezra and Nehemiah.

65:11 **But you who forsake the LORD,**
      who forget my holy mountain,
   who set a table for Fortune
      and fill cups of mixed wine for Destiny;
  ¹² **I will destine you to the sword,**
      and all of you shall bow down to the slaughter;
   because, when I called, you did not answer,
      when I spoke, you did not listen,
   but you did what was evil in my sight,
      and chose what I did not delight in.

These verses return to the hard-line judgment of verses 1–7. Again, we are not prepared for such harshness after verses 8–10, except that we are now aware of the intensity of internal dispute within the community. There are those, so the party of obedience insists in the name of Yahweh, who "forget and forsake" Yahweh, Yahweh's Torah, and Israel's identity. The indictment of them in verse 11 echoes that of verses 3–5. These are the ones who worship other gods. Scholars commonly conclude that "Fortune" and "Destiny" (in Hebrew, *Gad* and *Meni*) are proper names of the gods of fate. That is, these members of the community have traded off the risky vitality of Yahweh for other gods whose decrees are taken to be settled and without elusiveness or risk. If so, they yield a kind of flat, one-dimensional certitude.

The sentence of decree in verse 12 picks up on the name of the god "Destiny," and now Yahweh says, "I destine you" (same verb). It is Yahweh and not any other who has the capacity to decree futures in Israel. This decree, moreover, unlike the imagined decrees of these other gods, is a brutal, violent death. The reason for such harshness, to return to earlier themes, is unresponsiveness to Yahweh. Stated negatively, the people did not answer; they did not listen. Stated positively, they disobeyed and displeased Yahweh. Yahweh is ready to intervene in behalf of this endangered community but will not do so for those who choose otherwise. The close juxtaposition of assurance and threat is logically difficult; but it is immediately sensible when we remember that we are dealing, not with a formula or a mechanism, but with a Person of intense requirement and even more intense commitment. It is clear that the God who says "Here I am" cannot say so to those who neither seek nor find, neither answer nor listen.

65:13 **Therefore thus says the Lord GOD:**
    My servants shall eat,
      but you shall be hungry;
    my servants shall drink,
      but you shall be thirsty;
    my servants shall rejoice,
      but you shall be put to shame;
    ¹⁴ **my servants shall sing for gladness of heart,**
      but you shall cry out for pain of heart,
      and shall wail for anguish of spirit.
    ¹⁵ **You shall leave your name to my chosen to use as a curse,**
      and the Lord GOD will put you to death;
      but to his servants he will give a different name.
    ¹⁶ **Then whoever invokes a blessing in the land**
      shall bless by the God of faithfulness,
    and whoever takes an oath in the land
      shall swear by the God of faithfulness;
    because the former troubles are forgotten
      and are hidden from my sight.

The sociopolitical-theological division in the community is now completely clear. This text is the voice of advocacy for "the good guys," the ones who seek and find Yahweh, who obey and who are the carriers of the marvelous land promises of Yahweh as an antidote to exile. The conflict is between "my servants" and "you." The "you" is not identified, but they are clearly the unorthodox members of the community who practice the abominations of verses 2b–5, 11. The contrast is elaborated in four symmetrical statements that echo the old covenantal cadences of blessing and curse. Each statement is introduced by "behold" (completely absent in the NRSV) that focuses dramatic attention on the statements. The fourfold statement is not unlike the rhetoric of Jeremiah 4:23–26, also an anticipation of the coming decisiveness of Yahweh, introduced by "behold." "My servants" shall eat/drink/rejoice/sing; that is, be blessed. But "you" shall hunger/thirst/be ashamed/cry out/wail; that is, be cursed. The two sequences of terms bespeak a *life under blessing* and a *life under curse*. The difference concerns both *material* resources for life as well as the *sociomoral* future of inclusion or exclusion. The poetry intends to bring every aspect of life under the aegis of Yahweh's blessing or curse.

The tight symmetry of verses 13–14 is further elucidated in verses 15–16. The "you" here condemned will become a tag word and a slogan for negativity; "you" shall be destroyed by Yahweh, contra verse 8. But the blessed shall receive a new name—a new identity, a new relationship. The new name is perhaps reminiscent of the renaming anticipated in 62:4, 12.

Verse 16 seems to provide a transition to the glorious promise that is to follow in verses 17–25. In this verse, all that is negative and destructive is left behind. Now the focus is singularly upon the sphere of blessing that is marked by Yahweh's *faithfulness*. In the long run, what will count is Yahweh's complete reliability, even in the midst of deep crisis. As a result of that overriding, determined, resilient, inexhaustible reliability, the "former troubles" will be completely forgotten. In this last formulation, two observations are in order. The "former troubles" are not identified, and in context the term probably refers to the Exile. If, however, we consider the completed book of Isaiah, then we may say that the phrase refers to the entire theme of judgment at the hand of Yahweh, a theme that has dominated early Isaiah (see 9:1 on "former time" and 43:18 on "former things"). This part of the book of Isaiah intends to move the imagination of the exilic community into a future governed by Yahweh, embraced by faithful Israel, free of vexation.

The reference to what is "former" invites us also to consider one other linkage to the earlier book of Isaiah. We have identified 7:9 and its summons to faith as definitional for early Isaiah. In that text, Ahaz and Jerusalem are urged to *trust* in Yahweh against risky circumstance. Here the same word is not a summons to Jerusalem to trust but an assertion that Yahweh is *trustworthy*. Indeed, it is the *trustworthy God* who is the ground and object of *Israel's trust*. The emergence of a blessed community out of the "former troubles" is in response to Yahweh's reliability.

The entire unit of verses 1–16 is a deep summons to the community of faith to decide. Although the rhetoric is daring, the theological structure of the passage is simple and direct, and echoes an ancient urging (Deut. 30:15–20). Those who seek Yahweh will live and be blessed, rejoicing in safe food, abundant drink, and exuberant singing. Those who choose otherwise will be "destined" (v. 12) by the God of all destiny. The poem as a whole is a powerful insistence that Yahweh continues to be the defining factor in the future shape of the life of Israel.

NEW HEAVENS; NEW EARTH; NEW JERUSALEM
65:17–25

These verses are commonly taken to be a new rhetorical beginning that offers an extended, exuberant divine oracle of the newness Yahweh is about to give. It is worth noting, however, that the promissory tone of these verses is especially appropriate after the affirmation of verse 16. In that verse, the faithful God of Israel promises to the obedient (who seek Yahweh) a newness in which "former troubles" are overcome. Our verses then portray in considerable detail the "latter time" about to be given that is in total contrast to "former troubles." Although the oracle itself is exceedingly large in scope, the structure of verses 1–15 concerning a sharp division in the community suggests that the newness here is not offered generally. It is, rather, an offer made only to the obedient. They are the ones now about to be inducted into a gospel newness.

65:17 **For I am about to create new heavens**
      and a new earth;
      the former things shall not be remembered
      or come to mind.
   18 **But be glad and rejoice forever**
      in what I am creating;
      for I am about to create Jerusalem as a joy,
      and its people as a delight.
   19a **I will rejoice in Jerusalem,**
      and delight in my people;

Here speaks the creator of heaven and earth, the governor of world history, whose peculiar attention—like the attention of the book of Isaiah—is fixed on Jerusalem. The initial particle, "For behold" (RSV), may refer back to verse 16; if so, a linkage is made to the former time used in both verse 16 and verse 17. Yahweh is now the unqualified, wondrous subject of sweeping verbs, faithful to the cosmic vision of the Isaiah tradition. The mood is anticipatory. The creator God is to work a newness beyond all that is old, former, previous, failed. Although the articulation is fresh, the theme is not new. We have already seen, early in this tradition, that Yahweh is moving beyond what is troubling and unresolved to what is wondrously new and life giving (see 2:1–4; 4:2–6; 9:2–7; 11:1–9). There is a steady push toward newness in the Isaiah tradition that intends to override the despair of Israel, especially the despair of exile.

The newness to be wrought by the inscrutable power and irresistible resolve of Yahweh is as large as heaven and earth. The old heavens are overrun with controversy. The old earth is burned out with violence. The new cosmic realm will be perfectly governed by Yahweh, and the cosmos will be perfectly responsive to that governance. As cosmic as the newness to come is, it is also as specific as Jerusalem. The Isaiah tradition accepts that the matrix of Yahweh's work in the world concerns Jerusalem above all. It is Jerusalem where Yahweh's powers are rooted. It is Jerusalem where the Torah now resides (2:2–4). It is Jerusalem where Yahweh's presence is assured. It is Jerusalem where are met together "the hopes and fears of all the years." But it is also Jerusalem that was so disobedient as to be destroyed. It is Jerusalem that becomes the venue of timid, fearful, compromising kings and wayward, disobedient priests. Jerusalem that might have been glorious has turned out to be ignoble and disappointing. So has said the Isaiah tradition.

But now there is newness in every way! It is no wonder that the vision of the new Jerusalem evokes joy unbound and delight beyond measure. Now, before the very eyes of Israel, all that had been sordid and compromised will be pure and singular as promised. The city known as *Jeru-Shalom* will be a city of *shalom*, given by the God of all peace. Such a *shalom* is for singing and dancing. The poet now proceeds to itemize the facets of newness about to be given.

65:19b **no more shall the sound of weeping be heard in it,**
     or the cry of distress.
   20 **No more shall there be in it**
     an infant that lives but a few days,
     or an old person who does not live out a lifetime;

for one who dies at a hundred years will be considered a youth,
     and one who falls short of a hundred will be considered accursed.
21 They shall build houses and inhabit them;
     they shall plant vineyards and eat their fruit.
22 They shall not build and another inhabit;
     they shall not plant and another eat;
   for like the days of a tree shall the days of my people be,
     and my chosen shall long enjoy the work of their hands.
23 They shall not labor in vain,
     or bear children for calamity;
   for they shall be offspring blessed by the LORD—
     and their descendants as well.

This new infrastructure of the city will be marked by peace, justice, righteousness, and faithfulness. That is the long-term vision of the tradition of Isaiah:

> Afterward you shall be called the city of righteousness,
>   the faithful city.
> Zion shall be redeemed by justice,
>   and those in her who repent, by righteousness. (1:26b–27)

Such qualities are not simply theological ideas but conditions that prevail in actual social relationships.

The first quality of the new city, stated negatively and then positively, is a stability and order that guarantees long life. As long as the city is both a practitioner and victim of violence and brutality, no life is safe and no one will last very long. Thus we may imagine a violent, threatening social circumstance of assault, threat, and fear, permeated by weeping and cries of distress (too familiar to us!). But no more!

Moreover, it is possible to think that infant mortality is an index of the quality of community life. In a disordered, uncaring community too many babies die too soon from neglect, from malnutrition, from violence, from poor health and bad medical service—but no more! This is a city that will have a sustained infrastructure in which life is not endlessly at risk. Positively, it is asserted that premature death will be an exception that constitutes a judgment; such death is not ordinary or taken as routine. It is to be insisted, I assume, that a guaranteed long life of well-being is not to be equated with "medical advances" that extend life expectancy in order to keep people "alive" in various states of misery and dysfunction. Such a vision of the future as conjured by our technological capacity would be completely incongruous with the coming *shalom* of *Jeru-shalom*. Thus the vision is not only of an extended quality of life but a quality of life congruent with the gifts of a generous creator. There will be a reordering of resources so that all may luxuriate in life as the creator intends.

A second facet of the reconstituted city is economic stability (vv. 21–22). It is assured that there will be economic continuity with enough civil order that there need be no fear for loss of the results of work. We have already seen in 62:8–9 that the produce of the land is not to be vulnerable to foreign usurpation. We saw in that context, moreover, that the assurance given is counter to something like the "futility curses" of Amos 5:11:

> You have built houses of hewn stone,
>   but you shall not live in them;
> you have planted pleasant vineyards,
>   but you shall not drink their wine. (see also Mic. 6:15; Zeph. 1:13)

The effect of the newness of Yahweh is to turn old curses into blessing, old community-destroying practices into community-enhancing assurances.

The loss of one's economic gain might indeed happen by foreign invasion and occupation, for such occupiers brazenly and indiscriminately seize everything; that is, they "devour" the land (Jer. 8:16; 10:25). It may also be that such usurpation happens internally by confiscation or tax policies whereby the "big ones" arrange the economy to take, in an exercise of "eminent domain," what the "little ones" have. Such would seem to be the social practice criticized in Amos 5:10–11a, which evokes the futility curses.

Against such social condition and economic practice, the new city will leave people free of threat from outside aggression and inside confiscation, especially the confiscation of "widows and orphans." Yahweh will be the guarantor of a viable, community-sustaining economy. We may imagine that the torah practice envisioned in 2:2–4 produces such an assured community, especially envisioned in the parallel text of Micah 4:4, which adds a note concerning the safety of the economically marginalized:

> But they shall all sit under their own vines and under their own fig trees,
>   and no one shall make them afraid;
>   for the mouth of the LORD of hosts has spoken.

Nobody is threatened. Nobody is at risk. Nobody is in jeopardy because the new city has policies, practices, and protective structures that guarantee what must have been envisioned as an egalitarian possibility.

The third provision, perhaps connected to verses 19b–20 (v. 23), concerns an agenda of well-being for children in the new city. This single verse appears to draw on two different ancient traditions in Israel. On the one hand, the first two lines are often thought to allude to the curse of Genesis 3:16, so that the new Jerusalem will be free of a long-standing threat to well-being. On the other hand, the last three lines are saturated with cadences of the ancestral tales of Genesis. The terms "offspring" and "blessing" surely recall those stories, so that this is an imaginative move from the ancient "story of curse" (Genesis 3—11) to the freshly enacted "story of blessing" (Genesis 12ff.). The city is resituated in the story of blessing; indeed, father Abraham is anciently linked to *Jeru-shalom* (Gen. 14:18–20), and now the old vision of Salem (*Shalom*) will become concrete. The accent is upon children, the most vulnerable members of the community. It is worth noting that in our violent, acquisitive society, children are deeply at risk. The new city will declare that every year is "the year of the child."

These three accents on guaranteed long life (vv. 19b–20), economic stability (vv. 21–22), and life under blessing (v. 23) all attest to a city in which the power for life given by the creator is fully available and operates in concrete ways. The poem is a vision, but it is a vision looking to a public practice.

65:24 **Before they call I will answer,**
　　　　while they are yet speaking I will hear.
　25 **The wolf and the lamb shall feed together,**
　　　　the lion shall eat straw like the ox;
　　　　but the serpent—its food shall be dust!
　　They shall not hurt or destroy
　　on all my holy mountain,
　　　　　　　　　　says the LORD.

The conclusion of this promissory vision sounds two remarkable themes. The first concerns the direct, immediate availability and attentiveness of Yahweh to the city (v. 24). There is no doubt that economic viability is crucial to the city, evidenced in verses 19b–23. But economic viability by itself is not enough for the city, a lesson yet to be learned in an acquisitive society like ours. Beyond economic viability, there is a more elemental hunger that economic development cannot satisfy. In the end, the work of the city is to make *communion with God's holiness* a genuine possibility.

Here it is affirmed in Yahweh's own promise that Yahweh will be engaged with and attentive to the city. Indeed, that was Yahweh's gracious, self-giving offer already at the outset of this long chapter: "I said, 'Here I am, here I am'" (v. 1). Yahweh is ready to be in sustained contact. As we have seen in verses 1–7, 11–15, however, negative conditions made that impossible. Now, in the new city, conditions are right and Yahweh will be attentive.

It occurs to me that in this offer, Yahweh is portrayed (as in 49:14–15; 66:13) as an attentive mother. Or at least in conventional gender roles, it is mother who is so attentive that she senses a child's need or danger or summons and responds ahead of time. So here Yahweh will be attentive beforehand, able to anticipate and respond. The offer of the new city is a wondrous communion! Calvin, in this connection, mentions Ephesians 2:28; 3:12; and Hebrews 4:16, which affirm the miracle of *access* to God.

The second motif here returns to the large accents of creation in verse 17 (v. 25). The new work of Yahweh is not simply Jerusalem but a whole new creation that is laid out in the radical reordering of Jerusalem. This promise is a direct, albeit somewhat modified, quotation from 11:6–9. In that passage, we observed two important matters. First, the renovation of creation is linked in 11:1–5 to the coming of the new David. Second, 11:1–9 functions as a rhetorical conclusion to chapters 1—11 and so enacts a promise already in the midst of the trouble of "former things." The newness does not wait until the end, but according to the Isaiah tradition is being given all along the way.

From the outset, the Isaiah tradition has pressed toward Yahweh's newness, which is local and cosmic. Here it is affirmed that the most elemental hostilities in creation will be overcome, and all ancient hostilities in the human city will be nullified. There will be no more hurt in the realm of Yahweh's governance. *Shalom* will be full and complete and pervasive.

The third line of verse 25, given such wonderful affirmation, is curious. Although the verse clearly follows 11:6–9 in its phrasing, this third line is altered. Whereas 11:8 would seem to include snakes in the renovation, in our verse the serpent is the only creature of Genesis 3 who continues under curse. Calvin suggests: "*The serpent*, satisfied with *his dust*, shall wrap himself in it and shall no longer hurt by his envenomed bite." Perhaps in the end the poet is realistic and understands that even in the new city the resolution of Yahweh's *shalom* is still qualified. The poet has not yet undertaken a flight to apocalyptic. Such an acknowledgment about the serpent, however, although it may qualify the newness, also resonates with the reality of faith. The comment on the snake suggests that the divine oracle speaks about life in the real world and not in a never-never land.

This poetic unit, of everything in the Isaiah tradition, may give us pause.

It is a glorious artistic achievement. It is also an act of daring, doxological faith that refuses to be curbed by present circumstance. This poet, and the Isaiah tradition more generally, knows that Yahweh's coming newness is not contained within our present notions of the possible. And although the work of urbanization is hard and daily and concrete, that work is situated in a vision unscarred. What this poet imagines for his treasured city, the subsequent people of faith have regularly entertained as a promise over every failed city. Here the old city is submitted to the wonder of the creator, the one who makes all things new.

"I AM COMING"
66:1–24

After the elegant hope voiced in 65:17–25 as promise to the "seekers after Yahweh," this complex chapter returns us to the disputatious life of emerging Judaism. Although the glorious vision of Yahweh's coming future may have been powerful and comprehensive enough to gain the assent of all parties in the community, the concrete response to the vision in practice evidently evoked deep disagreements. This chapter, seemingly made up of a series of smaller units, testifies to the fractured and fractious character of the community addressed by these texts.

66:1 **Thus says the** LORD:
    Heaven is my throne
       and the earth is my footstool;
    what is the house that you would build for me,
       and what is my resting place?
  ² **All these things my hand has made,**
       and so all these things are mine,
                    says the LORD.
    But this is the one to whom I will look,
       to the humble and contrite in spirit,
       who trembles at my word.

Judaism became increasingly a cultic community, largely precluded from any significant exercise of political power. As a consequence, the character of right worship became an urgent topic, as we have already seen in chapter 58. These two verses, in the form of a divine oracle, articulate a vision of true worship of Yahweh from Yahweh's side. We have already seen that Yahweh, in awesome sovereignty, is said to dwell in heaven (63:15). Here the notion is more fully explicated to identify heaven as Yahweh's throne room and the earth as a mere footstool for convenience of the Holy One. The purpose of this statement, however, concerns neither God in heaven nor earth as footstool. Its purpose, rather, is to minimize the importance of the Jerusalem temple as an artifact that can hardly mean much to such a great and awesome God.

This grand statement probably reflects a dispute with an alternative opinion, as for example with Haggai, who regarded the temple and its rebuilding as the quintessential act for the faith of Judaism. The dismissive attitude of our text toward the temple is surely designed to resist an overemphasis. It is paralleled by the critique of the temple placed in the very context of the temple dedication under Solomon: "'But will God indeed dwell on the earth? Even heaven and the highest heaven cannot contain you, much less this house that I have built!'" (1 Kings 8:27). More generally, such a critique may be a warning about the church taking itself too seriously on any issue. The awesomeness of Yahweh, who fills heaven and occupies earth, assures that every church agenda—liturgical, doctrinal, moral—is deeply penultimate and does not deserve the passion of ultimacy.

The wonder of the vision of Yahweh offered here is enhanced by the assertion of verse 2 (see 57:15). Yahweh's attention is on the "humble and contrite," that is, those who are not stylishly situated in the environs of establishment religion. The double placement of Yahweh, "high and holy," with the "humble and contrite" sharply dismisses all religious pretense and all one-dimensional claims made on behalf of God.

66:3 **Whoever slaughters an ox is like one who kills a human being;**
     whoever sacrifices a lamb, like one who breaks a dog's neck;
   whoever presents a grain offering, like one who offers swine's blood;
     whoever makes a memorial offering of frankincense, like one who
       blesses an idol.
   These have chosen their own ways,
     and in their abominations they take delight;
   [4]**I also will choose to mock them,**
     and bring upon them what they fear;
   because, when I called, no one answered,
     when I spoke, they did not listen;
   but they did what was evil in my sight,
     and chose what did not please me.

The eloquent positive articulation of Yahweh vis-à-vis "religion" in verses 1–2 has as a counterpart a sharp critique of bad religion (vv. 3–4). The rhetorical strategy of verse 3 is to identify a seemingly routine ritual activity and push it into the orbit of gross practice by which even conventional practice is scandalized. Thus slaughtering an ox or sacrificing a lamb may be routine, but now those acts are recharacterized along with murder and the offer of a pig. The practical outcome of the rhetoric is to reclassify all such worship activity as "abomination," an act deeply affrontive to Yahweh. This massive critique of worship of the wrong kind at the end of the book of Isaiah has its counterpart and antecedent in 1:12–15 at the beginning.

In both cases, the worship acts themselves may not be intrinsically evil, though the rhetoric is deliberately inflammatory. What is wrong with such worship in 1:12–15 is that the ethical mandates of Yahweh are neglected (see 1:16–17). In our text, the effectiveness and significance of these liturgical acts are completely undermined by the fact that the worshipers were not in truth attentive to Yahweh, did not answer, and did not listen. The judgment culminates with a quotation of 65:12. What Yahweh wants is responsive, direct engagement, for which external acts of worship are no adequate substitute. It is possible that this harsh critique of "wrong worship," like the critique of the temple in verses 1–2, is a dispute with the temple-priestly party that exercised strong leadership in the community of early Judaism.

66:5 **Hear the word of the LORD,**
     you who tremble at his word:
   Your own people who hate you
     and reject you for my name's sake
   have said, "Let the LORD be glorified,
     so that we may see your joy";
     but it is they who shall be put to shame.

Whereas verses 1–4 would seem to be a polemic against "the other," that is, the opponent of those who speak in the text, in this verse the allies of this textual claim are addressed. They are the ones who "tremble at his word," that is, who are zealous and devoted to the most serious claims of Yahwism. They are deeply contrasted with the targets of critique in verses 1–4, so that we can detect here an ongoing division and dispute in the community. In this verse, the seriously devout are warned that they may expect rejection at the hands of their opponents, who prattle about Yahweh but whose phoniness is evident. Thus the text affirms that right practice of faith is a costly affair. Its proponents can expect to be treated negatively. This is the same warning that Jesus subsequently issued to his disciples, who would pay dearly for their serious faith:

"Blessed are you when people revile you and persecute you and utter all kinds of evil against you falsely on my account. Rejoice and be glad, for your reward is great in heaven, for in the same way they persecuted the prophets who were before you" (Matt. 5:11–12).

There is no easy way for serious faith.

66:6 Listen, an uproar from the city!
    A voice from the temple!
 The voice of the LORD,
    dealing retribution to his enemies!

 7 Before she was in labor
    she gave birth;
 before her pain came upon her
    she delivered a son.
 8 Who has heard of such a thing?
    Who has seen such things?
 Shall a land be born in one day?
    Shall a nation be delivered in one moment?
 Yet as soon as Zion was in labor
    she delivered her children.
 9 Shall I open the womb and not deliver?
    says the LORD;
 shall I, the one who delivers, shut the womb?
    says your God.

10 Rejoice with Jerusalem, and be glad for her,
    all you who love her;
 rejoice with her in joy,
    all you who mourn over her—
11 that you may nurse and be satisfied
    from her consoling breast;
 that you may drink deeply with delight
    from her glorious bosom.

12 For thus says the LORD:
 I will extend prosperity to her like a river,
    and the wealth of the nations like an overflowing stream;
 and you shall nurse and be carried on her arm,
    and dandled on her knees.
13 As a mother comforts her child,
    so I will comfort you;

you shall be comforted in Jerusalem.

14 You shall see, and your heart shall rejoice;
      your bodies shall flourish like the grass;
   and it shall be known that the hand of the LORD is with his servants,
      and his indignation is against his enemies.
15 For the LORD will come in fire,
      and his chariots like the whirlwind,
   to pay back his anger in fury,
      and his rebuke in flames of fire.
16 For by fire will the LORD execute judgment,
      and by his sword, on all flesh;
   and those slain by the LORD shall be many.

17 Those who sanctify and purify themselves to go into the gardens, following the one in the center, eating the flesh of pigs, vermin, and rodents, shall come to an end together, says the LORD.

Verses 1–5 have made a clear distinction between *right obedience* and *irresponsible worship*. The sharp division is further extended to affirm (a) the "humble and contrite" (v. 2), and (b) those who "tremble at the word" (vv. 2, 5), and to warn those who practice abomination (vv. 3–4). The community is deeply divided into conflicting parties. But these verses only *describe* the actual situation in Judaism.

In the present verses, what has been heretofore *described* is now subject to the fierce and determined *intervention* of Yahweh, whereby both parties receive their deserts. The intervention of Yahweh is characterized in classic terms of Yahweh's disruptive epiphany (v. 6). That coming is characteristically accompanied by blasts of a trumpet, a signal for invasive military activity; the coming characteristically arises from "the city," for the Divine Warrior is known to dwell in Jerusalem (see Amos 1:2). Thus the whole earth—and most particularly the community of faith—is about to be subjected to the decisive adjudication of Yahweh, who has the power to implement the verdicts we have already witnessed.

The positive verdict is given for those who are devout in their worship and obedience of Yahweh (vv. 7–14a). The good news is that Yahweh will intervene forcefully and effectively to do good for the faithful. That promised good is announced in a variety of images:

1. The newness will be as a sudden, miraculous birth that will happen so immediately that it violates all normal sequence and procedures for birth. Verses 7–9 are saturated with birth language, signifying the radical

and abrupt newness that will be caused only by the power of Yahweh. The word "labor" is used twice, and the verb for birth ("deliver") is used five times. Something completely new is about to happen. The birth imagery plays against the motif of barrenness (= hopelessness) that is rooted in the old ancestral narratives and is used in Isaiah 54:1. Yahweh will now override the barrenness and hopelessness of devout Judaism.

2. The newness will evoke unrestrained joy (vv. 10, 14), partly because of the sheer astonishment at the newness and partly because of the substance of the newness. The poem keeps the response of joy intimately linked to the metaphor of birth. Thus the contrast of joy and mourning is correlated with birth and barrenness. The joy is that of birth, for the newborn child—newborn Jerusalem—will nurse and be satisfied and comforted (see 40:1). The imagery suggests that Yahweh is the birth-mother, the one who suckles and satisfies and comforts the newborn. The connection of *abrupt birth* and *unrestrained joy* is reiterated in the promissory statement of Jesus to his disciples:

> "Very truly, I tell you, you will weep and mourn, but the world will rejoice; you will have pain, but your pain will turn into joy. When a woman is in labor, she has pain, because her hour has come. But when her child is born, she no longer remembers the anguish because of the joy of having brought a human being into the world. So you have pain now; but I will see you again, and your hearts will rejoice, and no one will take your joy from you" (John 16:20–22).

In our text, as in John 16, the abruptness of birth is a move toward apocalyptic, a move already suggested in verse 6.

3. The substance of the abrupt newness assured by the power of Yahweh is that Jerusalem will be a "river of *shalom*" (v. 12). But we should not be pious or romantic about this use of the word *shalom*, for it entails not only peace but also material security and affluence. Thus the poem picks up on the earlier images of all the wealth of the nations "streaming" into Jerusalem (see 60:5–14; 61:5). The metaphor of river bespeaks a flow of goods and cargo that floods into the city like a mighty stream, so that Jerusalem, so long humiliated and impoverished, will be the new trade center and commercial pivot point of the world.

But the poet cannot for long resist the dominant imagery of birth, and so in verse 12b the imagery is again of a cherished, caressed, valued, suckled child. The imagery of a suckled child is so crucial and so overwhelming that it is used in a double entry. The statement of verse 12 appears to pick up on the theme that foreign leaders will be reduced to nursemaids, in a completely subordinate posture (see 49:23; 60:4). But in verse 13, it is Yahweh, the God of all comfort, who will comfort Jerusalem as a mother comforts a child. The poet makes daring use of the metaphor by casting Yahweh in the role of the comforting mother. The poet will stop at nothing to enumerate the wondrous miracles of newness that are about to emerge amid this community without prospect.

4. Joy and prosperity in the end are only signals (sacraments) of the elemental claim of this promise. It is Yahweh who is with "his servants." We have already seen in 65:13–14 that "servants" is the correct identity of the Yahweh-fearers. And now it is evident, known, and acknowledged that Yahweh is in solidarity with this community, with all of the power for newness and all the resolve and attentiveness of a nursing mother. The metaphor guarantees intimacy in a context of stark need. Quite clearly, the metaphors of birth and nursing are essential for speaking of the elemental newness now in store for this community.

But the decisive action for the city is not only a great positive promise. It is also a devastating threat (vv. 6, 14c–16). The poem moves abruptly from affirmation to threat. It is payback time against those who mock Yahweh and practice abominations (vv. 3–4). Yahweh will come like a ferocious warrior and will violently exterminate those who violate and resist and dismiss. This violent threat surely has theological rootage in the very character and self-announcement of Yahweh. But we should also notice that the entire passage is deeply freighted with ideological bias. This is no neutral statement about Yahweh. The oracle is surely on the lips and in the ears of "the good guys" who anticipate payback time against their opponents who are seen to be opponents of Yahweh. But then, all such moral indignation in the name of Yahweh is characteristically shot through with self-interest. As is usual, the matter is not an either/or. It is a blend of legitimate theological, moral passion and partisan advocacy.

Verse 11 appears to be a late, heavily loaded prose refinement of the judgment made against the abominators in verses 3–4. The verse exploits the theme of 65:3–4, already itself a summary indictment. The "gardens" are treated as places of self-indulgent religion where the severe holiness of Yahweh is completely absent. The earlier indictment of 65:4 had mentioned the eating of pork as a quintessential violation, and this is now reinforced by "vermin and rodents." The point is the ritual impurity of the ones judged, a ritual impurity undertaken cavalierly and without any thought or sensitivity. It is no wonder, in the eyes of the devout, that Yahweh must come ferociously, for such deliberately embraced ritual contamination will in the end drive Yahweh away and jeopardize the entire community. The threat must be eliminated and will be eliminated in urgent, brutal fashion.

> 66:18 **For I know their works and their thoughts, and I am coming to gather all nations and tongues; and they shall come and shall see my glory,** [19] **and I will set a sign among them. From them I will send survivors to the nations, to Tarshish, Put, and Lud—which draw the bow—to Tubal and Javan, to the coastlands far away that have not heard of my fame or seen my glory; and they shall declare my glory among the nations.** [20] **They shall bring all your kindred from all the nations as an offering to the LORD, on horses, and in chariots, and in litters, and on mules, and on dromedaries, to my holy mountain Jerusalem, says the LORD, just as the Israelites bring a grain offering in a clean vessel to the house of the LORD.** [21] **And I will also take some of them as priests and as Levites, says the LORD.**

These verses, unlike the internal polemics of the preceding, are a prose vision of Yahweh's future, Yahweh's coming to establish sovereignty. The language is epiphanic, at the edge of apocalyptic: Yahweh will be all in all. But Yahweh not only *comes;* Yahweh comes *to gather.* "The God who gathers the outcasts" (56:8) will gather "all nations and tongues." This is apparently a great inclusive, universal reach of Yahweh to claim sovereignty over all peoples and to include all nations in the protected, blessed, covenanted community. The purpose, moreover, is that all nations shall see "my glory," that is, recognize Yahweh's majestic sovereignty. Indeed, as long ago as 40:3–5 the purpose of Jewish emancipation is that "all flesh" may see the glory of Yahweh. Calvin observes:

> This is a remarkable passage, which teaches us that God is not confined to any people, so as not to choose whomsoever he pleases, by casting off unbelievers whom he formerly called to himself (*Isaiah* IV, 431–432).

Yahweh will dispatch "survivors," that is, restored Jews, to all parts of the known world. These messengers (missionaries?) will go where the news of Yahweh has never been before. There they shall "declare my glory." They shall witness to the cosmic splendor of the one who inhabits eternity and dwells among the humble and contrite. They shall let all know of Yahweh's governance.

And all kindred ("your kindred") shall bring an offering to Yahweh in Jerusalem. The text envisions a great ritual procession of people in every kind of transport imaginable; they shall all come to Jerusalem to submit to

Yahweh. They shall be included "just as the Israelites" and shall be reckoned "clean," just as are good Jews. The rhetoric is congruent with the advocacy of 56:3–7. All are welcome who engage torah obedience and covenantal solidarity.

Then, as the ultimate imagery of inclusiveness, in verse 21 it is asserted that from among these *goyim*, these Gentile nations, some will be designated and ordained as priests and Levites, priests to handle Jewish holy things and Levites to interpret Jewish torah. This paragraph is a most astonishing refusal to settle for sniggling, punctilious sectarianism. The vision is as large and comprehensive as the invitation to Pentecost (Acts 12:1–13). If we push the birth metaphor of verses 7–9 back into the book of Genesis, it will not surprise us to remember that the promise to father Abraham and mother Sarah was "in you all the families of the earth shall be blessed" (Gen. 12:3). Here they are blessed as true insiders in the community of Yahweh.

66:22 **For as the new heavens and the new earth,**
  which I will make,
 shall remain before me, says the LORD;
  so shall your descendants and your name remain.
 23 **From new moon to new moon,**
  and from sabbath to sabbath,
  all flesh shall come to worship before me,
 says the LORD.

 24 **And they shall go out and look at the dead bodies of the people who have rebelled against me; for their worm shall not die, their fire shall not be quenched, and they shall be an abhorrence to all flesh.**

These final verses of the book of Isaiah pick up on themes we have already encountered. In verse 22a, the new heavens and new earth of 65:17 are recalled, a glorious vision of Yahweh's large newness as sovereign over a fully healed cosmos. But in verse 22b that large vision is kept close to Jewish self-awareness, for it is "your descendants" and "your name," referring to the chosen, covenanted community of Jews, who are guaranteed sustenance and maintenance.

In verse 23, the large vision of verses 18–21 is reiterated, for it is "all flesh" that are welcomed in worship. Indeed, from verse 21, we can imagine Gentiles presiding over the festivals of the Jews. But in verse 24, the focus is on the "rebellious," the party in the community that has violated the requirements of nascent Judaism (see 65:2). These are the ones who will be slain by the sword (see v. 16). In a passion that sounds almost like contemporary ethnic hatred, moreover, it is not enough that they die. They must *keep* dying, endlessly destroyed, perpetually humiliated, ever-lastingly remembered scornfully. The lines are imaginative in their capacity to conjure ways to keep the polemic alive: worms to eat endlessly on their bodies, fire to burn endlessly in their bones. The final term, "abhorrence," is used only one other time in the Old Testament, to speak of those who are raised to an eternal negative state: " 'Many of those who sleep in the dust of the earth shall awake, some to everlasting life, and some to shame and everlasting *contempt*' " (Dan. 12:2). No wonder Westermann can say, "This is the earliest idea of hell as a state of perdition" (*Isaiah 40–66*, 428).

Interpreters observe that these final verses of the book of Isaiah exhibit a profound tension between magnanimous *inclusiveness* and intensely felt *exclusiveness*. It is evident, moreover, that there have been continuous, disputatious editing and additions to the book, as though each of the contending parties of inclusiveness and exclusiveness was determined to have one more say, and even to have the last say.

Clearly, the disputatious editing is not finished. It was not finished in ancient Judaism, which continued to struggle about the relationship between membership and serious torah keeping. The surest sign of the unfinished arrangement of the testimony is the later scribal note that in synagogue reading, after verse 24 is read, verse 23 must be repeated as the last word in order to overcome the venom of verse 24.

The issue is, moreover, not finished in the contemporary life of the church, for the struggles concerning inclusion and exclusion continue. It is not clear who will have the last word in the church, or indeed if there will ever be a "last word." The community of faith, anciently and now, is the carrier of a large vision of inclusiveness, a vision carried in a community that perceives itself in deep jeopardy. Like those ancient text-makers, we have an amazing capacity to draw Yahweh into our deepest fears. The fears are checked and perhaps ultimately will be healed by the God who abruptly births newness and then gently nurses us amid our palpable fragility. More than that we cannot know. That much we can trust.

For Further Reading

Commentaries Cited

Calvin, John. *Commentary on the Book of the Prophet Isaiah*. Volumes 1–4. Grand Rapids: Baker Book House, 1979.

Hanson, Paul D. *Isaiah 40–66*. Interpretation: A Bible Commentary for Teaching and Preaching. Louisville, Ky.: Westminster John Knox Press, 1995.

Kaiser, Otto. *Isaiah 1–12*. Old Testament Library. Philadelphia: Westminster Press, 1972.

———. *Isaiah 13–39*. Old Testament Library. Philadelphia: Westminster Press, 1974.

Muilenburg, James. "The Book of Isaiah, Chapters 40–66." Vol. 5 of *The Interpreter's Bible*, pp. 381–773. New York: Abingdon Press, 1956.

Seitz, Christopher R. *Isaiah 1–39*. Interpretation: A Bible Commentary for Teaching and Preaching. Louisville, Ky.: Westminster John Knox Press, 1993.

Watts, John D. W. *Isaiah 34–66*. Word Commentary. Waco, Texas: Word Books, 1987.

Westermann, Claus. *Isaiah 40–66*. Old Testament Library. Philadelphia: Westminster Press, 1969.

Wildberger, Hans. *Isaiah 1–12*. Continental Commentary. Minneapolis: Fortress Press, 1991.

———. *Jesaja Kapitel 13–27*. Biblischer Kommentar. Neukirchener-Vluyn: Neukirchener Verlag, 1978.

———. *Jesaja Kapitel 28–39*. Biblischer Kommentar. Neukirchener-Vluyn: Neukirchener Verlag, 1982.

Other Works Cited

Berrigan, Daniel. *Isaiah: Spirit of Courage, Gift of Tears.* Minneapolis: Fortress Press, 1996.

Brueggemann, Walter. *Biblical Perspectives on Evangelism: Living in a Three-Storied Universe.* Nashville: Abingdon Press, 1993.

———. *Cadences of Home: Preaching Among Exiles.* Louisville, Ky.: Westminster John Knox Press, 1997.

Buechner, Frederick. *The Longing for Home: Recollections and Reflections.* San Francisco: Harper, 1996.

Childs, Brevard S. *Introduction to the Old Testament as Scripture.* Philadelphia: Fortress Press, 1979.

Clines, David J. A. *I, He, We, and They: A Literary Approach to Isaiah 53.* JSOT Supp. 1. Sheffield: JSOT Press, 1976.

Donner, Herbert. "Jesaja lvi 1–7: ein Abrogationsfall innerhalb des Kanons—Implikationen und Konsequenzen." *Supplements to Vetus Testamentum* 36 (1985): 81–95.

Evangelical Catechism. St. Louis: Eden Publishing House, 1961.

Gaiser, Frederick. "A New Word on Homosexuality? Isaiah 56:1–8 as Case Study." *Word & World* 14 (1994): 280–93.

Gottwald, Norman K. *All the Kingdoms of the Earth: Israelite Prophecy and International Relations in the Ancient Near East.* New York: Harper & Row, 1964.

Hanson, Paul D. *The Dawn of Apocalyptic: The Historical and Sociological Roots of Jewish Apocalyptic Eschatology.* Philadelphia: Fortress Press, 1975.

Levenson, Jon D. *Creation and the Persistence of Evil: The Jewish Drama of Divine Omnipotence.* San Francisco: Harper & Row, 1988.

Lifton, Robert Jay. *The Nazi Doctors: Medical Killing and the Psychology of Genocide.* New York: Basic Books, 1986.

Melugin, Roy F., and Marvin A. Sweeney, eds. *New Visions of Isaiah.* JSOT Supp. 214. Sheffield: Sheffield Academic Press, 1996.

Melville, Herman. *Moby Dick: Or the Whale.* New York: Penguin Classics, 1992.

Miller, Patrick D. *They Cried to the Lord: The Form and Theology of Biblical Prayer.* Minneapolis: Fortress Press, 1994.

Milton, John. *Paradise Lost.* New York: McGraw-Hill, 1969.

Moberly, R. W. L. *The Old Testament of the Old Testament: Patriarchal Narratives and Mosaic Yahwism.* Overtures to Biblical Theology. Minneapolis: Fortress Press, 1992.

North, Christopher R. *The Suffering Servant in Deutero-Isaiah: An Historical and Critical Study.* Oxford: Oxford University Press, 1956.

Plöger, Otto. *Theocracy and Eschatology.* Richmond: John Knox Press, 1968.

Reich, Charles. *Opposing the System.* New York: Random House, 1995.

Reventlow, H. Graf. *Gebot und Predigt im Dekalog.* Gutersloh: G. Mohn, 1962.

Ringe, Sharon H. *Jesus, Liberation, and the Biblical Jubilee: Images for Ethics and Christology.* Overtures to Biblical Theology. Philadelphia: Fortress Press, 1985.

Sawyer, John F. A. *The Fifth Gospel: Isaiah in the History of Christianity.* Cambridge: Cambridge University Press, 1996.

Steinbeck, John. *The Grapes of Wrath.* New York: Viking Penguin, 1992.

Stuhlmacher, Peter. *Reconciliation, Law, and Righteousness: Essays in Biblical Theology.* Philadelphia: Fortress Press, 1986.

Terrien, Samuel. *The Elusive Presence: Toward a New Biblical Theology.* San Francisco: Harper & Row, 1978.

Tuchman, Barbara W. *The March of Folly: From Troy to Vietnam.* New York: Ballantine Books, 1984.

Whybray, R. N. *Thanksgiving for a Liberated Prophet: An Interpretation of Isaiah Chapter 53.* JSOT Supp. 4. Sheffield: JSOT Press, 1978.

For Further Study

Achtemeier, Elizabeth. *The Community and Message of Isaiah 56–66: A Theological Commentary.* Minneapolis: Augsburg Publishing House, 1982.

Barton, J. *Isaiah 1–39.* Old Testament Guides. Sheffield: Sheffield Academic Press, 1995.

Clifford, Richard J. *Fair Spoken and Persuading: An Interpretation of Second Isaiah.* New York: Paulist Press, 1984.

Emmerson, Grace I. *Isaiah 56–66.* Old Testament Guides. Sheffield: Sheffield Academic Press, 1992.

Seitz, Christopher R., ed. *Reading and Preaching the Book of Isaiah.* Philadelphia: Fortress Press, 1988.

Seitz, Christopher R. *Zion's Final Destiny: The Development of the Book of Isaiah: A Reassessment of Isaiah 36–39.* Minneapolis: Fortress Press, 1991.

Whybray, R. N. *The Second Isaiah.* Old Testament Guides. Sheffield: JSOT Press, 1983.